Essays in American Historiography

PAPERS PRESENTED IN HONOR OF

ALLAN NEVINS

Essays in
AMERICAN
HISTORIOGRAPHY

PAPERS PRESENTED IN HONOR OF

ALLAN NEVINS

Edited by

Donald Sheehan & Harold C. Syrett

COLUMBIA UNIVERSITY PRESS

New York   1960

Publication of this work has been made possible by a gift from Mr. Marcellus Hartley Dodge and by grants from the William A. Dunning Fund and the Edgar A. and Frederic Bancroft Foundation, made available by the generous cooperation of the Department of History, Columbia University, and of the Columbia University Libraries.

ALLAN NEVINS — AN APPRECIATION

by John Allen Krout
COLUMBIA UNIVERSITY

IN THIS RATHER AUSTERE era of historical writing it is not often that a professional historian elbows his hard-won notes off his desk and sets himself the task of defining the nature and scope of history. Fortunately for us that is exactly what Allan Nevins did almost a quarter century ago. The result was published in 1938 under the title *The Gateway to History*. A gateway it has been ever since to generations of college and university students, intent upon teaching as a career, and also to a host of amateurs merely seeking "a very Doric entrance to the historical domain." Its pages are bright with the qualities which Professor Nevins over the years has exemplified: erudition, enthusiasm, clarity, and brilliance. "History," he writes, "in its protean forms touches the realm of ideas at more points than any other study, and in the best of its forms it is compact as much of ideas as of fact."

One doubts that he fully realized this truth when, as a boy in an Illinois farmhouse, his imagination was first stirred by the events recorded by Macaulay and Prescott and Parkman. But he learned it quickly as newspaperman, teacher, biographer, and editor. His life long he has been trying to persuade his fellow countrymen that if history is read "by the blazing illumination" of an aroused intellectual curiosity, it will richly provide the materials out of which each successive generation may fashion the philosophy it so sorely needs.

Allan Nevins was already at home in the world of letters when Professor Carlton J. H. Hayes persuaded him in 1928 to join the Department of History at Columbia University. His editorials in the New York *Evening Post, The Nation,* and the New York *World* had shown how happily were combined in him the talents of the painstaking scholar and the literary artist.   His interest in aspiring students quickly became highly personal and stubbornly enduring.   He was concerned not only to guide the young historian toward an understanding of historical method but also to make him aware of the opportunities which history, as a form of literature, offered to the writer, the editor, the critic.   For almost two decades he carried the responsibility for all those in the Department of History who were candidates for the master's degree and were writing a master's essay; and yet he found time to give a hand to scores who were preparing doctoral dissertations for publication.   When his colleagues protested that he was carrying too heavy a load, he would reply with a wry smile that no task had really seemed burdensome since he left the Illinois farm.

What moments he could call "spare," he devoted to his own writing.   And most of it was exciting.   In 1933 the Pulitzer Prize for biography came to him for *Grover Cleveland: a Study in Courage,* and again in 1937 for *Hamilton Fish: the Inner History of the Grant Administration.*   Ten years later he received the Bancroft Prize and the Scribner Centenary Prize for the first two volumes of *The Ordeal of the Union.*   Now in the fifth of ten volumes, the *Ordeal* portrays on a heroic scale the cruel testing of American national unity from the Compromise of 1850 to the close of the Reconstruction Era.   To appreciate Professor Nevins's monumental achievement one needs only to compare his volumes with James Ford Rhodes's *History,* so long regarded as the classic interpretation of this period in American life.

His inquiring mind, fortified by his enduring energy, has led Allan Nevins into many bypaths off the main highways of history; but his chief concern about mankind's story is unmistakable.   He has given it monolithic form in the address which he delivered to the American Historical Association, as its President, in December, 1959.   He would have the professional historians and the popular historians forget their earlier recriminations and join in a common effort to give greater attention to a humanized and at-

tractive presentation of the record of the past.   In the last analysis, he insists, the historian is the servant of the great democratic
public.   "That public has come through a terrible period of confusion, effort and disaster, and lives on in a period of intense
strain.   It needs all the sense of pattern, all the moral fortitude,
all the faith in the power of liberty and morality to survive the
assaults of tyranny and wrong, that historians of every school can
give it."

The contributors to this *Festschrift,* all of them recipients of
the doctorate under Professor Nevins's supervision, have had in
the present enterprise the benefit of the encouragement and
guidance of Donald Sheehan, Associate Professor of History and
Assistant to the President at Smith College, and Harold C. Syrett,
now Professor of History at Columbia and editor of the Alexander
Hamilton papers.   They represent hundreds of students who
would honor Professor Nevins as scholar, author, and teacher.
They have enjoyed his exciting lectures, have learned of new areas
for historical research in his seminars, and have been instructed
by the way in which he has applied his concept of the nature and
scope of history to the subjects on which he has written.   Most of
all they have been moved by his ability to show them how en-
grossing the pursuit of history can be.

The late Stuart P. Sherman of the University of Illinois once
remarked that Allan Nevins in his younger days was a remarkable combination of St. Vitus and Benjamin Franklin.   If the observation be true, surely the Franklin strain has grown stronger
with the passing years.   Indeed, one might say today of Professor
Nevins what Carl Van Doren said of Franklin: "More than any
single man, a harmonious human multitude."

March 1, 1960

CONTENTS

Essays in American Historiography

PAPERS PRESENTED IN HONOR OF

ALLAN NEVINS

SCIENTIFIC HISTORY IN AMERICA:
ECLIPSE OF AN IDEA

by Edward N. Saveth
THE GRADUATE FACULTY
NEW SCHOOL FOR SOCIAL RESEARCH
NEW YORK

THE PROSPECT of a science of history that would chart the past and enable the future to be projected has invariably intrigued the historian. Technically, this would leave history unencumbered by its mass and the historian concerned only with lines of development delineated by historical science. With the road map of the future before him, the status of the historian would grow as indispensable counselor of politicians and statesmen, bringing the science of human development to bear upon his deliberations. Henry Adams, in "The Tendency of History" written in 1894, imagined a situation in which state and church, capital and labor, and all other important social groupings and institutions, would ask anxiously of the historian: Am I justified in history and will I live on?

The movement toward a science of history, which had its most significant development toward the last two decades of the nineteenth century, coincided with the professionalization of historical study. Throughout most of the nineteenth century and before, history had been the province of those who regarded it as primarily a branch of literature. The best of the literary historians did no injustice to the muse, since they were as discriminate in their use of sources as they were careful in their stylistic presentation.

The last quarter of the nineteenth century witnessed the development of the professionally trained American historian, many

of whom attended German graduate schools. The professional
American historians were inclined to associate the development of
a science of history with the growth of professional prestige and
aspired to a utilitarian history in an increasingly practical era.
They were less interested in attracting and entertaining a relatively large reading public than were their predecessors such as
Francis Parkman and William Hickling Prescott. Indeed, the
strain of romanticism which had attracted the public to early nineteenth-century historiography was considered by the professional
historian to be superfluous, if not unsuited, to a scientific era.

Scientific historiography had larger ambitions than narrative
pace, dramatic presentation, or a large readership—goals considered unimportant in relation to the discovery of a law, comparable
to Darwin's in biology, that would unify all of human history.

Although the heyday of scientific history was the late nineteenth century, the belief that there was law in history, even if not
necessarily scientific law, existed earlier. George Bancroft wrote
of God as manifest in American history and national destiny as
controlled by His law. History is "swayed by general laws," Bancroft wrote, "event succeeds event according to their influence." [1]
Even in the literary histories of Prescott, Parkman, and John
Lothrop Motley, the triumph of the Anglo-Saxon, the Protestant,
and democracy over the non-Anglo-Saxon, the Catholic, and mon-
archism, of moral law and progress, if not exactly determined by
historical law, was inherent in the unfolding of events.[2]

Toward the middle of the last century, the ideas of Jeremy
Bentham and Auguste Comte began to influence American historiography and made themselves apparent particularly in the
work of Richard Hildreth, John W. Draper, and, somewhat later,
in the writings of Henry Adams. Hildreth's *History of the
United States, 1497–1789,* which was published in 1849, was background for a more comprehensive effort to create an "Inductive
Science of Man" in accordance with the principles of Benthamite
utilitarianism. Comte's positivism and Henry T. Buckle's theory
of the relation between environment and human evolution had
important influence upon John W. Draper's *Intellectual Development of Europe* (1863) as well as on Draper's work in American
history.

The scientific historiography of the late nineteenth century reflected these earlier patterns. John W. Burgess, with a doctorate from Göttingen and an interest in scientific history, wrote of God's will in history manifest in the victory of the North in the Civil War. The Newtonian universe of John Fiske, who was a popularizer of scientific history, if somewhat more complex than the world which "the Lord's Remembrancers" described for Puritan readers, was none the less providentially determined. Fiske's God was a master mechanic governing through natural law rather than by direct, personal intervention as did the God of the Puritan historians. The Anglo-Saxon, Protestant, and democrat were no less triumphant in the deterministic sequences of the late nineteenth-century scientific historians than in the more leisurely teleology of Parkman and Motley. Certain hypotheses which were applied to American history by scientific historians during the twentieth century—regionalism, sectionalism, and geographic determinism; the frontier theory; economic determinism—were at least anticipated by earlier nineteenth-century historians. Finally, fact-finding and the intelligent, accurate, and discriminate use of sources, essentials of scientific historiography, were not altogether wanting in earlier American historiography.

There were also important differences between the older historiography and the newer scientific pattern which grew out of the cumulative impact of developments in nineteenth-century science. Bancroft, Parkman, Prescott, Motley were more philosophers of history than believers in natural law, more interested in the working out of an eternal principle, in propounding *das Weltgericht,* than in positivistic formulations. The scientific historiography of the late nineteenth century aspired to oneness with Lyell's *Principles of Geology* (1830–33), Lamarck's theory of development, von Baer's law in embryology, and finally, Darwin's *Origin of Species* (1859), which rooted man in nature and biological evolution and encouraged the study of mankind along naturalistic lines. History was also influenced by revolutionary discoveries in physics, particularly in thermodynamics, which resulted in the integration of biology and physics, the organic and inorganic, in a common energy system representing the primal force of an interrelated universe.

Gustav Fechner, a year after the publication of Darwin's epic work, announced that man's mind could be studied scientifically and measured quantitatively, a premise of the science of psychology. In 1874, Ernest Brucke in his *Lectures on Physiology* developed the theory of the living organism as a dynamic system governed by the laws of chemistry and physics. Brucke exerted an important influence on Freud, who, in the 1890s, began to evolve a dynamic psychology which, according to Calvin Hall, "studies the transformations and exchanges of energy within the personality." [3] An aspiration of later nineteenth-century scholarship was to create a physiobiological synthesis embracing mankind and the stars. The mechanistic world systems evolved by European scholars like Edward Buchner, Jacob Moleschott, Wilhelm Ostwald, Ernst Haeckel, and Herbert Spencer had their counterparts among American historians in the work of John Fiske and Henry Adams. To these men, history represented a continuum with the universe of nature, and like nature, was supposedly governed by law.

It is understandable, therefore, that Charles McLean Andrews wrote retrospectively of this era as a time when the historian pursued "his experiments just as does the investigator in the scientific laboratory." [4]

As a preliminary methodological step, the historian, like the scientist, had to assemble the facts. In gathering data, the American scientific historian made a point of deriving facts from original sources, a technique which was stressed by their German mentors—Bluntschli and Erdmannsdorffer among others—in whose seminars they studied. As has been pointed out before, this was by no means an original development since earlier American historians like Bancroft and Hildreth were not inclined to play fast and loose with historical data. What scientific methodology contributed at this time was less the kind of factual accuracy which the best of the earlier historians took for granted, but a mystique about historical data in which the facts would yield meaning to the impartial historian provided his researches were sufficiently painstaking. As monograph succeeded monograph, it was almost assumed that, as a result of so much diligent research into narrow segments of the past, an historical law inherent in the data of history would emerge as a result of the additive process alone.

Secondly, the scientific historians had implicit faith in the comparative method enabling them to classify data "to the fullest extent possible." The comparative method had been used by Cuvier in zoology, Lyell in geology, Muller in philology, and was now being applied to history. In 1874, the English historian Edward Augustus Freeman predicted that the comparative method would open a new world to the historical investigator, "and that not an isolated world, a world shut up within itself, but a world in which times and tongues and nations which seemed parted poles asunder, now find each one its own place, its own relation to each other, as members of one common primaeval brotherhood." [5]

Employing the comparative method, scientific historians discovered seeming similarities between American, German, and English institutions, leading them to conclude that these institutions had a common origin among prehistoric Aryan peoples whose very existence the scientific historians postulated rather than proved. American institutions were derived supposedly from this original race as a consequence of Aryo-Teutonic migrations from an original Aryan homeland to Germany; thence to England by Anglo, Saxon, and Jute invaders in the seventh century; and ultimately, to New England by the Puritans in the seventeenth century. The United States, therefore, was regarded as the latest homeland of the Aryo-Teutonic peoples who deposited the Aryan institutional seed upon New England's shores. History, concluded Herbert Baxter Adams, the most ardent proponent of the Teutonic hypotheses, "should not be content with describing effects when it can explain causes. It is just as improbable that free local institutions should spring up without a germ along American shores as that English wheat should have grown here without planting." [6]

As Adams's statement indicates, analogies borrowed from biology were crucial to the theory of the Aryo-Teutonic theory of the origin of American nationality. Racial continuity among the Aryo-Teutonic peoples, it was argued, insured recapitulation of

the original Aryan political heritage in each new homeland.   The
first generation of American scientific historians, committed to
the theory of the Aryo-Teutonic origins of American nationality,
wrote in terms of the biological evolution of the Aryan institutional "seed," its being "transplanted" to Germany, England, and
the United States, and "germinating' into the institutions of the
New England town, the New England states, and, finally, into the
Constitution of the United States.   More than one scientific historian saw the American Constitution as culmination of Aryan
political evolution.[7]

The stronghold of this theory was Herbert Baxter Adams's
seminar in the graduate school of Johns Hopkins University.   It
was also taught by Moses Coit Tyler and Andrew D. White at
Cornell and by Albert Bushnell Hart at Harvard.   Through the
widely read histories of John Fiske, the Teutonic theory became
familiar to general readers.   So wide has been the acceptance
of Teutonism, wrote Charles McLean Andrews, "and so strongly
installed is it in the minds of both students and readers that it
might seem more bold than discreet to raise the question regard-
ing the soundness of the theory." [8]

"If the historian," wrote Henry Adams in 1876, "will only
consent to shut his eyes for a moment to the microscopic analyses
of personal motives and idiosyncracies, he cannot but become
conscious of a silent pulsation that commands his respect, a steady
movement that resembles in its mode of operation the mechanical operation of nature herself."   One of the aims of Adams's
*History of the United States during the Jefferson and Madison
Administrations* (1889–91) was to grasp this "silent pulsation," to
ascertain the natural laws underlying the development of the
American nation between 1800 and 1817, and to predict lines of
future national evolution.   Adams assumed that there was linear
progress in history that was not only measurable in the past but
predictable in the future.   "With almost the certainty of a mathematical formula, knowing the rate of increase of population and
wealth, [the American people] could read in advance their economical history for at least a hundred years. . . . [The] movement
of thought was equally well defined . . . the character of people

and government was formed; the lines of their activity were fixed." [9]

Despite the great expectations of those who tried to make a science of history, the late nineteenth-century attempt to apply the laws of the physical and biological universe to history yielded no impressive results. Critics soon pointed out that there was no necessary continuum between nature and society and that even if there was, the laws applicable in one field were not necessarily valid in another. In addition, the comparative method, a mainstay of scientific history, began to be recognized as a device of dubious value to the historian. Analogies, wrote Edward Channing, between American institutions and the institutions of the primitive Germanic tribes were not identities, nor were analogous institutions descended from one another. "The argument," said Channing, "that, because a New England town and a German village were each surrounded by a defensive wall, the one is descended from the other proves too much. A similar line or argument would prove the origin of New England towns to be the Massai enclosure of Central Africa." Gradually, critical scholarship undermined the main props of the Teutonic theory of the origins of American institutions. Within a very few years, the Teutonic hypothesis survived mainly as an historical archaism, cropping up occasionally, and as late as 1918, in unexpected places like James Truslow Adams's *History of Southampton*.[10]

Henry Adams's attempt to apply the laws of physics to history was equally unproductive. It is true that Adams's history has been much read and admired, but mainly for reasons other than its scientific pretensions. It is difficult to determine, moreover, how serious Adams was about the ideas of scientific history. In his *History,* Adams appears to take the concept of science seriously, then to lose the theme, revive it and play with it for a bit, and then drop it. Amidst the swirl of facts detailing the Jefferson and Madison administrations, the theme of scientific history recurs and again goes nowhere for all its bold and well-stated promise. And yet, Adams's application of the law of nature to history was more than a literary device. He toyed with the problem throughout his lifetime and, towards the end, pounced upon the theme of historical law with a degree of stubbornness that could result only from the desire to match the disintegration of the world with the destructive furies that raged within him.

This is not the place to set forth in detail Adams's inverted social Darwinism and his belief that civilization, like the universe, was progressively losing energy in accordance with the principle of the second law of thermodynamics promulgated by Lord Kelvin. Viewed in the perspective of scientific history, and apart from their subjective meaning to Adams, the "Letter to American Teachers of History" (1910) and "The Rule of Phase Applied to History" (1909) represent the last gasp of that phase of late nineteenth-century historiography which attempted to establish a science of history based upon the laws of the physical universe.

In the present century, the effort toward a science of history continued sporadically and with the bulk of the historical profession unconvinced. William M. Sloane, in 1912, comparing history and the natural sciences with respect to predictability, argued that the sciences which claimed to be the most exact achieved "at best but a more or less close approximation to prediction, a higher or lower degree of probability." History, Sloane went on to say, might approach and even match the probability of the natural sciences, if research revealed enough of the factual background. A few years later, Edward Cheyney revealed six inherently moral, as distinct from mechanical or biological, historical laws: law of the continuity of history, law of impermanence in history, law of the interdependence of mankind, law of the inevitability of democracy, law of the necessity of free consent to government, and the law of moral progress. Cheyney also believed that once the historian grasped the laws of history he could act "with the same intelligence and precision and anticipation of success as the physicist, engineer and cattle breeder." [11] The last important effort to establish a science of history was by the Marxists who, mainly in the 1930s (there were earlier efforts in this direction), attempted to hitch American development to their universal dialectic, again without success and without significant following.

Opposition to the principle of historical law by the bulk of the historical profession derives from the belief that the great diversity of factors entering into a given historical situation makes prediction or extensive generalization impossible. It is also argued that the data of nature are static and repeatable and may be stated in terms of law, whereas the data of history are progressive, cannot be repeated, and, owing to contingencies inherent in the historic situation, cannot be expressed as a formula.[12] Finally, there are some historians, fewer in number than those taking the above positions, who view historical knowledge as inherently subjective—so subjective, in fact, as to provide insubstantial foundation for objective historical law.

The foundation stone of the scientific history of the Teutonists was the fact. The latter, in addition to being immutable, allegedly possessed a natural order. Consequently, when the disciples of the so-called New History, circa 1910, challenged not only the manner in which the Teutonists ordered the facts, but also "the being of a fact," they mounted a two-pronged attack upon the scientific concepts of their predecessors.

Writing to Frederick Jackson Turner in 1910, Carl Becker recalled that when he was Turner's student, the latter had given him to understand "that no one . . . knew 'exactly what happened,' " and Turner replied that he had wanted to accomplish just that. In questioning "the being of a fact," by describing the fact "as not planted on the solid ground of fixed conditions," as "itself a part of the changing currents, the complex and interacting influences of the time, deriving its significance as a fact from its relation to the deeper-seated movements of the age," Turner was challenging the basis of scientific history as evolved by the Teutonists. If the facts were not fixed phenomena, then any theory of order in history that was based upon them must be flawed. To Becker, the "facts of history whatever they once were" are to the investigator "only mental images of pictures which the historian makes in order to comprehend it." The continuity of history was largely subjective with the historian.[13]

Extreme historical relativism, however, not only ruled out the possibility of historical law, but also of historical knowledge. Neither Becker nor Turner pushed this position to its ultimate and, from the point of view of historiography, negative conclusion.

Instead, Turner, in his presidential address to the American Historical Association in 1910, used relativism as a springboard for attacking not "the being of a fact," but those who derived historical law from *a priori* evidence and exploited history for "justificatory appendices." "The pathway of history," Turner warned, "is strewn with the wrecks of 'known and acknowledged truth' ... due not only to defective analyses and imperfect statistics, but also to the lack of critical historical methods, of insufficient historical mindedness ... to failure to give due attention to the relativity and transience of the conditions from which ... laws were deduced."

Although the historian could not tell for certain what went on in the past, continued Turner, he could at least try honestly to find out. This required conscientious effort to understand the material of history and, along with such an effort, use of the hypothesis (more tentative than historical law), to guide the historian's probings. In formulating and refining the hypothesis, the historian would be aided by concepts derived from the social sciences: economics, sociology, psychology, and anthropology. The gist of Turner's statement is that if history could not be made into a science, it might at least be infiltrated by the social sciences to the end that true understanding might be achieved.[14]

The hypothesis, if less ironclad than historical law, was still more of a commitment to a point of view than simple induction from facts. It assumed that the process of inquiry in historical research began less with a problem of interpretation presented by a body of empirical data and more with a theory, the validity of which had been established. The hypothesis seemingly committed the historian more to a point of view than the "neutralist" claim that the facts of history spoke for themselves. It also challenged the notion of the Teutonists that there was a natural order and meaningfulness in history which the mere unearthing of facts would unfold.

Did the use of hypotheses make for more or less bias in historical writing? The pledges of impartiality that adorn the prefaces of historical studies are not always redeemed in the texts, and historians who deliberately avoid a philosophy of history,

like James Ford Rhodes, are by no means unprejudiced.[15]   On
the other hand, it cannot be said that the major hypotheses of the
last fifty years of historical writing have lived up to what the disciples of the "New History" anticipated of them when the century was young.   The frontier hypothesis, geographical, sectional,
and regional interpretations, the economic interpretation, and
the urban explanation provide necessary rather than sufficient explanations of American development.   Or else, as in the case of
the frontier, regional, and urban interpretations, they subsume
so many factors as to be useless to the historian in search of causes.
Hardiest of the major historical hypotheses has been the economic
interpretation—mainly because it is an explanation of human behavior and, as such, was compatible with the economic orientation of twentieth-century liberalism.

To its chief proponent, Charles A. Beard, the economic interpretation of history was "as nearly axiomatic as any proposition
can be."   If, said Beard, you were to find that "men owning substantially the same amounts of the same kind of property were
equally divided on the matter of adoption or rejection—it would
then become apparent that the Constitution had no ascertainable
relation to economic groups or classes, but was the product of
some abstract causes remote from the chief business of life—gaining a livelihood."   But on the other hand, if you discovered "that
substantially all of merchants, money lenders, security holders,
manufacturers, shippers, capitalists, and financiers and their professional associates are to be found on one side in support of the
Constitution and that substantially all or a major part of the opposition came from the non-slaveholding farmers and the debtors
—would it not be pretty conclusively demonstrated that our fundamental law was not the product of an abstraction known as
'the whole people' but of a group of economic interests which
must have expected beneficial results from its adoption?" [16]

Even before the enormous development of the behavioral sciences in the last two decades, historians were aware of the limitations of this kind of an approach, as was Beard himself in the
preface of the 1935 edition of *An Economic Interpretation of the
Constitution* and in other of his writings.   The impact of more

sophisticated concepts of political behavior further weakened
Beard's position as they did the entire fabric of economically ori-
ented liberal philosophy in America. Still, for many historians,
Robert E. Brown's line-by-line analysis of Beard's work—conclud-
ing with the indictment that "if historians accept the Beard thesis
. . . they must do so with the full knowledge that their acceptance
is founded on a 'act of faith' not an analysis of historical method,
or that they are indulging in a 'noble dream' not history"—was
something of a revelation.[17]

Critical of historical law and historical hypothesis, less prone
than scholars in other fields to pursue Marxian and Freudian fan-
tasies, there has been a tendency, less pronounced among those
writing American history than among the philosophers of history
in our midst, toward an antiscientist position. This is reenforced
by the current political climate wherein historical determinism is
looked upon as an aspect of the denial of free will and free choice
in human affairs and, if not actually antidemocratic, as having
the potential of being so. It is ironic that the search for historical law began on a note of expectation in the late nineteenth century, anticipatory of the triumph of democracy and intelligence
over nature and social forces. Times and attitudes have changed
to the extent that within the past few years, Karl Popper dedicated *The Poverty of Historicism* to the "memory of the countless
men and women of all creeds or nations or races who fell victim
to the fascist and communist belief in Inexorable Laws of Historical Destiny"—which levies, in my opinion, a disproportionate burden of guilt upon historical law for the ills of the world.

There has been emphasis, prideful emphasis, upon the uniqueness of the subject matter of history and its emancipation from
the positivistic philosophy that gave rise to the concept of historical law. Thus, Dr. Lloyd Sorenson is of the opinion that the
late nineteenth-century impetus in American historiography toward historical law will be succeeded in our time by the antisci-
entific historiographical tradition of "historismus" and "an un-
named development beyond *Historismus*" which he finds rooted in
the work of Wilhelm Dilthey, Heinrich Rickert, Ernst Troeltsch,
and Frederick Meinecke.[18] But he also speaks of the need to

"analyze what historians do in much the same way that we have already analyzed what scientists do. Perhaps then history and nature can be taken into a single system that encompasses both by transcending both" [19]—a conclusion which seems to suggest a revival of scientific history. Indeed, the murkiness of this conclusion is in keeping with the character of the definitions variously assigned to historismus.[20]

There has developed over the years a widening breach between the theory and philosophy of history (including the conception of scientific history), on the one hand, and the writing of history on the other. Carl Becker, perplexed about the nature of a fact, nevertheless wrote brilliant narrative history. Charles A. Beard, convinced of the invalidity of the concept of cause in history, did not write history without reference to cause.[21] If the practicing historian was to take seriously the ruminations of the philosophers of history, he would risk being traumatized by philosophic objections to the essentials of his task. Unquestionably, awareness of the ultimates involved in their work has contributed a certain maturity to historiography, although precisely how this has come about and what is meant by maturity is a little hard to describe. However, the American historian, producing as much as he does and as well as he does, does not give the impression of being frustrated either by a heavy burden of theory or the fact that an ahistorical American public could not be less interested.

With respect to the imponderables of history propounded by the philosophers, most historians are willing to arrive at practical compromises. With few exceptions, like Mr. James C. Malin, the guild is willing to accept the position stated by Oscar Handlin a few years back that, recognizing that objective truth is unobtainable, historians are content to work as honestly as they can with materials that entail subjective involvement.[22] Regardless of the ultimate philosophic validity of this position, it has proven eminently practical. The American historian has managed his materials with such restraint that the influence of relativism has not had the disintegrating effect upon the American historical tradition which Hannah Arendt claims—and the claim, like Karl Popper's, may be exaggerated—has had upon the European.[23]

It is possible, too, that the idea of a science of history has been chewed over too much; that whatever the philosophic implications of the problem, the sum of which only the rare historian is qualified to grasp, it has lost relationship to the practice of historiography. Reading the literature of the subject, the impression is that all that can be said about scientific history seems to have been said; that there have been, over a period of years, reformulations of the concept of historical law and of a science of history which strike an initial exciting note, are developed by intellectual acrobatics that are fascinating to watch, and end disappointingly without anything new having been added to knowledge of a subject which seems a little tired. Predictions about historiography are as hazardous as those about history; but barring a major breakthrough in thinking one does not anticipate new understandings in this area.

Historians who once aimed at historical law and then lowered their sights to the less all-embracing field of historical hypothesis are now, even more modestly, inquiring as to the validity of their generalizations. Louis Gottschalk concludes that "no honest scholar need feel ashamed because his generalizations are not golden or may not even glitter." [24]

Armed by this half-hearted note of positivism, the historian, in generalizing, is tempted and expected to employ more and more the methodology of the social sciences. Although this emphasis has increased in recent years, the historian's exploitation of allied fields and disciplines is as old or older than the promulgation of the New History, circa 1910. This kind of an approach differs from the earlier concept of historical law insofar as it does not seek to bend the entire stream of history into a given channel but to derive new meanings from relatively limited factual sequences.

Although two Pulitzer Prize-winning volumes in American history, Oscar Handlin's *The Uprooted* and Richard Hofstadter's *The Age of Reform,* owe in large measure their success to the authors' skill in the use of social science concepts, by and large American historians remain conscious of the barriers to effective integration between history and the social sciences arising out of the differences between them.[25] The social-science approach is essentially microcosmic centering in the relationship, frequently lending itself to quantitative expression, between a relatively few phenomena in a limited and, for the most part, contemporary time sequence. The historian's approach, on the other hand, is macrocosmic, embracing a great number of variables distributed widely in space and time, whose interaction can rarely be precisely determined and, as a rule, cannot be measured quantitatively.

Consequently, historians argue that generalizations which are valid in social-science sequences might not hold for historical sequences. It is also true that certain of the methods of the social and behavioral sciences such as interviewing, polling, and other forms of inquiry which require the presence of the subject, are useless to the historian who, concerned with mankind's past, cannot ask questions of the dead. In addition, the historian has certain reservations about the methods and techniques of the social sciences. The historian tends to be more skeptical than the behavioral scientist of the values of psychological and psychoanalytical techniques, of the superiority of the quantitative measurements of the social scientist to his own informed guesses. The reaction of Dr. Henry David is typical of that of many historians when he asserts that the pollsters, had they been around in 1800, could not have done a better job of estimating popular attitude in the United States than did Henry Adams by using the historian's traditional sources.[26]

There can be little doubt that to the extent that American historians have resisted the reduction of their discipline to a science and have resisted the social science incursion, the public prestige of history is diminished. Society's demand that its experience be analyzed so that essential tasks like predicting election returns, measuring opinion, and selling deodorants might be performed—has been met by others than the historians. Government and industry make use of sociologists, anthropologists, psychologists, economists, and political scientists while, apart from a few areas of government service and an occasional business history, the historian can only teach and write books which, for the most part, do not sell well. The social scientists with their analyses of such intriguing subjects as sex, delinquency, suburbia, and status have captured the public imagination. When Louis

Gottschalk asserts that one of the historian's most important functions is to "check the looseness of others' generalizations about human experiences," [27] he is describing a very necessary function. But it is not likely to impress even the informed public which has been conditioned by a certain amount of vulgarization of the social sciences to think in terms of formula explanations of diverse social phenomena.

Nor, apart from the exceptional institution, will the historical approach find favor among those empowered to make research grants and who have a manifest preference for projects that are set up on a problem-solving basis with hypothesis, procedure, and tentative conclusions strait-jacketed into the application.

The trend in the social sciences toward the quantitative methods and techniques of the natural sciences—a trend strengthened by the development of an elaborate statistical methodology and the looming presence of IBM machines which cry out to be used if only to demonstrate, on occasion, banal and self-evident conclusions—has no counterpart in historiography. The historian's broad-gauged approach to subject matter and his concern with a myriad of conditioning, if not determining factors, causes him to look askance at the fragmentation of experience that is involved when the sociologist isolates social phenomena for the purpose of measuring relationships between variables with a seeming disregard of other factors.

Not all sociologists go along with this approach which C. Wright Mills has dubbed, "abstract empiricism." Mills himself has raised the standard of revolt with the slogan: "The sociological imagination is the ability to grasp history and biography and the relations between the two within society." And while the historian can only regard this as most encouraging, he must also recognize how little history has been used by sociologists to clarify differing conceptions of social organizations; to illuminate issues that divide sociologists such as the extent to which power is concentrated in American society and whether the pattern of American social mobility is unique or similar to that of the industrialized nations of Western Europe.[28]

C. Wilson Record speaks for many historians when he complains that sociologists "have failed to develop a coherent body of theory that would provide durable principles on which historians and others might draw in reshaping their approaches and interpretations." [29] This view coincides with that of David Riesman when he writes that compared to the new specialties that have emerged at the juncture of physics and chemistry or of physics and biology, the social sciences have been curiously static in their relationships.[30] To which, I would add, that the relationship between history and the social sciences has been more static still.

The historical craft is an ancient one with a long and frustrating experience with historical law—a tradition and experience which the sociologists have not shared.   When I, as an historian, read even so cautious a statement as that by Ralph Ross and Ernest Van Der Haag: "History probably cannot be a science in the full sense of the word until there is a unified social science.   And even then, its laws might be thought of as 'belonging' to unified social science rather than to history itself," [31] I begin to feel as old as Herodotus and that these two sociologists were born yesterday.

Scientific historiography, despite three quarters of a century of practice, still means little more than a conscientious search for facts and an attempt at their interpretation so as to discover what went on in the past.   Plainly, historians today know that they are further from the concept of all-embracing historical law than John Fiske and John W. Burgess considered themselves as being circa 1890.   Frederick Jackson Turner, in 1910, sounded more sanguine of the results of history's borrowings from allied fields than do the guildsmen of today of the contribution of the social sciences.   We estimate, and no sensible man will deny, that our historical judgments have become better informed—but it is also clear that we can make no final reckoning on that score.   We can console ourselves that the conclusions of science lack certainty, but the degree to which history is more or less uncertain than science is impossible for a finite mind to evaluate.   Perhaps, in a universe without hitching posts, we can ask no more of scientific method than that it remain a somewhat undefined means whereby honest men seek the truth of what happened in history.

NOTES

Sections of this article have appeared in *Diogenes*, **XXVI** (Summer, 1959), 107–22.

1. Cited in Michael Kraus, *A History of American History* (New York, 1937), p. 232.

2. David Levin, *History as Romantic Art* (Stanford, Calif., 1959), pp. 24–25.

3. Calvin Hall, *A Primer of Freudian Psychology* (New York, 1955), pp. 13–14.

4. A. S. Eisenstadt, *Charles McLean Andrews* (New York, 1956), p. 29.

5. E. A. Freeman, *Comparative Politics* (London, 1873), p. 302.

6. H. B. Adams, "The Germanic Origin of New England Towns," *Johns Hopkins University Studies in Historical and Political Sciences,* 1st Ser., No. 2 (1882), p. 8.

7. Edward N. Saveth, *American Historians and European Immigrants, 1875–1925* (New York, 1948), pp. 16–31.

8. C. M. Andrews, "The Theory of the Village Community," *Papers of the American Historical Association,* V (New York, 1891), 47.

9. W. H. Jordy, *Henry Adams: Scientific Historian* (New Haven, Conn., 1952), pp. 74, 80–81.

10. Saveth, *American Historians and European Immigrants,* pp. 26–31.

11. Herman Ausubel, *Historians and Their Craft* (New York, 1950), pp. 216, 232–36.

12. Robert L. Schuyler, "Contingency in History," *Political Science Quarterly,* LXXIV (September, 1959), 330–31.

13. Charlotte W. Smith, *Carl Becker: On History and the Climate of Opinion* (Ithaca, N.Y., 1956), pp. 46, 71–75.

14. F. J. Turner, *The Frontier in American History* (New York, 1920), pp. 322, 331–33.

15. M. A. De Wolfe Howe, *James Ford Rhodes, American Historian* (New York, 1929), pp. 149–50, 277.

16. C. A. Beard, *An Economic Interpretation of the Constitution of the United States* (New York, 1913), pp. 16–17.

17. Robert E. Brown, *Charles Beard and the Constitution* (Princeton, N.J., 1956), p. 93.

18. L. R. Sorenson, "Historical Currents in America," *American Quarterly,* VII (Fall, 1955), 246.

19. L. R. Sorenson "[Review of] *Nature and Historical Experience* . . . by John Herman Randall, Jr.," *American Historical Review,* LXIV (October, 1958), 70–71.

20. Dwight E. Lee and Robert N. Beck, "The Meaning of Historicism," *American Historical Review,* LIX (April, 1954), 577, discusses a variety of meanings ascribed to historicism.

21. William A. Williams, "A Note on Charles Austin Beard's Search for a General Theory of Causation," *American Historical Review,* LXII (October, 1956), 59–80.

22. James C. Malin, *Essays on Historiography* (Lawrence, Kan., 1946), Chap. IV, pp. 109–68; Richard D. Challener and Maurice Lee, Jr., "History and the Social Sciences," *American Historical Review,* LXI (January, 1956), 331.

23. Hannah Arendt, "History and Immortality," *Partisan Review,* XXIV (Winter, 1957), 11–35.

24. Louis Gottschalk, "The Historian's Use of Generalization," in Leonard D. White, ed., *The State of the Social Sciences* (Chicago, 1956), p. 450.

25. For reservations by historians concerning the social-science approach of Handlin and Hofstadter in certain of their books, see *American Historical Review,* LXII (July, 1957), 927; *ibid.,* LXI (April, 1956), 667. Handlin's severest and most effective critic has been Dr. John Higham.

26. Mirra Komarovksy, ed., *Common Frontiers of the Social Sciences* (Glencoe, Ill., 1957), p. 271.

27. Gottschalk, "The Historian's Use of Generalization," in White, ed., *The State of the Social Sciences,* p. 441.

28. C. W. Mills, *The Sociological Imagination* (New York, 1959), p. 6; Leonard Reissman, *Class in American Society* (Glencoe, Ill., 1960), pp. 196–203; S. M. Lipset and Reinhard Bendix, *Social Mobility in Industrial Society* (Berkeley, Calif., 1959), p. 11. See the review of this book by Oscar Handlin in *American Historical Review,* LXV (January, 1960), 339.

29. C. W. Record, "Of History and Sociology," *American Quarterly,* XI (Fall, 1959), 427.

30. David Riesman, "Some Observations on the 'Older' and the 'Newer' Social Sciences," in White, ed., *The State of the Social Sciences,* p. 339.

31. Ralph Ross and Ernest Van Der Haag. *The Fabric of Society* (New York, 1957), p. 250.

THOUGHTS ON THE CONFEDERACY

by Robert C. Black, III

TRINITY COLLEGE
HARTFORD, CONNECTICUT

AS WE PASS the middle years of the twentieth century, it would, seem as if American historiography, American folklore, even the American mind itself, were revolving about a dominant center of gravity called the "Civil War." It is a striking phenomenon, and it evidently springs from something more significant than the imminence of centenary observances. Our hearts seem not, in these days, to belong to the contemporary world at all. Somehow, amid the by-products of nuclear fission, we sniff the smoke of Shiloh.

Nor is the current interest in the Civil War an unprecedented thing. Americans never have been disposed to forget their national tragedy. They vicariously have assaulted—or defended— Marye's Heights for more than ninety years. Andersonville has remained, since 1864, a favorite theme for the exercise of the national indignation. Moreover, the fascination of the period has commanded the attention of the professional historian quite as strongly as that of the layman. In fact, the War of the Rebellion has been subjected to so much serious scholarship that other areas of United States history have suffered real neglect. The Wilderness of Spotsylvania County long since has choked the life from the Argonne Forest; already Leyte Gulf lies submerged in Hampton Roads.

But if today's obsession with the Civil War is but the climax of an established tradition, it is nevertheless marked by certain characteristics of its own. Fifty years ago, the emphasis lay upon easily understood symbols like Grant, Sherman, and Lincoln the Humanitarian. Nowadays the dominant features are Lincoln the distracted War President and—rather conspicuously—the Confederate States of America.

Much of the recent proliferation of Confederate material lies, to be sure, beyond (or below) the scope of the serious historian, and, if the book review supplements are frequently gaudy with Southern battle flags, it does not necessarily indicate that we know a great deal more about the Confederacy than we did a quarter-century ago. But serious historians have been examining the subject for nearly a hundred years, for as long as they have been studying the Civil War itself. Thanks to their labors, anyone with sufficient time and energy will soon possess a wider knowledge of the Confederacy than the Confederates themselves. He even may come to understand the Confederacy.

Such understanding is not easy to acquire; it demands not merely reading, but critical reading. Confining oneself to serious historians is no short cut, for a serious historian is not always a satisfactory one. As everyone knows, he may be prejudiced with respect to party, nationality, society, or economics. He may be afflicted with the heinous habit of "present-mindedness." Or he may so neglect the conceptions and beliefs of his own time as to be nearly unintelligible. He may marshal disciplined armies of facts, without explanation of what they may mean. Or he may be so intent upon esoteric implications and trends as to produce an invertebrate essay, quite devoid of proper framework. He perchance may go so far as to waste everyone's time by asking unnecessary questions and providing equally unnecessary answers. Serious historians of the Confederacy have been guilty of all these things; but they have most commonly committed two offenses: the sin of prejudice and the sin of the unnecessary question.

Early chroniclers of the Rebellion tended toward personal prejudice. It was inevitable; they had lived through the crisis themselves. Prejudice of this sort was frequently marked by nothing more vigorous than a tacit assumption of moral or legal superiority, but a few authors let themselves go. There were Northerners like Henry Wilson, who, in three fat volumes, contrasted his New England standards to those of the Southern slave power—and found them good.[1]   There were Southerners like the Richmond editor, Edward A. Pollard, who was possibly less satanic in his opinion of Yankees than of Jefferson Davis, but who could assert that the war was "brought on by Northern insurgents against the authority of the constitution." [2]   Even a moderate like Alexander H. Stephens could scarcely be expected to bestow unqualified praise upon his recent enemy; as a matter of fact, his *Constitutional View of the Late War between the States* is not history at all but an *apologia* in which everyone but the author is in the wrong.   And this influence of memory lingered to the turn of the century and beyond.   It is all too evident in James Schouler, who goes so far as to refer to "slavery's grand levy of war against the United States." [3]   It even is discernible amid the blunt and honest paragraphs of James Ford Rhodes.[4]

It must not be assumed that these earlier writers composed briefs in lieu of history; the great majority endeavored to be fair, and most of them to a degree succeeded.   But not until there appeared a generation which was free from vivid recollections of the Confederate period could efforts at impartiality begin to produce steady yields.   This was especially true of Southern authors; it is easier for a victor to achieve post-bellum lucidity than for the vanquished.   Indeed, there is almost no recognized Civil War historian of the first generation who is also a Southerner.   The writers of Confederate military memoirs were not, strictly speaking, historians, nor was the oddly brilliant Pollard.   The Charles W. Ramsdells, Douglas Southall Freemans, and Avery Cravens who finally did appear were not of the Confederacy at all.   The publication of acceptable Civil War history was thus a conspicuously Yankee enterprise until nearly 1900, and there is more Yankee prejudice than Rebel venom in the superseded volumes that line the stacks.

It was easier in the twentieth century.   Youthful historians could at last respect—if not admire—the men who had shot their grandfathers.   They could, moreover, put their new-found impartiality to work under conditions undreamed of by their predecessors.   The official records, Army and Navy, Union and Confederate, stood in massive, complete rows upon the shelves of every sizable public library. The harvest of memoirs and reminiscences—political, military, and social—had been gathered in. Papers, letters, memorabilia of every sort, were being swept from the desks and attics of the recently deceased and into conveniently located state, federal, and university archives. In such a milieu, it was inevitable that pens should scratch and typewriters clack from the Laurentian Shield to the Florida Keys. It likewise was inevitable that a percentage of the work turned out should be of a superior quality.

It is also, to a commendable extent, fair-minded history, history produced by a people reunified, if not wholly among themselves, at least in the face of the outer world. The sin of sectional prejudice, where it is evident at all, is chiefly of the venial sort, more whimsical than meaningful. There are disagreements, to be sure, and numerous bookish arguments over details, but no longer are they inevitably based upon the position of an author's childhood home with respect to the Ohio River. A major historical failing had been expatiated, and Clio herself must have been pleased—whereupon a number of her leading devotees turned with obvious gusto to the commission of another, and more serious, offense.

This was the afore-mentioned sin of the unnecessary question. More specifically, they undertook to inquire whether secession, the Confederacy, and the Civil War were inevitable, or, in the approved jargon of the guild, "irrepressible." It was from the first an insecure point of departure for an exercise in mature scholarship; the question itself was not even original. It had been raised as early as 1858 by Senator William H. Seward, who presently wished he had not done so. But it was a fascinating question, and it was not long before whole battalions of "repressibles" and "irrepressibles" were snatching at each other's banners along a flaming Cemetery Ridge of argument, to the unconcealed delight of the observers posted upon the Round Tops of learned journalism. It was, and continues to be, an exciting show. But it is a most inefficient way in which to apply serious historical standards to the problems of secession, the Confederate States and the Civil War. And it has gone on too long; what at first resembled a promising Gettysburg has become a Stone's River of sterile indecision.

Indeed, does not this whole concern with what is "repressible" and what is "irrepressible" fail utterly to face up to the *fact* of secession and of the Confederacy? Is it not time to view the Confederacy, and the war it occasioned, from quite another outlook? One would think so, and if the more logical alternatives have been examined already, they may at least afford the advantage of a solid foundation.

Let us begin by considering anew our particular subject. The Confederacy has been many things to many people, historians included, but upon two facts everyone seems agreed. It *existed*. And it *failed*.

Two questions come immediately to mind. *Why* did it exist? *Why* did it fail? These are, to be sure, very simple questions. But they are cogent; they strike at the heart of the matter. There is no skirting of the periphery, no fruitless inquiry as to whether the Confederacy *should* have existed or *should* have failed.

These questions furthermore confront us with no inconvenient historical vacuum. They already have been answered and answered repeatedly. Practically every delver in the Confederate garden has tackled them at one time or another. The difficulty is chiefly one of emphasis; there has been too little recognition of essentials; the straight and obvious questions have not elicited straight and logical answers. The stuff of such answers is there, but it has been left in ill-assorted array upon the bank, while we have gone floundering off across the marshes of "irrepressibility." It behooves us, I think, to attempt a rearrangement, to classify our jumbled information under two understandable headings. One portion will appertain to the first of our fundamental queries: Why did the Confederacy exist? The other will reflect the second question: Why did it fail?

Once the sorting has been completed, it will be most convenient to consider first the assembled replies to the second question. For one thing, it is the less difficult of the two. Moreover, a fairly careful examination will reveal a rather strong sense of agreement among the replies that have been given to it.

It is not of course to be assumed that writers of history have spoken with a single voice upon the problem of the Confederate failure. Quite the contrary: they have proposed, at one time or another, an almost infinite number of explanations, ranging from the alleged provincialism of Mrs. Jefferson Davis to a chronic shortage of draft horses. Some of these explanations are impressive; others are patently frivolous; not all are by any means consistent with each other. But a number of them have come, over the years, to stand out from their fellows. Authors past and present, Northern and Southern, keep returning to them; they seem nearly, if not quite, unavoidable. Furthermore, the majority of them are scarcely controversial at all; to the experienced connoisseur of the Confederacy they appear both simple and unexceptionable. Certain of them will occur at once to any neophyte.

A case in point is the universally recognized superiority of the Federal physical strength. There is hardly a commentator upon the Confederacy who fails either to cite this or at least to assume its validity. From Rhodes to Allan Nevins, the chorus runs very much the same. There is a vague tendency among earlier writers to discuss Yankee omnipotence in terms of numbers of men and quantities of guns; since 1900, it has been mildly fashionable to emphasize the Federal industrial potential. But it is all cut from the same obvious cloth. There is no question but that the South was overwhelmed. "The preponderance of power on the part of the North was so great," declares Robert Selph Henry, "that nothing short of perfect performance by Southern statecraft and Southern command could have reversed the result." [5]

The performance, of course, was not perfect. Students of the Confederacy have been almost equally conscious of the deficiencies of Southern finance. The war was hardly over when Pollard asserted that they influenced the result as potently as "any other cause." [6] No one has seriously disagreed with him since. To be sure, some writers have contended that a more vigorous and intelligent management could have prevented the chaos. Pollard himself thought so, as did Alexander H. Stephens.[7] Thirty-five years later, John C. Schwab was not quite so sure, though he could think of little that was good to say of Treasury Secretary Memminger.[8] Nathaniel W. Stephenson, writing against the disconcerting background of the First World War, wondered if the Richmond government should not have conscripted wealth as well as men, though he admitted that in the 1860s "such an idea was too advanced for any group of Americans."[9] More recently, E. Merton Coulter and Clement Eaton have suggested that there might have been much heavier taxation and rather less borrowing.[10] But differences of this sort are, after all, minor. There is no dispute over the essentials: Confederate finance *did* fall into appalling condition, and it *was* a major element in the Southern defeat.

Even less controversy seems to have arisen over the matter of Confederate morale. That it finally disintegrated, and that it was a serious factor in the ultimate failure, appear seldom to be questioned. It is particularly noteworthy that responsible Southern writers show little disposition to evade the issue, despite its implicit denial of a major doctrine of the United Daughters of the Confederacy. Pollard (who was no descendant, but the real thing) openly admits to a steady decline in the will to fight. "After all," he concludes, "the main condition of the success of the Confederacy was simply *resolution,* the quality that endures."[11] Clement Eaton even views the war as a race against declining morale on *both* sides, and concedes that the South lost decisively.[12] "Morale was the most potent weapon the South had," adds E. Merton Coulter. "They lost their weapon, and, therefore, the war."[13] Subscribers to the decaying-morale concept comprise an impressive list. Included are Rhodes, Schouler, Edward Channing, Charles A. Beard, A. B. Moore, William E. Dodd, Frederick L. Paxson, Arthur C. Cole, and James G. Randall. There are numerous others. Against weight of this kind, the United Daughters of the Confederacy cannot hope to make headway.

Anyone who has troubled to read the Confederate record in the original will have been struck by the bad feeling that developed between the Davis administration and certain of the States. It was an obviously unfortunate situation from the Southern point of view, and it involved sooner or later a large proportion of the Southern leadership. But it seems to have been accepted as a matter of course, and this is possibly the reason why the "states' rights" explanation of the Confederate defeat received so little emphasis at the hands of early investigators. To be sure, constitutional quarrels were alluded to from the beginning, but they did not achieve major historiographic stature until the first decade of this century. Since then, the "states' rights" vogue has flourished unchecked, and if the endorsement of every important worker in the field over a period of fifty years can be taken as proof of authenticity, it is clear that we must accept as valid the idea that the Confederacy died, in part, of states' rights.

Of the more frequently cited reasons for the secessionist failure, only one has become a matter of notable dispute. This is the question of the adequacy of President Jefferson Davis. The Southern chief executive was of course one of the most conspicuous of Confederate figures. One might even speculate whether the superior publicity nowadays enjoyed by Robert E. Lee and Stonewall Jackson were not essentially a post-bellum product. It was Davis, not Lee, who appeared upon Secretary John H. Reagan's postage stamps; it was Davis, not Stonewall Jackson, whom the more enthusiastic Yankees threatened to hang from a sour-apple tree. It was Davis who had the more extensive wartime press, who loomed largest as a controversial personality, South as well as North.

He remains controversial to this day. To be sure, no one has seriously attempted to translate his martyrdom into sainthood; his critics, both hostile and friendly, seem in basic accord as to his personal weaknesses. But the naked claim that the Southern Confederacy died of Jefferson Davis is another matter. It is here that we encounter a sturdy academic give-and-take.

The thesis is of ancient vintage; it dates back to the Confederacy itself. It cannot be wholly ascribed to any single source, but the venomous pen of Edward A. Pollard had much to do with it, and it likewise was Pollard who did most to keep the tradition

alive after Appomattox.[14]   Alexander H. Stephens soon provided
a semiofficial endorsement, as did the rationalistic memoirs of a
number of former generals, particularly Joseph E. Johnston.[15]
That later historians should be affected by the legend was probably inevitable.   James Schouler was one of the first; he in fact
went quite overboard, describing Davis as arbitrary, impatient,
and dictatorial, the very image of a military despot.[16]   Another
was Rhodes, though his criticism was far more restrained.   Mut-
terings of disapproval have continued to the present.   Clement
Eaton and Allan Nevins endeavor to be fair, but are clearly of
the anti-Davis persuasion.[17]   Coulter is more sharp: "The American Revolution had its Washington; the Southern Revolution
had its Davis.   Therein lay in part the historic fact that the one
succeeded and the other failed." [18]

On the other hand, there has been much variation in the intensity of the theme.   The initial bitterness of Pollard has experienced a good deal of dilution.   Moreover, the Confederate
executive has not lacked a few positive accolades.   At the turn of
the century, John W. Burgess thought that the selection of Davis
was "the best that could have been made" and implied that disaster came in spite of, not because of, his leadership.[19]   Edward
Channing is even warmer in his praise; Davis, he thinks, ranks
high above his associates in terms of "power and sincerity." [20]
Indeed, there never has been any general agreement upon the
Davis issue, at least insofar as he can be cited as a positive factor in
the ruin of his own government.   But one thing does remain
clear: the Confederate president, with all his tight-strung intelligence, his rigid courtliness, his iron dedication, had not the stature of the Civil War President of the United States.

We have by no means examined the full list of Southern defects, nor would such an exercise prove useful.   A thousand writers have been finding things wrong with the Confederacy for
many years; their comments vary as the patterns of snow crystals.
Yet it may be asserted that students of the Confederate failure do
agree upon certain fundamentals.   The military potential of the
North (in its broadest sense) was too great for the South.   Southern financial resources and techniques were wholly inadequate.

Southern morale failed under pressure. Southern conceptions of states' rights (and local rights) proved inconsistent with the war effort required. Here, in brief, are the principal answers to the second principal question—why did the Confederacy fail? And if historiographic favor can confer verity, the answers are valid.

To cope with the first principal question is not so easy. Historians have been dealing with the problem of the origins and nature of the Confederacy since before Appomattox. Upon it they sometimes agree—and often disagree. Their results are compounded of an infinite variety of the good, the bad, the indifferent, and the bizarre. There at first seems little that can be arranged into a discernible pattern; there is much that is open to argument. He who would resolve the matter merely by classifying books will risk losing himself amid the fire and brimstone of an antiquarian Chickamauga.

Let us examine for a moment the more striking issues. Here James G. Randall points to a popular, "nationalist" movement, an instance of a romantically conscious minority, wherein the old instinct for "union" had become geographically reduced to apply to Southerners only.[21] Goldwin Smith, a classic expounder of late nineteenth-century liberalism, naturally agrees, but nevertheless chooses to emphasize the sins of a plantocratic despotism, a slave power that "flaunted its banner in the face of humanity." [22] George Fort Milton features a common revolt in the Abraham Lincoln tradition; there was, he declares, "no secession, only an unsuccessful revolution, a fight that failed." [23] Woodrow Wilson wonders if it were not all a sham, a device to frighten Yankees into accepting Southern concepts of the "Old Union." [24] Charles A. Beard reduces everything to simple profit and loss; to him, "Southernism" is merely agrarianism turned militant against encroaching high finance and high industry.[25] John W. Burgess preaches mystical stuff of an American nation that first must suffer to the utmost in order that it may rise again: "This, then, was in the plan of universal history, the meaning of secession: The hastening of emancipation and nationalisation . . . Slavery and 'State Sovereignty' were the fetters which held them back, and these fetters had to be screwed down tight in order to provoke the nation to strike them off at one fell blow, and free itself, and assert its supremacy forevermore." [26]   "The Confederacy was a plot!" cries French Ensor Chadwick.   "The movement . . . [was] one of the politicians and not of the people." [27]   "It was nothing of the kind! " retorts Professor Coulter.   "Secession . . . merely recognized a division of the country that already was almost complete except for the bonds of government." [28]   And, as if all this were not enough, the scene is further confused by the presence of assorted cavaliers, conservatives, Nordics, discredited politicians, and the clearly mad.

Nor have the historians gathered conspicuously about any particular standard.   Certain arguments, to be sure, have enjoyed a greater following than others.   The defense-of-slavery concept has always attracted a crowd.   So too has the defense-of-states'-rights idea.   Economic determinism can claim numerous friends, though many subscribe to the faith with reservations.   Southern Nationalism has had a powerful appeal.   Complex emotion, simple fear, deficient statesmanship, mob psychology, all frequently are hailed as Confederate fundamentals.

It is so very complicated!   Indeed, we may ask if the present question, the nature of the Confederacy, can be answered at all by an historiographic exercise.   We may ask if the study of the Confederacy itself will not be more rewarding than any comparing of books about the Confederacy.   We may ask if it is not high time to renounce the academic arena and to assume an alternative position of our own, to examine the receding Civil War against the clear background of the whole of American history.   For as we stand in the midst of the twentieth century, it is becoming evident that the Confederacy was neither a semi-isolated phenomenon nor the climax and dénouement of a self-centered "Middle Period."   It marked no historical Great Divide, separating the story of the United States into two unrelated watersheds.   It was something less, and it was something more.   The Confederacy was in essence a chapter in the long story of the South.

One may express it in yet another way: he who would understand the Confederacy must first understand the South.

What, then, is the South?   Wherein does it differ from a

North, an East, or a West? The answer is not so simple as may
at first appear. It is not an ordinary case of geocentric latitude.
The valley of the Shenandoah is bisected by the lately notorious
thirty-eighth parallel; so also is the valley of the Upper Gunni-
son in the Colorado Rockies. The former is traditionally reckoned as Southern; the latter is not Southern at all. Charleston
and San Diego are nearly equidistant from the equator. Charleston is not merely Southern; it is very deeply so. San Diego, for
all its palms and sunshine, is no more Southern than Seattle.

Nor is it simply a question of geographic environment. Land-
scapes can play confusing tricks. Natural forces have produced
basically similar results upon the banks of both the Connecticut
and the James. Yet one is Northern; the other belongs to the
South. On the other hand, the Piedmont hills and the Okefeno-
kee Swamp are conspicuously dissimilar, yet both appertain to
the South, indeed, to a single Southern state. By a similar token,
Boston, Massachusetts, and Prairie View, Kansas, possess a common *mystique*, which we regard as Northern.

Is it a case of economics? It is a temptation to think so;
there is a hidden Charles A. Beard in most of us, and the concept
of an industrial North locked in mortal combat with an agrarian
South is strikingly colorful. It is upsetting to recall that it is
not valid. But we cannot argue with facts. We know in our
hearts that the North was still, in 1861, far more agricultural
than industrial. And we are obliged to concede that the Bir-
minghams and Atlantas of today have so far done precious little
to remake the South into the authentic Yankee image.

What, then, is this Southern foundation? What has been
common to this enormous land, these million square miles, which
nature patterned so variously and which man has made more varied still?

The answer, of course, is all around us. It crowds the pages
of contemporary newspapers with dispatches from Tuscaloosa,
Little Rock, Clinton, and Richmond. It pours from our loud-
speakers. It is the special nightmare of a thousand political candidates. Yet it is least of all a new thing. We discover it deep
in our public libraries. It starkly colors the census maps, decade

upon decade. It lies in half-forgotten archives, bearing dates a century, two centuries, old. It is quite traditional, very American, and altogether terrifying. It is the race problem.

In short, what we call the South has been rendered unique upon this continent by the presence there, in close association with Europeans, of *large numbers* of persons of African descent. And without such large numbers of Negroes, the South we have known—the half-manorial tidewater, the half-capitalist cotton kingdom, the New South of Henry Grady, the still newer South of the kudzu, Brahma cow, and branch factory—simply would not have come to pass. Without the Negro, the South would long since have joined the North to become the East. Without the Negro, there would have been no Wilmot Provisos, no compromise measures, no Alabama Platforms. Without the Negro, there would have been no Confederate States.

This may seem a gross oversimplification. It likewise will be remarked that it all has been said before. So it has; there is scarcely an historian of the Confederacy who has not referred to it, albeit a clique of economic determinists has endeavored to minimize its importance. But fundamentals are frequently worth repeating, and a reassertion of Confederate fundamentals would seem particularly timely. For the Confederacy, as a grand crisis chapter of Southern history, may yet possess the capacity to instruct.

Why did eleven Southern States secede? Why was there, by 1860, something that could fairly be described as "Southern Nationalism"? Was it the presence of the "plantation" as a characteristic socioeconomic unit? It seems incredible; the farms of the Old Northwest were fully as agrarian. Was it that old chestnut, the tariff? Hardly—the rates of 1860 were among the lowest on record, and the times were reckoned prosperous. Was it a simple plot, conceived in infamy? The idea is reminiscent of a Republican radicalism that is seventy-five years in its grave. What, then, *was* the issue? The primary sources—the newspapers, letters, orations, diaries, pamphlets, and tracts of the time—fairly thunder an answer: slavery.

On the other hand, the Confederacy was more than a simple

manifestation of an institution. The South defended slavery bitterly, but an unprejudiced consideration of the whole matter renders inescapable the conclusion that it was not of itself the ultimate ark of the Confederate covenant. Indeed, a majority of students, from Pollard to Nevins, have made clear the basic role of slavery as a device to assure the supremacy of the white race in a half-Negro society. To protect that device, half-a-million slaveless Southerners stood in line of battle from the Ozarks to the Chesapeake. They and over four million slaveless neighbors thought that device *indispensable*.

Therein lay the tragedy, the monumental error, of the Confederacy. For slavery was not a *sine qua non*. There were, in fact, numerous alternatives, all of them consistent with the white supremacy principle, and a number of intelligent Southerners came to realize it while yet a Confederacy remained. These were the leaders who sought to prop the distintegrating structure by placing arms in the hands of the slaves, and there was a certain wisdom in their apparent madness. To be sure, *armed* Negroes necessarily meant the end of the "peculiar institution," but they also represented a possible instrument of defense, which, if successful, would enable the Southern white to face the consequent reorganization of his society upon his own terms, without reference to the demands of any Northern radical.

If these be valid considerations, is it not reasonable to regard the Confederacy as basically an effort to maintain a system of race control? Is this not the ultimate substance, the nucleus of a complex atom? Are not the other factors—the "Southern way of life," the dislike of Yankee money grubbing, the chivalry concept, the gentry obsession, the platform oratory, the slavery institution itself—mere satellite particles, quite under the influence of the dominant thing? Again we may ask it: Without the Negro difficulty, could there have been a Confederate States?

One may express it yet another way. *The Confederacy was peculiarly a white man's republic.* Its primary mission was to protect the asserted interests of the white race across a broad belt of North America. It was not of itself fundamental; it was but one of a number of Southern incarnations. It represented one possible way of achieving a goal, and it turned out to be an in-effective way.   But if the Confederacy lost its battle and died, we cannot assume that the whole campaign was wrecked, that the *South* was destroyed.   Reconstruction to the contrary notwith-standing, despite burgeoning cities, crop diversification, and pro-gressive "Zeitgeists," real and imaginary, the *South* has remained. That this should be so was grasped as early as 1868 by the shrewd, if uncritical, Pollard.[29]   And if the South no longer responds to disapprobation with rifle bullets, that has little to do with the underlying reality.

In fact, after the passage of nearly a century, it is becoming increasingly clear that the Southern Confederacy was no more than a very intense and vivid episode and that its destruction did not seriously affect the basic *Southern* substance.   An obsolete engine of white supremacy—slavery—was legally condemned; an emergency rig for keeping it in operation—secession—was dem-onstrated to be impractical.   That was all.   The essential sub-stance survived rather easily.

These are not, to repeat, new conceptions.   They have been broadly appreciated for a long time, and not alone by historians. But they deserve constant reemphasis.   For if the Southerner of a hundred years ago unwisely placed too many of his eggs in the worn-out basket of slavery, his Northern cousin was guilty of an equally profound lack of circumspection.   Together they pro-duced the greatest American disaster.

The War between the States was, indeed, a calamity so ter-rible as to justify every bit of the attention that since has been lavished upon it.   To this day, nothing can be so instructive as the contemplation of so great a crisis, and it is good that Ameri-cans should be committed so irresistably to its study.   Most espe-cially should we welcome the present vogue for *Confederate* his-tory.   For though the Confederacy is dead, the South which gave it birth is with us still.

NOTES

1. Henry Wilson, *History of the Rise and Fall of the Slave Power in America* (3 vols., Boston, 1872–77).

2. Edward A. Pollard, *The Lost Cause; a New Southern History of the War of the Confederates* (New York, 1866), pp. 43–44.

3. James Schouler, *History of the United States of America under the Constitution* (6 vols., New York, 1880–99), VI, 619.

4. James Ford Rhodes, *History of the United States from the Compromise of 1850* (9 vols., New York, 1900–29). See, for example, his attitude toward the secession of South Carolina, III, 117.

5. Robert Selph Henry, *The Story of the Confederacy* (New York, 1943), p. 1.

6. Pollard, *The Lost Cause,* p. 416.

7. *Ibid.,* p. 428; Alexander H. Stephens, *Constitutional View of the Late War between the States,* II, 569.

8. John C. Schwab, *The Confederate States of America, 1861–1865; a Financial and Industrial History of the South during the Civil War* (New York, 1901), p. 312.

9. Nathaniel W. Stephenson, *The Day of the Confederacy; a Chronicle of the Embattled South* (New Haven, 1919), p. 45.

10. E. Merton Coulter, *The Confederate States of America, 1861–1865* (Baton Rouge, 1950), p. 182; Clement Eaton, *A History of the Southern Confederacy* (New York, 1954), pp. 233–39.

11. Pollard, *The Lost Cause,* p. 659; see also pp. 728–29.

12. Eaton, *A History of the Southern Confederacy,* Chap. XIII.

13. Coulter, *The Confederate States of America,* p. 83.

14. See especially his *The Lost Cause,* pp. 386–87, wherein he particularly condemns Davis's choice of subordinates.

15. Stephens, *Constitutional View of the Late War,* II, 307–8, 500–1; Joseph E. Johnston, *Narrative of Military Operations, Directed, during the Late War between the States* (New York, 1874).

16. Schouler, *History of the United States of America under the Constitution,* VI, 65, 167, 169, 293.

17. Eaton regards Davis as thoroughly honest and courageous, but lacking in warmth; Nevins speaks of "two fatal qualities, selfishness and obstinacy." See Eaton, *Southern Confederacy,* pp. 49–50, and Allan Nevins, *The Emergence of Lincoln* (2 vols., New York, 1950), I, 23–24.

18. Coulter, *The Confederate States of America,* p. 105.

19. John W. Burgess, *The Civil War and the Constitution, 1859–1865* (2 vols., New York, 1901), I, 120.

20. Edward Channing, *A History of the United States* (6 vols., New York, 1905–25), VI, 626.

21. James G. Randall, *The Civil War and Reconstruction* (Boston, 1937), pp. 338–39.

22. Goldwin Smith, *The United States; an Outline of Political History, 1492–1871* (New York, 1893), p. 243.

23. George Fort Milton, *Conflict; the American Civil War* (New York, 1941), p. 4.

24. Woodrow Wilson, *A History of the American People* (5 vols., New York, 1902), IV, 208–9.

25. Charles A. and Mary R. Beard, *The Rise of American Civilization* (2 vols., New York, 1927). See, for example, II, 4.

26. Burgess, *The Civil War and the Constitution*, I, 135.

27. French Ensor Chadwick, *Causes of the Civil War, 1859–1861* (New York, 1906), p. 150.

28. Coulter, *The Confederate States of America*, p. 18.

29. Edward A. Pollard, *The Lost Cause Regained* (New York, 1868). See especially p. 164.

RADICAL RECONSTRUCTION

by Donald Sheehan

SMITH COLLEGE

NORTHAMPTON, MASSACHUSETTS

RECONSTRUCTION HISTORIOGRAPHY has been handicapped by even more than the usual quota of obstacles to objectivity.[1] Emotional tension and chaotic upheaval formed the background of the first accounts; unresolved questions about the position of the Negro in Southern society condition present writing. Indeed, the ancient issue of "states' rights" is still a lively one because of circumstances which have direct parallels in the Reconstruction period. It is difficult to separate contemporary judgments from historical analysis.

Yet sectional loyalties have declined in intensity. The first generation of commentators grappled with few of the complexities which bedevil today's writers. For such Northerners as Sidney Andrews and Henry Wilson,[2] the facts were simple and straightforward. The Southerners were traitors defeated in war and untrustworthy in peace. The Republican Party was the bulwark of patriotism whose domination of the South was essential to human decency and national survival.

The vanquished South spoke principally through the ballot box and the Ku Klux Klan while Reconstruction was in progress. When its viewpoint was presented in literary form in the 1880s, few could have been surprised. In a comprehensive volume edited by Hilary Herbert called *Why the Solid South?* [3] the Southerners defended their culture, asserted their respect for the best interests of the Negroes, and attacked the North for despotism, corruption, and violation of the constitutional rights of individuals and states. Those "carpetbaggers" who weren't thieving opportunists were misguided idealists whose subversive influence was at least as harmful.[4]

It was the Northern view which first underwent revision, and the journalists among the Northern writers who initially called attention to the disparity between Republican theories and Reconstruction practices under Congressional laws. Writing as eyewitnesses, James Pike and Charles Nordhoff,[5] among others, recorded their disappointment, even disgust, with the Southern governments. Basic to the failures they recorded were the revolutionary advance of the Negroes and the corruption of their carpetbag allies.

General historical developments tended to confirm this trend towards a Northern view more sympathetic to the Southern interpretation. Such writers as James G. Blaine and Green B. Raum continued in the 1880s to echo the arguments of the radical Republicans, but with less conviction and for a less enthusiastic audience.[6] The war and its memories were fading. The reforming zeal which had sustained the fight for Negro rights now focused upon the complex problems of easing the adjustment to an urban, industrial society. By a systematic but erroneous application of Darwinism, the Anglo-Saxons of the world were uniting to uphold the doctrine of their own racial superiority. The concept of the "white man's burden" to "civilize" inferior races was more in keeping with Southern views than Northern ones. In such an environment, the evaluation of black Reconstruction was likely to decline.

Spokesmen for the new historical viewpoint included James Ford Rhodes and William Dunning.[7] Rhodes's staunch Republican affiliations proved to be no barrier to a thorough denunciation of his party's Reconstruction policies. He condemned the partisanship of the motivation and deplored the results— "the worst government ever known in the United States." [8] He ascribed these evils to universal Negro suffrage. Dunning was even more significant in this revisionist school, chiefly because of the large number of productive scholars he trained in his seminar at Columbia University. Like Rhodes, he was a Northerner with what appears to today's historians to be a fundamental racial bias. The two writers also shared a somewhat ineffectual desire to integrate the study of Reconstruction with the national scene and to broaden it to include economic and social factors, as well as the political and ethical considerations on which their predecessors had dwelt almost exclusively.

Dunning's revisionism carried over into the period after the First World War. It was sustained, in part, by a natural division of labor which resulted in a predominance of Southerners in the field of Reconstruction history. Yet many arose to challenge this interpretation and it no longer represents, as it once did, a national synthesis. What support it retains may be found on both sides of the Mason-Dixon Line. Its most congenial soil is in the South, among spokesmen for the traditional sectional viewpoint. For example, in *The South during Reconstruction,* E. Merton Coulter explicitly attacks the efforts of the "revisionists" to depart from what he considers to be long-established facts.[9] A considerable body of non-Southern historians agree with this judgment.   J. G. Randall, in the highly respected *The Civil War and Reconstruction,* concluded his analysis by quoting, without comment, a passage from James Ford Rhodes identifying the Restoration of 1877 as the triumph of "respectable people," the "escape . . . from usurpatory rule," the "reestablishment of . . . intelligence and property." [10]

The reasons for the attack on this interpretation, mounting since the 1930s, are as complex as those for its creation and perhaps even more difficult to measure. The doctrine of Anglo-Saxon superiority, so respectable in the 1890s, has been relegated to the dustbin. And while a second-line defense has been founded on the Negroes' ignorance, as opposed to their innate inferiority, a retreat took place which undermined the South's basic position. Further, the historians' increasing disposition to think in broad economic and social terms has turned attention from "blame" and reduced the need for attacks and apologetics. If conservatives have rallied to Dunning, new social forces have produced in every section writers antagonistic to the "Old South," even in its newer forms. Among them can be found Southerners such as C. Vann

Woodward, David Donald, and Francis B. Simkins,[11] whose willingness to lay bare the South's shortcomings is as pronounced as the wish of Dunning's followers to exaggerate its virtues.

The explanation for the rejection of "Dunning-ism" becomes more explicit when one examines the work of Negro historians and the Marxists. As early as 1915, the Association for the Study of Negro Life began a general reevaluation of the role of Negroes in American civilization. Many individuals have contributed to the same end. However specialized the perspective, the writing of such men as Horace Mann Bond and John Hope Franklin [12] pointed to basic flaws in the traditional Anglo-Saxon picture of Reconstruction which had exaggerated the faults of Congressional Reconstruction and overlooked the shortcomings of the Restoration of 1877.

Marxists like James Allen, Herbert Aptheker, and William Du Bois [13] have seen Radical Reconstruction as a bright interlude between the disintegration of the agricultural autocracy of the slaveholders and the consolidation of power of the industrial bourgeoisie. As a democratic revolution, it was necessarily limited in scope and duration because of the immaturity of the working-class movement and because of the controlling self-interest of the industrialists. The latter theme is shared by non-Marxist writers, both liberal and conservative.

Thus, the present range of interpretation is wide, suggesting an accumulation of three quarters of a century rather than an approach to an accepted synthesis. The two sectional views in the first decades after the Civil War gave way to a single analysis in the Dunning period. But that unity has long since disappeared. An identifiable Southern thesis forms a continuous thread but many Southerners have repudiated it. Northern writers have little interest in defending the actions of the radical Republicans but can find many nonsectional reasons for attacking their opponents. There are still those who share Thaddeus Stevens's view that radical Reconstruction was not radical enough; others who echo Wade Hampton and the Klansmen.

Analysis remains comparatively simple at each end of the spectrum of interpretation—that is, for the traditional white Southerner and for the Marxist. But the area in between forms the main stream of historical belief, and within that stream there are so many crosscurrents that it is difficult to detect the direction of the flow. Perhaps it is fair to suggest that those who are not firmly committed to either extreme attempt to take both sides, sometimes in alternate paragraphs. Few there are who do not find some things to applaud and others to censure. Historians are firm in evaluating details and somewhat fuzzy in drawing final conclusions. The monographists take refuge in complexities; the textbook writers in indecision. It is this aspect of Reconstruction writing, not certainly its only characteristic, to which this paper draws attention.[14]

The reasons for this ambivalence, apart from the subject matter itself, lie deep in the American conscience. Reconstruction presented problems which could not be solved without violating some traditional ideals at the same time that others were implemented. Minority rights for the white Southerners sat on one end of the seesaw; the individual liberties of millions of Negro citizens on the other. A preference for gradual change was challenged by a situation which was intrinsically and unavoidably revolutionary. The general assumption that property rights and liberty were inseparable offered no guide to solve the problems of people whose liberty could be secured only by depriving other people of property. Neither the American Constitution nor the American experience could produce a formula. There was ample room for confusion then just as there is an understandable lack of finality about historians' opinions today.

But indecision is not only the product of ideological confusion; it arises also from professional training. At mid-century, historical method continues to be dominated by openmindedness rather than by precision. The receptivity of historians is not balanced by a capacity to reject. Objectivity has become a barrier to selectivity. It follows that most American historians are eclectic, impressed more by the variety of the past rather than by its unity. Every historical situation can thus be accorded its full measure of uniqueness. Theoretically, at least, the facts are never prearranged or prejudged. However, the eclecticism of many can be called a philosophy of history only be default. Too often it represents not a choice but a lack of choice. It is a way of believing yet remaining uncommitted.

It is a short step from openmindedness to fairness. Yet the eagerness to do justice to both sides, certainly a virtue of our trade, is also one of our greatest weaknesses. By confusing means with ends, we have managed often to permit moderation to take the place of judgment. A willingness to look at all the facts before drawing conclusions has been joined to the easy theory that the truth must lie somewhere between two extremes. At this point eclecticism becomes simple "middle-ism," and a method of arriving at truth becomes truth itself. If compromise is impossible in this form, there is the alternative of conceding to each side the truth of at least a part of its arguments and assuming that there is no conflict between them. Finally, "fairness" may require keeping in suspense what history decided long ago.

The Reconstruction period especially invites suspended and divided judgments. Not only does it present an irreconcilable conflict among American ideals; the facts themselves are confusing, incomplete, and incapable of speaking for themselves.

Thus the period has come to be described in balanced terms and in dualities which are often left unresolved. One of the most traditional of the latter asserts that although radical Reconstruction was managed by thieves, opportunists, and illiterates, it managed to produce constructive constitutional reforms. When James Ford Rhodes wrote that the period witnessed "the worst government ever known in the United States," [15] he observed also that the "constitutions which they adopted were on the whole moderate." [16]   Even E. Merton Coulter, speaking for the South in 1947, reported that "the constitutions were much better than the Southerners had even hoped for; in fact, some of them were kept for many years after the Southern whites again got control of their government." [17]   Accounts more favorable to Congressional Reconstruction naturally speak well of the constitutions, and it is difficult to find in the modern literature any author who does not have something positive to say of them.

This praise is often accompanied by surprise that anything

good could come from people so foul. To some historians, the constructive aspects of Reconstruction seem "miraculous"; others find them merely "strange." Such words do not seem to be included for literary effect. Indeed, coming after the typical description of radical legislatures, the reaction is most appropriate. Yet to consider such legislation so unexpected as to be "miraculous" raises serious questions about the adequacy of the analysis as a whole. Either the author means that readers will be surprised but he is not, in which event it would appear that something has been kept from the readers; or the author means that he himself is surprised, which is tantamount to an unintended confession of an incomplete understanding. What appears to be indicated is a reinterpretation of the forces which produced these fundamental laws. Dishonesty and opportunism could not. Neither could ignorance, vengeance, or hatred. By balancing infamous legislators with basic reform, historians have been "fair" at the cost of logic.

Then another set of opposites is usually added. It is common also to distinguish sharply between constructive laws and the manner in which those laws were put into effect. Necessary railroads were provided for, but corrupt men filled their pockets with money intended for their building. Government was made democratic, but the new office holders made a travesty of the legislative processes. There is no denying that facts support this analysis. But it is questionable that they make up a balance sheet quite so neat as we have become accustomed to. The implication that the personal manners of a state representative were as important as his voting record is certainly false, yet it is still current. James Pike's horror at the scene in South Carolina's capital, the inevitable list of that state's "legislative supplies" (including the Brussels carpets and ornamental cuspidors)—these are given weight in most of today's textbooks equal to that accorded the establishment of public schools or the abolishing of imprisonment for debt.

After an uneasy equilibrium has been established between good and bad, yet another set of weights is placed on the scale to change the force of the negative part of the appraisal and to make

suspect what has gone before.   Having explained the evils of Reconstruction in terms of the Southern situation, historians go on
to say that they were really national evils to be accounted for by
national trends.   Abuses originating in the ignorance and vindic-
tiveness of carpetbaggers, scalawags, and ex-fieldhands, become
instead the product of urbanization, expansion, and technology.

The attempt to link the South with national developments
was obviously necessary; Reconstruction scarcely took place in a
vacuum.   Yet the connections can be made in so indiscriminate a
manner as to add more confusion than light.   Today's need is
not the need to which the critics of nineteenth-century historians
responded.   These years of Southern history are blurred beyond
recognition when the uniqueness of the problems of the postwar
South is not fully recognized.   References to Boss Tweed and
Oakes Ames and the society which gave them their opportunities
create more problems of analysis than they solve when they are
used to explain Reconstruction.   The connection is real but as
yet poorly defined.

The efforts of the Southern whites to regain control are described in terms which leave the reader in another state of doubt.
Did they succeed with legitimate weapons or were criminal tactics employed?   It is easy to say both, which is what most historians assert.   But rarely does one see an attempt to measure
the comparative importance of votes and violence.   Even a final
evaluation of the Ku Klux Klan is left dangling.   We are told
that it is extralegal but are reminded of the vigilante committees
of the West and of the need for maintaining social order.   Its activities in persuading Negroes are mentioned in the same paragraph as those of the Union League, whose propagandizing activities are sometimes put forth to justify it.   As a further hedge,
it is usual to make a sharp—perhaps excessively sharp—distinction
between the Klan of the 1860s and the Klan of the twentieth century.   Only after it had deteriorated and officially disbanded is
the original Klan clearly condemned.

Parenthetically, a similar balance is commonly struck in the
analysis of the black codes of presidential Reconstruction.   They
were bad, but their kinship with the vagrancy laws of Northern

states is offered in explanation or extenuation. Their purpose of retaining a system of legal inferiority for the freedmen is coupled with a statement of the North's refusal to recognize the magnitude of the chaos created by the Thirteenth Amendment.

The fundamental question of the amount and character of the aid given by the federal government to the Negroes involves historians in further indecisions. It is not unusual for an individual writer to believe both that too much was done and that too little was done for them. Washington pampered the Negroes, but deserted them. They received excessive political prerogatives, but little or none of the land necessary for their sustained progress. The Freedmen's Bureau abused what power it had by becoming political, but it should have had more power.

Basic to this ambiguity are two factors mentioned above: a desire to be "fair" to both Negroes and white Southerners, and a difficulty in reconciling traditional democratic forms with the civil rights of millions of individual ex-slaves. Obviously, this is not wholly an historical problem. The present gropings for a practical application of the Supreme Court's decisions on desegregation mirror not only Reconstruction itself, but also historians' efforts during three quarters of a century to appraise it accurately.

Another favorite theme about the Reconstruction years erects still another dualism. The radicals, so most historians hold, can be divided into two parts according to their motives in supporting the Congressional solution to the problem of how and under what terms the South was to be readmitted to the Union. The first group—Charles Sumner is usually made its spokesman—is distinguished by its genuine concern for Negro rights. These were the humanitarians, the crusaders, the latter-day abolitionists eager to complete the job only begun by the Thirteenth Amendment. The second category—Roscoe Conkling, Benjamin Wade, and Oliver Morton are named to typify it—consists of the Republican partisans and the spokesmen for banking and industry. Having little regard for the freedmen except as pawns, they were willing to oppress the South but were uninterested in carrying out a genuine reform program. Presumably, they gained control of

Reconstruction policies some time after the original acts were passed in 1867.

To some extent these "new radicals" offer a refuge to historians unable to decide between the primacy of Negro rights and Southern rights. While the "old radicals," the Charles Sumners, deserve some kind of respect, the self-seeking spoilsmen are the ideal whipping boys. Perhaps this is one reason why they tend to be emphasized increasingly. It is left to the Marxists to find the largest place within Reconstruction for "democratic idealism."

But to condemn the new radicals, however much they may deserve it, is not to make a judgment about the whole of Reconstruction but only about a part of it. The present tendency to make them the central fact of Reconstruction leads not only to oversimplification, but to distortion and even to a "conspiracy" thesis. The latter involves asserting that Reconstruction ended in 1877 because Northern industrialists already had penetrated the South economically and decided to substitute white economic allies for Negro political allies. Hence, the withdrawal of troops. The analysis rests on the assumption that the new radicals, in and out of office, actually were in a position to control policy and to continue Congressional Reconstruction if they wished to. The facts are quite different. The return of the Southern states to "conservative" government resulted from many forces and came not because of the new radicals but largely despite them. It did not occur suddenly in 1876 or 1877 after decisions were reached in smoke-filled rooms by powerful individuals; it was the product of innumerable votes cast in North and South over a considerable number of years. Hayes did not institute a policy; he contributed merely a final step to a long evolution that began when the first Southern state overcame Republican rule in 1869.

Looked at from the standpoint of Negro rights, the failure of Congressional Reconstruction cannot be attributed to the indifference of Northern capitalists and politicians. Regardless of their motivation, they were willing to go farther in the 1870s than popular opinion would permit them to go. For better or worse, the American people made the decision to have the white South substantially control its own destinies. The operations of the new radicals in 1876 are better thought of as salvaging operations than as policy-making. Hayes was not their candidate, and his Southern policies scarcely met with their approval.

What needs to be emphasized in connection with the end of Reconstruction is not the machinations of businessmen but the bases of public judgment. The problem was not a devil named "greed" or "industrialism." Rather, it was a commitment to long-standing national ideals. Americans preferred civil government to military government. They were concerned with democratic processes in their traditional senses. These included a regard for local self-government and a federal structure, a nonpartisan basis for the franchise and a free choice of leaders. There was also a distaste for "bloody shirts" and a monolithic majority based upon a single standard of hatred and distrust.

Self-interest was present, too, but not most significantly in the form of railroad lobbies. Reconstruction faded during depression years. The people who voted it out were not "robber barons" or their lieutenants. Instead, they were people angry at the failures of industrialism. The Democratic majority elected to the House of Representatives in 1874, and again in 1876, reflected a political alliance new to the postwar world. One segment consisted of farmers, Northern and Southern, more impressed with the problems of agriculture than the problems of Civil War sectionalism. In 1890, a similar coalition was to defeat another "Force Bill," sponsored by latter-day new radicals, because of a common interest in monetary reform.

Thus, Reconstruction ended not for cabalistic reasons but for democratic ones. Its end did not represent the triumph of industrialism over idealism; the converse is more nearly correct. Yet Reconstruction conceived as a popular decision involves us in the dilemma with which we began. How do we evaluate a situation in which good American principles consigned millions of people to second-class citizenship?

One of the solutions has been equivocation to which reference has been made. This has not made easy a final judgment. It would be inaccurate to record either a complete success or a complete failure. Historians have felt free to criticize its shortcomings from a number of viewpoints; most of them have been less than willing to acknowledge the impossibility of a solution consistent with all the national ideals.

There is general agreement, then, that for a variety of reasons this was a "tragic era." But the awareness of tragedy is relieved by the knowledge that conditions could have been far worse. The words of James Bryce lend comfort: "There was never a civil war or rebellion . . . followed by so few severities." [18] It seems curious that the solace is offered only to one end of the seesaw, extending just to the white Southerners who are asked to remember that no one was hanged for political crimes, that practically no land was confiscated, that the sequels of other civil wars were far more painful for the losers. But what shall historians say to the Negroes who have yet to receive the full benefits of constitutional amendments passed three quarters of a century ago? For them the "tragic era" began at the moment it ended for ex-Confederates.

NOTES

1. I am indebted to a Columbia University Master's essay by Elaine Englander entitled Reconstruction in Historical Thought for a general survey of interpretations since 1865, and to the following articles for summaries of recent trends: Howard K. Beale, "On Rewriting Reconstruction History," *American Historical Review*, XLV, 807–27; John Hope Franklin, "Whither Reconstruction Historiography?" *Journal of Negro Education*, XVII, No. 4 (1948), 446–61; Francis B. Simkins, "New Viewpoints of Southern Reconstruction," *Journal of Southern History*, V (February, 1939), 49–61; T. Harry Williams, "An Analysis of Some Reconstruction Attitudes," *Journal of Southern History*, XII (November, 1946), 469–86.

2. Sidney Andrews, *The South since the War* (Boston, 1866); Henry Wilson, *History of Reconstruction Measures of the 39th and 40th Congresses, 1865–1868* (Hartford, 1868); and his *History of the Rise and Fall of the Slave Power in America* (Boston, 1872).

3. Hilary A. Herbert, ed., *Why the Solid South?* (Baltimore, 1890).

4. Myrta Avary, *Dixie after the War* (New York, 1906), p. 312.

5. James S. Pike, *The Prostrate State; South Carolina under Negro Government* (New York, 1874); Charles Nordhoff, *The Cotton States in the Spring and Summer of 1875* (New York, 1876).

6. James G. Blaine, *Twenty Years of Congress* (Norwich, 1893); Green B. Raum, *The Existing Conflict between Republican Government and Southern Oligarchy* (Washington, 1884).

7. James Ford Rhodes, *History of the United States* (New York, 1900); William A. Dunning, *Essays on the Civil War and Reconstruction* (New York, 1904), and his *Reconstruction, Political and Economic, 1865–1877* (New York, 1907).

8. Rhodes, *History of the United States,* VI, 324.

9. E. Merton Coulter, *The South during Reconstruction, 1865–1877* (Baton Rouge, 1947).

10. James G. Randall, *The Civil War and Reconstruction* (Boston, 1937), p. 858.

11. See, for example, C. Vann Woodward, *Reunion and Reaction* (New York, 1956); Simkins, "New Viewpoints of Southern Reconstruction"; David H. Donald, "The Scalawag in Mississippi Reconstruction," *Journal of Southern History,* X (November, 1944), 447–60.

12. Horace Mann Bond, *Negro Education in Alabama* (Chicago, 1937); Franklin, "Whither Reconstruction Historiography?"

13. James Allen, *Reconstruction: The Battle for Democracy, 1865–1876* (New York, 1937); Herbert Aptheker, *To Be Free—Studies in American Negro History* (New York, 1948); William Edward Burghardt Du Bois, *Black Reconstruction* (New York, 1935). The last author, a Negro, seems occasionally to permit social considerations to intrude upon formal Marxist ideology.

14. This essay does not attempt to summarize trends in monographic studies of Reconstruction, already adequately surveyed in the articles (see note 1) of Beale, Simkins, Williams, Franklin, and others. For the most part, it is concerned with generally prevailing ideas rather than with specific new viewpoints. While reflecting specialized studies, it also gives attention to textbook treatments of the Reconstruction era, a large number of which do not incorporate revisionist interpretations.

15. Rhodes, *History of the United States,* VI, 324.

16. *Ibid.,* VI, 90.

17. Coulter, *The South during Reconstruction,* p. 135.

18. Quoted in Arthur M. Schlesinger, *The Rise of Modern America* (4th ed., New York, 1951), p. 21.

THE NEW SOUTH

by Jacob E. Cooke
COLUMBIA UNIVERSITY
NEW YORK

"THE LAST QUARTER of the nineteenth century," wrote Philip A. Bruce of the history of the South, "is certain to be pronounced in the future to be, from many points of view, the most honorable period in their history, illustrious as that history has been made by achievements in war as well as in peace." [1]   Bruce's pronouncement, made in 1905, has not materialized.   Historians not only have failed to find the history of the South from Reconstruction to the First World War honorable or meritorious, but often have ignored it.   Books on the ante-bellum South, on the Civil War, and on Reconstruction exist in abundance, for a later period we have excellent studies, but the story of the integration of the post-Reconstruction South into the economy and politics of the nation has been, at least until recent years, a neglected one.

The paucity of works on the New South is perhaps explained by this preoccupation of historians with other periods of Southern history.   The ante-bellum South attracted historians because, contrasting it to the North and West, they assumed that the uniqueness of the South was then developed and affirmed.   The Civil War, perhaps because it represents the most conspicuous failure of American democracy, and Reconstruction, because of the attempts to change the pattern of Southern society and politics, have held a perennial fascination for historians.   But the South after 1877, its position of preeminence in the councils of the nation gone and its economy and social order evidently conforming ever more closely to the national pattern, seemed to many an unrewarding study.

This lack of interest is nowhere better revealed than in the pages of the *Journal of Southern History,* the one scholarly publication devoted exclusively to the South's history. In a review of fifteen years of its history, 1935–49, David M. Potter examined 245 articles by 169 authors. Although he considered the period from the end of Reconstruction to the present as a unit and made no separate calculations for the years 1877–1914, his statistics are revealing. Omitting 30 articles which he found difficult to classify, he found that "17 deal with colonial subjects, 40 with the Revolutionary and early national period—that is to 1830—76 have their primary focus in the three decades before the Civil War, 29 in the Civil War and Confederacy, 18 in Reconstruction, and 35 in the period from Reconstruction to the present." He concluded that "for the 45 years, approximately, from 1830 to the end of Reconstruction, there are 123 papers for an average of 27 per decade . . . but for the seventy-odd years since Reconstruction, there is an average of only 5 papers per decade." [2]

It is unfortunate that this period of Southern history has been neglected, for it was then that the pattern of society, politics, law, and race relations which have prevailed in the South to the present day were established. When one attempts to trace developments and influences on subsequent Southern history and thought, he finds the starting point of many ideas and practices in this era. As C. Vann Woodward has said, "In the long range of more than three centuries of the white and black man's history in the South . . . Reconstruction, like the Confederacy, was an ephemeral experiment." The work of the leaders of the New South, he asserts, was more enduring.[3]

The New South does not readily lend itself to a historiographical discussion, for few historians have presented a monistic interpretation which gives unity and meaning to the varied facts of Southern experience. An emphasis on economic development has characterized the work of some writers, the uniqueness of political development has concerned others, and many have explained the South in terms of racial attitudes and conflict. Yet few have argued that any single interpretative key would unlock the door of this vast storehouse of historical material. Finding it difficult to interpret the New South, writers have tended to compartmentalize its history and to discuss separately its economic growth, political history, and record in race relations. The pattern they have imposed on the past must dictate the organization of a historiographical essay; the historiography of the New South may best be discussed by relating the various interpretations that have been made of these aspects of the New South's history. It will be seen that authors fall into two groups: contemporary journalists and historians who, however different their method or purpose, usually revealed the same preconceptions and reached the same conclusions; and the historians of more recent years who, removed in time from the events they interpret, have questioned the assumptions and conclusions of previous interpreters. Such a categorization is perhaps too general to be especially meaningful, for it only indicates the truism that each generation reinterprets the past. Whatever interest a historiographical essay on the New South has lies, finally, not in distinguishing many schools of historians but in describing the change which has occurred during the last few decades in the interpretation of its history.

A description of the interpretations of contemporary and later historians leaves unanswered, of course, the question of *why* they differed, a question whose answer would have to be sought both by an analysis of their preconceptions and an examination of the extent to which they reflected the prevailing ideas of their time. It is the purpose of this essay to describe how, not why, historians differed; it does implicitly suggest, however, that the most satisfactory explanation of the reason why interpretations of the New South have changed is the most obvious one. Its very remoteness has allowed recent historians more objectively to evaluate its history. The nearness of the Civil War and Reconstruction, the agricultural depression of the eighteen-eighties and nineties, the almost religious fervor with which the process of industrialization was viewed—all these factors certainly influenced those who, from 1877 to 1914, wrote on the New South. When to the collective memory of historical tragedy and exaltation of industrialization was joined fear and hatred of the Negro, the attitude which underlay contemporary interpretations was established. The last four decades have witnessed in those who write Southern history, if not in those who read it, a marked alteration of attitude. The Civil War and Reconstruction became subjects to be investigated rather than experiences one recalled; the industrialization of the South, as it gradually was accomplished, became a process the benefits and costs of which should be examined rather than a prize to be sought; the Negro a subject of compassion rather than an object of contempt. These changes, it should be emphasized, were not characteristic of most Southerners and possibly not most Americans; they do seem to have characterized the work of those who, in recent decades, have written on the history of the New South.

The correctness of the designation "the New South" has itself been questioned. Although it probably did not originate with him, it was Henry W. Grady who popularized the phrase. In an address entitled "The New South," Grady, in 1886, announced to a New York audience that the South, having found victory in defeat, was entering upon a new era of history. "The Old South," he declared, "rested everything on slavery and agriculture, unconscious that these could neither give nor maintain healthy growth. The New South presents . . . a hundred farms for every plantation, fifty homes for every palace—and a diversified industry that meets the complex need of the complex age." [4] Along with Grady, many contemporary observers considered a diversified economy—more specifically the increase of cotton mills—the essential component of the newness of the South. But as used by the New South promoters, the term soon became a slogan, connoting a belief in progress, a hopeful nationalism, an abandonment of the ideals of a rural society.

Subsequent historians have challenged the concept of a New South. As early as 1919, Holland Thompson declared that the New South was not so new, for, he wrote, "The Civil War changed the whole organization of Southern society . . . but it did not modify its essential attributes." [5] Robert S. Cotterill, in a more specific challenge to users of the term, declared in his presidential address before the Southern Historical Association in 1949, that "there is, in very fact, no Old South and no New. There is only The South." If, Cotterill argued, one pointed to cotton manufacturing as an example of "newness," it was only necessary to determine if it was new. "The difficulty writers have experienced in explaining the origin of the 'Industrial Revolution' in the South," he told his audience, "may be primarily owing to the fact that there was no industrial revolution to explain. The so-called Revolution was, in fact, not a Revolution, but an evolution from the Old South to the New." [6] Other writers, too, have challenged the newness of the post-Reconstruction South. Wilbur Cash, for example, in his interpretation of the mind of the South, maintained that there was little difference between the Old and the New South. Although he described the economic changes in the post-bellum South, he concluded that they merely reinforced the mental traits characteristic of Southerners before the War.[7]

Other historians have assumed a middle ground and argue that the South after Reconstruction was in some respects new, in other ways similar to the ante-bellum South. Such is the position of William B. Hesseltine, author of a popular text on the history of the South, who believes that after Reconstruction there was a conflict of ideals between those who wished to recreate the Old South and those who wished, through industrialization and progress, to build a New. Neither ideal triumphed, he maintains, for there remained proponents of each: while Robert E. Lee and Henry Grady represented the tradition which "has been responsible for the industrialization of the South," the traditions of the Old South "were realized to a large extent, in cotton, sugar and rice." But this equipoise was short-lived, Hesseltine concludes, for "by the beginning of the twentieth century the forces of the New South had almost achieved their victory over the traditions of the old plantation." [8] C. Vann Woodward, like Hesseltine, would subject the newness of the New South "to considerable qualification." Those who have written of the New South, he argues, "have not always been careful to dissociate themselves from the implications of the phrase as a popular slogan," and he would, if possible, dispense with the term. Woodward questions that the South from 1877 to 1944 had lost those unique characteristics which earlier had distinguished it. The mind of the New South, he believes, was divided: it accepted at once the pronouncements of the spokesmen of the New South—Grady, Tompkins, and Edmonds—and glorified the romantic tradition of the ante-bellum South, its own invention.[9]

Differences over terminology perhaps have obscured preoccupation with a question not always asked but implicit in every study of the South: was the post-Reconstruction South, whether new or not, sufficiently different from other sections of the country to warrant separate study? The justification of sectional history is the conviction that an area was separated not only geographically from the rest of the United States but that it possessed social or cultural differences worthy of special study. Why have students of the New South considered it unique? How is its experience and history different from that of other sections of the country? Historians reveal the difficulty of the question by assuming it is unique and failing to give any clear explanation of the nature of the uniqueness.[10]

While many contemporary historians accepted the uniqueness of the South as an irrefutable premise on which one based research rather than an assumption to be proved or disproved, others attempted to define it by describing distinct Southern personality or character traits. "The fact is," wrote Samuel Childs Mitchell, one of the authors of a thirteen-volume history of the South which exemplified the best scholarship of the New South movement, "that local attachments seem to strike deeper rootage in this soil, than in some other portions of our country, due perhaps to the warmth of our natures and to the large part that sentiment plays in our lives." [11] No historian of the time, North or South, dealt with the problem more extensively than A. B. Hart, professor of history at Harvard University, who, in 1907-8, traveled through the South and published his conclusions in *The Southern South*. The work is representative. Hart concluded that there had developed in the South a distinct "temperament."

"There is," he said, "a subtle difference of temperament hard to catch and harder to characterize, which may perhaps be illustrated by the difference between the northern 'Hurrah' and the 'Rebel yell'; each stirring, each lively, yet each upon its separate key." But Hart, like his fellow historians, found it impossible to define with any exactness the origins of this unique temperament.[12]

Most contemporary historians, while probably agreeing with Hart and Mitchell that the Southern nature or temperament was different, emphasized geography and climate as the most important determinants of Southern uniqueness. They assumed that "the imprint of sun, rain, and wind," to use Rupert Vance's phrase, had created a distinct social and political order. A variant of this geographical determinism was the conviction of other writers that the uniqueness of the South was the product not of climate but of the predominance of agriculture.

Perhaps the most generally accepted interpretation of Southern uniqueness—often implicit and usually regarded as axiomatic —was offered in its most succinct form by Professor U. B. Phillips, who, noting that it is difficult to explain sectional solidarity in terms of geography or of economic or cultural forces saw white supremacy as "the central theme" of Southern history. It was so, he believed, because the presence of many Negroes led the whites to assume "in the interest of orderly government and the maintenance of Caucasian civilization" their superiority over all Negroes. To Phillips this attitude made the South unique, for if it were to disappear the section would be one with the rest of the United States.[13] The literature on the New South demonstrates conclusively that other historians, whether following Phillips or reaching the same conclusion independently, also have found the presence of millions of Negroes and the attendant caste system sufficient proof of Southern uniqueness.[14]

As many historians have assumed that the coming of the Industrial Revolution distinguished the New from the Old South, it is not surprising that they have discussed in detail the rise of the cotton mill, the most conspicuous example of Southern industrialism in the last decades of the nineteenth century. The question of the extent and significance of Southern industrialism has been beclouded because, from the beginning until the present, industry has been considered by many a cure-all for the economic problems of the South, and the attempt to secure it has partaken of the nature of a moral crusade. Contemporary apostles of the New South—Henry W. Grady, Richard H. Edmonds of the *Manufacturers' Record;* Francis W. Dawson of the Charleston *News and Courier;* Henry Watterson of the Louisville *Courier-Journal* —encouraged the South's industrialization and praised its results. They made industry, and the cotton mill in particular, the symbol of a New South, a South in which magnificent opportunities for investment existed, a section which had adopted the idea of progress, which had rejected the out-dated notions of an agrarian region and embraced the doctrine of salvation through industrialization. They popularized the idea that the Southern mills were of indigenous growth with capital raised through local subscription, that the owners and managers were local men of prominence and of planter antecedents. In stressing the economic advantages of the South for manufacturing, they praised a tractable labor force and urged the factory as the solution to the problem of economic opportunity. Since to them cotton mills were the panacea for the economic difficulties besetting the "poor whites," it was assumed that their development would ameliorate the poverty characteristic of the small farms and mountainsides from which the workers came.[15]

But the doctrines of industrialization and progress were not accepted unanimously in the New South. To many Grady and his fellow promoters were seeking after false gods and their protest against the "new order" was vigorous if ineffectual. George Washington Cable, Edgar Gardner Murphy, Alexander J. Mc-Kelway were representative of those whose indictment of the prevailing situation in the South paralleled the attacks of muckrakers in the nation at large. Murphy, a native of Arkansas and minister in Montgomery, Alabama, reflected the sentiments of those reformers when he expressed distrust of the philosophy of material progress; he believed that the words business and prosperity had become symbols of Southern patriotism, and he courted

apostasy in criticizing them.   Like other dissenters, too, Murphy
was critical of labor conditions in Southern cotton mills, of child
labor, of wage slavery, and of squalor and poverty in mill villages.   Although no ardent supporter of labor unions, he declared
that "upon the one most vital, most practical, most popular industrial issue before the South today labor unionism has got upon
the right side, and 'capital' has too often been upon the wrong
side." [16]   Cable, who had been forced to leave his native Louisiana because of hostile public opinion, expressed his dislike of the
new gods of progress and industrialization even more strongly.
He criticized concentrated wealth, and warned that "a lasting
prosperity cannot be hoped for without a disseminated wealth,
and public social conditions to keep it from congestion." [17]

Unlike Cable and Murphy, who believed that to the extent
that industry raised the standard of living it was beneficial to
the South, other critics of the New South movement rejected it
and argued that the South should remain an agrarian section.
The Reverend Robert Lewis Dabney and Dr. J. William Jones of
Virginia followed the lead of Alfred T. Bledsoe, editor of the
Sewanee Review who, until his death in 1877, was the bitter foe
of all who favored the South's industrialization.   They regarded
science as the enemy of religion, democracy the product of a
fraudulent humanitarianism, and industrial growth as the necessary enemy of refinement and culture, and they wished to preserve a rural, conservative, religious South.

The controversy over the benefits of industrialization has followed the lines established by contemporary authors.   Grady and
his fellow editorial propagandists propounded an interpretation
of the South's Industrial Revolution which one group of subsequent historians has followed; Bledsoe and Dabney are the mentors of those who deprecate it.

The most detailed study of the growth of the cotton industry
has been made by Broadus Mitchell in *The Rise of Cotton Mills
in the South,* and by the same author, in collaboration with
George Mitchell in *The Industrial Revolution in the South.*
Their work is representative of that which has followed the interpretations of the editorial proponents of the New South move-

ment. The year 1880 marked the beginning of Industrial Revolution in the South, Mitchell believes, for "the South by 1880 was ready to be no longer negative, but affirmative; not just the passive resultant of its past, but the conscious builder of its future." The defeat of General Winfield S. Hancock, on whose election Southerners had pinned their hopes for curing "Southern sorrows," led them to the resolution that "out of our political defeat we must work . . . a glorious material and industrial triumph." And the wish, we are told, was father of the deed, for, having willed the triumph of industry, they strove to make it materialize. The cause of the Industrial Revolution in the South, Mitchell argues, was not merely political, it was moral; for industrialization "was emphatically in response to a moral stimulus." [18] While the reasons for England's Industrial Revolution were "narrowly economic," in "the South they were moral as well." [19]

Historians who, like Mitchell, praise the advent of industrialization, also follow the interpretations of earlier editorial proponents of industry in their description of labor in the cotton-mill villages. Although it is often asserted that conditions were deplorable, a comparison is inevitably made between the plight of small farmers and agricultural laborers, the group from whom the mill workers were drawn, and the labor in the mill villages. No matter what the difficulties, it is argued, the mill meant an economic improvement and was a change gladly accepted by the workers. Coupled with this explanation of the enviable lot of the mill workers is the explanation that investors in the factories were often philanthropically motivated men who wished to promote economic opportunities for the South's poor. These historians, of course, vary in the degree of evil which they find in the South's rapid industrialization and the plight of the workers, but they agree that whatever the hardships of the transition from farm to factory, the result, an enhanced prosperity in the section, justified them.[20]

If many historians have reflected the propaganda of Grady, the Southern agrarians are the best example of those who have followed in the tradition of Bledsoe. In the early nineteen thirties, the twin doctrines of industrialization and progress, for so long the accepted gospel of Southern leaders, was subjected to scrutiny and emphatic rejection by this group of Southern intellectuals. In *I'll Take My Stand* these writers protested against the growth of Southern industry as a betrayal of Southern tradition. An industrial civilization, they believed, stifled the amenities of life—"manners, conversation, hospitality, sympathy, family life, romantic love." John Crowe Ransom attacked the "blandishments of such fine words as Progressive, Liberal, and Forward-Looking"; Donald Davidson doubted that art ever could flourish in an industrial society, which, he argued, choked rather than promoted its cultivation; and Herman C. Nixon considered the term "the New South" the slogan of those who had exploited the agrarian interests. They concluded that the South should repudiate the industrial invasion and revive its agrarian tradition.[21]

More recently C. Vann Woodward, attacking the facts of the New South proponents rather than their preconceptions, has challenged the traditional interpretation of the growth of Southern industry and its meaning. "The dramatic elements in the rise of the Southern cotton mill gave the movement something of the character of a 'Crusade,'" he writes. "Burdened with emotional significance, the mill has been made a symbol of the New South, its origins and its promise of salvation. Facts that embarrass this interpretation of cotton-mill history have been somewhat neglected." Professor Woodward's facts refute at almost every point the assertions of the New South promoters and the historians whose interpretations have followed their lead.[22]

The political history of the New South has attracted more attention than any other phase of its history, for it was during this period that white supremacy was institutionalized and "the Solid South" emerged. Historians agree that the major peculiarities of Southern politics revolved around the Negro, that the fear of Negro suffrage led to the one-party system, and that the alleged threat of Negro domination was the major theme in the political history of the period. But on the extent of Negro suffrage in the

eighties and nineties and the motives for subsequent disfranchisement interpretations differ.   There are differences, too, in historians' interpretation of the role of the "Bourbons" in post-Reconstruction politics, the significance of Southern Populism and
the extent to which progressivism invaded the South.

Historians who wrote during the period emphasized the contrast between Reconstruction and the governments which followed.   They contrasted the extravagances of Reconstruction to
the economy of the new regime, its experiment in Negro suffrage
to white supremacy.   The end of radical Reconstruction brought,
in the opinion of these authors, the restoration of Home Rule,
the ouster of carpetbaggers, the end of profligate and corrupt legislatures, and the elimination of Negroes from political life.   They
regarded the leaders who effected this change as benefactors of
the South and described them as "conservatives" who had led the
Confederacy in battle or directed its civil government and who
had returned to power after the defeat of the hated radical governments.   These leaders are frequently referred to as "Bourbons," a term first used by Northern Republicans and soon applied indiscriminately by many Southern politicians to all who
differed from them.   The Bourbons of the New South, like the
Bourbons in the Europe of 1815, were supposed to be those who
"never forgave and never forgot"; who refused to accept the results of the war and the war amendments; and who, longing for
the past, refused to adapt themselves to a changing world.[23]   Contemporary historians, although they sometimes used the appella-
tion, did not accept its connotations.   The leaders of the New
South, they argued, preached sectional reconciliation and urged
Southerners to forget the past by turning to the economic recovery of the region.   In the interest of recovery, historians related,
these leaders fostered the growth of industry, not only by encouraging investment but by stressing its importance to sectional prosperity.

The Bourbons, contemporary historians believed, gave the
South economical government.   "It may be said," wrote Philip
A. Bruce, "that no other commonwealths of the Union are better
governed in their local affairs. . . .   In no part of the Union have

State finances been more conservatively managed than in the South. . . . Nowhere has there been so little peculation and defalcation on the part of officials in charge of the public treasuries; nowhere has the public income been expended with a stricter consideration for the principles of economy, so necessary, during so many years, to be rigidly observed in the Southern States." [24] Such economy, of course, necessitated a minimum of government expenditures both in salaries and for social services. Aware of this, contemporary historians, while sometimes deploring it, regarded it as a necessary incident to economical government. The honesty of conservative leaders seldom was challenged; they were regarded as the disinterested servants of the South's interest and their concern for its industrialization considered a public benefaction. That their support of industry benefited them personally seldom was charged.

To contemporaries, the signal accomplishment of the Bourbons was the elimination of the Negro from political life. They argued that whatever the theoretical arguments in favor of Negro suffrage, it was a divisive issue in Southern politics, one which paralyzed economic development and hampered progress in all other areas. They agreed that the whites were virtually unanimous in wishing the suppression of Negro voting and asserted that the Bourbons were only reflecting the opinions of their white constituents in urging it.

During the decades since the First World War books and articles by countless biographers and state historians have challenged the conclusions of earlier historians; a major revision of their descriptions and assessments of Bourbon politics has occurred. Although many can be named, C. Vann Woodward's study of the New South—based not only on a thorough knowledge of what other revisionists have written, but on a new study of the sources —is the most significant reinterpretation to appear.

Woodward, following the thesis propounded in his *Reunion and Reaction,* argues that the South was redeemed from Reconstruction by a resuscitative Whiggery which assumed, because of its monopoly of public office and economic privilege, a dominant position in the South.[25] The Redeemers, who themselves were usually identified with industrial concerns of some kind, represented the industrial, capitalistic classes. Their attempt to remake the South in the image of the North, redounded to the benefit of the business men and, incidentally, made the South a colony of the industrial and financial imperialism of the North.

The leaders of the new order, Woodward asserts, found it convenient to emphasize their loyalty to the traditions of the Old South and Confederacy. Confederate generals lent their names to the letterheads of Northern firms, and the Redeemers draped their economic activities in the folds of the Confederate flag. The greater the commitment to the new order, the louder their profession of loyalty to the old.

To the assertion frequently made by earlier historians that Bourbon governments were characterized by scrupulous honesty, Woodward enters a denial. In Virginia, Georgia, Tennessee, Louisiana, and Kentucky, he finds records proving embezzlement or defalcation of public funds by state treasurers and concludes that "personal honesty came at a discount among Redemption circles." Neither does he accept the contention that the Bourbons were totally disinterested in their advocacy of white supremacy. It was an issue they skillfully used to prevent the development of independent political movements, a means of fitting all whites into their Procrustean politics.

Economical governments, and the maintenance of low taxes, became, as we have seen, a standard defense of the Redeemers. But Woodward finds that all was not what it appeared on the surface. For one thing, state services were often shifted back to the counties, with little change in local taxation and, further, the systems of taxation resorted to were generally deplorable. Although he sees retrenchment as a natural extravagance of radical Reconstruction, he believes that the retrenchment of funds for education and other social services were often accompanied by unusual concessions to railroads, utility and insurance companies.[26]

Historians have agreed that Populism was the agrarian challenge to the Bourbon leadership of the New South and their description of the details of the movement and the reasons for its failure are similar.   As the same statistics on farm income, cotton prices, and railway and interest rates are generally cited, they give similar accounts of the economic plight of the farmer during the decades of the eighties and the first part of the nineties.   The depressed state of agriculture was, of course, not peculiar to the South as evidenced by the success of the Farmers' Alliance in the West.   But historians believe that Populism in the South differed in important respects from Western Populism.   They agree that the impact of the Populist party on the South's single-party system and on a society in which racial antagonism was intense warrants separate study.

Perhaps because only time could reveal its importance in the history of the South, historians writing during the period 1900–17 did not emphasize Populism.   Of course their interpretations of it sometimes reflected the partisanship of the times, but it was regarded merely as the farmers' attempt to ameliorate their economic position and little significance, real or symbolic, was attached to it. Since the 1920s the literature on Southern Populism has grown enormously.   It is not necessary, however, to summarize the work of all who have written state histories of the movement and biographies of its leaders, for authors disagree on only minor details.   It is accepted that the Negroes received a recognition unknown to them since the days of Reconstruction and that fusion politics—the co-operation of Republicans and Populists, and occasionally of Democrats, with Negro Republicans—was the order of the day.   There is accord, too, that the aftermath of Populism saw white supremacy finally institutionalized in the South by the creation of an elaborate network of legal devices designed to circumvent the Fifteenth Amendment.   Disagreement emerges, however, in their assessment of the significance of Southern Populism—its influence on political developments, its true meaning in the perspective of subsequent history, and its successes or failures.

The leading authority on Populism, John D. Hicks, believes that its significance stems from its platform.   "The party itself did not survive," he writes, "but Populist doctrines showed an amazing vitality."   The Populist platform, according to Hicks, revealed a fundamental change in the attitude of American farmers. He approvingly quotes Frederick Jackson Turner's statement that "the defences of the pioneer democrat began to shift from free land to legislation, from the ideal of individualism to the ideal of social control through regulation by law." Writing specifically of Southern Populism, Hicks argues that, paradoxically, the demands for popular government produced the disfranchisement of the Negro. With the Negro voter eliminated by suffrage laws, he concludes, "it became possible for the rural whites of the South to resume the struggle for a voice in public affairs that they had begun in the days of the Alliance and had continued under the banner of Populism." In brief, Hicks believes that Populism promoted democracy.[27]

Writing four years later, Kendrick and Arnett, professors of history at the University of North Carolina, failed to see that Populism represented the victory of the idea of social control over an older ideal of individualism, or to find any paradox in the promotion of democracy through the disfranchisement of the Negro and the enhanced political power of the "lower class" Southerners. Perhaps influenced by the then current emphasis on the merits of Southern agrarianism, they argued: "In so far as the Alliance men and Populists had stood for agricultural as against industrial, commercial, and financial interests and for the old coalition of South and West in national politics, they may be said to have represented the Old South group." And their defeat meant not only an increased dependence upon Northern business but the imitation of Northern manners and customs. The best traditions of the South were lost in the attempt, Kendrick and Arnett concluded, for "Washington and Lee had given place to Babbitt," and "the South had become the willing and almost humble disciple of its one-time foe."[28]

One of the most distinguished authorities on Southern history, Francis Butler Simkins, sees no contradictions between the interpretation of Hicks and that of Kendrick and Arnett. In *The South Old and New,* Simkins argues that "The agrarian revolt in the South merely served as an awkward interlude in the forward march of business." After 1898, he writes, "urbanism, industrialism, and commercialism achieved a firmer grip." But,

echoing Hicks and Turner, he also believes the agrarian revolt
had an important and permanent effect on the attitudes of Southern farmers.   They clearly were moving toward the abandonment
of their traditional individualism.[29]

The Populist revolt, some historians argue, caused the down-
fall of Bourbon domination and ushered in a new type of leadership, that of the demagogues.   Leaders like Vardaman and Bilbo
of Mississippi and Cole L. Blease of South Carolina represented,
historians relate, the lower classes in a class movement against the
Bourbons; they stirred the people to democratic revolt, using the
techniques of class agitation and race hatred to get and maintain
power.   The Southern demagogues elicited the criticism, and
often condemnation, of historians, who regarded them as power-
driven politicians who maintained themselves in office not by pro-
moting the enactment of legislation benefiting the classes who
elected them but by skillfully playing on the themes of small
farmer superiority and the necessary subjugation of the Negro.
More recently it has been argued that while they were rabid Negro
haters and fanned the fires of racial intolerance, they nevertheless
sometimes served the interests of Southern farmers and occasionally carried through progressive measures.   This is the conclusion
of the best study of the politics of a Southern state to appear in
many years.   Albert D. Kirwan, in his study of Mississippi politics
from 1876 to 1925, rejects the usual interpretation of the Mississippi demagogues, Vardaman and Bilbo.   Agreeing that they appealed to prejudice and passion, he suggests that they also "awakened the social consciousness of the people" and provided the
leadership for the enactment of constructive social legislation.[30]

In the era following McKinley, a new form of protest, as much
urban as rural, succeeded Populism.   Historians of the progressive movement have revealed their interpretation of its role in
the South by omission; although the statement is often made that
Northern and Western progressivism had a counterpart in the
South, Southern progressivism is considered a backwash of the
Northern reform movement.

The authors of two recent articles have argued that progressivism in the South has been deemphasized.   Arthur S. Link in

the *North Carolina Historical Review* and Herbert J. Doherty in the *Mississippi Valley Historical Review* [31] have provided a reevaluation of progressivism in the South. Link takes issue with the popular notion that progressive democracy did not exist in the South from 1870 to 1914 and accuses most writers of ignoring Southern progressivism. There was, he maintains, a far-reaching progressive movement there, expressed first in the membership of the Grange, then in the popularity of the Farmers' Alliance and the People's Party and, after 1900, a progressivism, similar to that in the nation at large, a movement whose base was as much urban as rural and which was primarily political in orientation. Progressivism in the South was nowhere better demonstrated, Link believes, than in the widespread support of Woodrow Wilson in 1912. Southern politicians were in the vanguard of the movement, for men who had been Bryan's spokesmen for nearly sixteen years—Daniels, Tillman, Gonzales, Hoke Smith, Robert L. Henry—found a new leader in Wilson. Doherty, studying a different aspect of Southern progressivism, demonstrates there were social critics in the South, who, like reformers in the North, exposed the evils in business and government. By examining the work of men like Thomas Fortune, George W. Cable, Walter Hines Page, Charles H. Oitken, and Edgar Gardner Murphy, he provides documentation for Link's political interpretation. Both men agree, however, that the forgotten man in the Southern progressive movement was the Negro.

Although, as we have seen, it is difficult to determine why writers considered the South unique, one does find a "central theme" in their work. However important may have been the rise of cotton mills, the difficulties of agriculture, the increased importance of the common man in politics, the great problem of the South—its *idée fixe*—was still the Negro. For every book that appeared on economics or politics there were ten on the Negro. Northern historians and journalists who interpreted the South to their fellow Americans spoke of industrial development but were chiefly concerned with the role of the Negro. The vast contemporary literature on him gave varying reasons for his plight and

proposed different solutions to his problems, but among most
white authors there was the common assumption that regardless
of his potentialities, he was inferior.   Writing in 1941, Gunnar
Myrdal found that those who defended a caste system for Negroes
believed:

(1) The Negro people belong to a separate race of mankind.
(2) The Negro race has an entirely different ancestry.
(3) The Negro race is inferior in as many capacities as possible.
(4) The Negro race has a place in biological hierarchy somewhere
between the white man and the anthropoids.
(5) The Negro race is so different both in ancestry and in characteristics that all white peoples in America, in contradistinction to
the Negroes, can be considered a homogeneous race.
(6) The individuals in the Negro race are comparatively similar
to one another and, in any case, all of them are definitely more akin
to one another than to any white man.[32]

Most of the white authors who during the period 1877–1910 discussed the Negro expressed these beliefs; it was then, after all, that
the rationale of the Southern caste system was elaborated.

The value judgments which served to defend the caste system,
although held by a majority, were not shared by all.   The controversy over the moral traits, personality characteristics, and capacities of the Negro, revealed great differences in opinion.   In
reconstructing the development and expression of the ideology of
white supremacy one can divide contemporary authors into two
categories, the Negrophobes and the moderates.[33]

The sentiments of the Negrophobes, expressed by countless
Southern orators and publicists, are too well known to require
elaboration.   They argued that the Negro was an uncivilized
savage, that because after centuries in Africa he had produced no
civilization, he benefited by the benign discipline and care of
white masters during slavery; that the freedom granted the Blacks
during Reconstruction revealed their shiftlessness and their unbridled sexuality; that to educate Negroes would be to prepare
for a bloody war between the races.   Speaking in the Senate on
the 23rd of March, 1900, Senator Tillman of South Carolina expressed, in his customary hyperbole, the position of the Negrophobes: "We have never believed him to be equal to the white

man, and we will not submit to his gratifying his lust on our wives and daughters without lynching him. I would to God the last one of them was in Africa and that none of them had ever been brought to our shores." [34]

Many contemporary Southerners, of course, deplored the assumptions of Negrophobes that Negroes were savages, strangers to the feelings and morals of white men. Their views varied from a belief in the Negro's permanent inferiority, accompanied by a wish to ameliorate his condition by providing economic and educational opportunity for him, to the gradualist position that through training and opportunity he might, always in the distant future, become the equal of the white man. The writings of the young humanitarian, Edgar Gardner Murphy, Episcopal clergyman of Alabama, best represent the position of the moderates. Murphy believed that the Negroes were "a backward and essentially unassimilable people" whom "the consciousness of kind . . . would forever set apart from the whites." By using, however, "the positive liberties and advantages of education and of industry, of religion and of political freedom," the Negro in America, Murphy thought, might by adopting "a programme of positive progress . . . enter into a larger heritage than is open to any like number of his race in any quarter of the world." [35] While his belief in the backwardness of the Negro and progress through education was one with many other moderates, Murphy argued that the problem was a white, not a Negro problem. He denied that the basic question was the capacity of the Negro and asserted it was the attitude of the whites toward him. To Murphy, it was as important that the whites be reeducated as the Negroes educated.[36] Afraid, however, of extending further this argument or of so alienating his fellow Southerners as to be refused a hearing, Murphy did not admit the possibility of complete equality. "The operation of the principle of the consciousness of kind," he assured his readers, "would forever prevent widespread social mingling and amalgamation." [37]

In a discussion of contemporary literature on the Negro, it is not necessary to make a distinction between historians and other writers, for the interpretations of historians are not suf-

ficiently different. Southern historians expressed the same preconceptions as other publicists of the region; while their ranks
included Negrophobes and moderates, there were no radicals
among them.[38] They, after all, shared to one degree or another
the common assumptions and prejudices of the time. But because they believed that they were objective, applying the principles of science to their observations of the past and present, it is
revealing to examine the extent to which their writings reveal
their bias or impartiality. Their attitudes on the Negro were
surprisingly similar, and birth or residence in the North or South
was of little importance.

Philip A. Bruce, Virginia historian, descendant of the planter
aristocracy, and author of the first survey of the post-Reconstruction South by a professional historian, spoke for those historians
who agreed, if with minor qualifications, with the Negrophobes
of the section. The Negro would, and at no distant date, he concluded, "revert to the African original. The return of the race
to the original physical type involves its intellectual reversion
also. . . . Every circumstance surrounding the Negro in the present age seems to point directly to his future moral decadence. . . .
The influences that are shaping the character of the younger generations appear to be such as must bring the blacks in time to a
state of nature." [39] Holland Thompson, a native of North Carolina who taught in New York, writing some years later, believed
in the possible progress of Southern Negroes through education
and hard work, but thought they were responsible for their own
plight. "Nowhere else in the United States," he wrote in his
survey of the New South, "has the negro the same opportunity to
become self-sustaining, but his improvidence keeps him poor.
Too often he allows what little garden he has to be choked with
weeds through his shiftlessness." [40] Although he attempted to be
unbiased, Thompson, like Bruce, reflected the anti-Negro prejudices prevalent in the South.[41]

If Southern historians assumed the congenital inferiority of
the Negro, so did many in other sections of the country. "Race
measured by race," wrote Albert B. Hart, influential professor of
history at Harvard University, "the Negro is inferior, and his past

history in Africa and in America leads to the belief that he will remain inferior in race stamina and race achievement." [42] Charles Francis Adams, descendant of New England's most prominent political family, assumed that "It is for the Afro-American as for the American descendant of the Celt, the Slav, or the Let, to shape his own future, accepting the common lot of mankind," and asserted that "we are confronted by the obvious fact . . . that the African will only partially assimilate and that he cannot be absorbed." [43]

Perhaps, as Charles S. Johnson has suggested, it is not by mere accident or inadvertence that the viewpoint of Negro Southerners was omitted from characterizations of the Southern point of view and histories of the New South.

Most Negro authors, as one would expect, protested against the prevailing pattern of racial segregation and discrimination. In 1883, George W. Williams published a two-volume history of the Negro in which he attempted to dispel many of the myths which white historians had accepted and popularized. In *The Aftermath of Slavery*, published in 1905, William A. Sinclair gave an excellent summary of the arguments in favor of extended privileges for the Negro and a plea for political equality. Kelly Miller of Howard University, author of countless magazine articles, a warm admirer of Booker T. Washington and hostile to the animadversions of Washington's critics, denounced the tortuous logic, employed by the Negrophobes, that used the results of inequality to establish the need of continuing it. "A wise and far-seeing statesmanship would not seek to isolate and perpetuate . . . incapacities in one race," he wrote the Atlanta editor, John Temple Graves. "Ignorance and vice are not racial attributes; knowledge and virtue are not racial endowments; they are the outcome of condition." [44]

But it was an ex-slave, Booker T. Washington, who became the recognized spokesman of his race and who framed the *modus vivendi* of race relations in the New South. Washington, famed not only for his educational theory but also for his social philosophy, preached a doctrine of moderation. Decrying any attempt to achieve immediate social equality, Washington urged Southern

Negroes to seek economic opportunity. His doctrine of industrial education or, more precisely, vocational education for the
South's Negroes was applauded by whites, North and South. During the two decades from 1895 to 1915, it was Washington's philosophy which dominated Negro thought and action in labor, education, business, and race relations. But Southern Negroes did
not unanimously accept his ideas. W. E. B. DuBois, a young
Negro trained at Fisk, Harvard, and Berlin, was the foremost op-
ponent of the Tuskegee philosophy; in books, essays and addresses he repudiated economic self-sufficiency as the chief desid-
eratum of cultural development. Washington's famous Atlanta
Exposition Speech, the address in which Washington announced
his widely quoted formula for the accommodation of the two races,
was to Du Bois the "Atlanta Compromise," "the most notable
thing in Mr. Washington's career." [45] It made the Tuskegee
philosopher, DuBois believed, the most distinguished Southerner
since Jefferson Davis.

      During the last three decades important changes have taken
place in the writing of the history of the Negro in the South. It
is not that facts have been altered, for his disfranchisement, social
ostracism, and economic plight were recognized by earlier as well
as more recent writers. But there has been an attempt to interpret his role in the history of the South, Old and New, without
the prejudice which led even the so-called scientific historians of
an earlier day to use the materials of history to support their
commitment to the idea of Negro inferiority. Of great importance to Negro history was the founding more than forty years
ago of the Association for the Study of Negro Life and History
by Dr. Carter G. Woodson. Dr. Woodson and the Association,
as John Hope Franklin has said, launched the era of "the New
Negro History." [46] This emphasis is reflected quantitatively by
the enormous number of studies of various aspects of Negro life
and history. During the last decade, for example, at least a half
dozen general histories of the Negro have appeared; in the preceding twenty-five years there was only one.

      The work of scholars, many of them born and trained in the
South, has thus during recent years provided for the first time an

unbiased account of the Negro in the New South.   Unburdened
by the assumption that the mission of the South is to keep the
Negro in subordination, relatively free of the convictions on which
the Southern caste system was for long premised, historians have
restudied the history of Southern Negroes.   Usually accepting
Lord Acton's dictum that it is not the role of the historian to
preside as judge over the past, censuring or praising as he is inclined, they have accepted the prejudice of most Southerners but
have tried also to understand the Negro.   Their work necessi-
tates a revision, in many particulars, of the accepted facts of
Negro history.   Vernon Wharton, for example, in an exemplary
study of the Mississippi Negroes has demonstrated that Negro
officeholders in that state were no more corrupt than their white
counterparts, and were, for the most part, as able.[47]   George B.
Tindall, in another carefully documented state history, has described sympathetically the history of South Carolina Negroes in
politics, agriculture, religion, and education.[48]   Such state histories, and the work of Woodward on the entire South, amply
show that recent scholars have attained that objectivity which an
earlier generation of historians assumed they had but which was
so conspicuously lacking in their writings.

Had one written a historiographical essay on the New South a
decade ago he would have faced an ineluctable problem: the literature was vast, but interpretations presented a monotonous
similarity.   As this study abundantly shows, any historiographical
discussion at this time must be heavily in the debt of C. Vann
Woodward's *Origins of the New South*.   Restudying the source
material available, he challenges many traditional interpretations
and provides the best study to appear on the subject.   But no
work of history is finally definitive nor can a volume fully relate
an era of history as complex and as significant as that of the New
South.
It would be presumptuous for one who has not studied the
New South long and diligently to give a reinterpretation of its
history.   He who does so must join insight and imagination to
extensive research.   But a study of its historiography leads one,

however immodestly, to point out defects in the works of others
and to suggest ways in which to improve our understanding of
this important era of Southern history.

Histories of the New South often have been characterized by
a provincialism which suggests that to some writers Southern history was not a branch but independent of national history.   One
may be justified in assuming that a history of the South, or a study
of a phase of its history, does not require a recital of events in the
national capital.   But neglect of national history too often prompts
the assumption that a development or phenomenon in the South
was unique when it was actually national and not peculiarly
Southern.   The interpretation of the disfranchisement of Southern Negroes offered by William G. Carleton, and discussed earlier,
is one example of the uses of comparative study.   Similar comparative studies might lead to significant reinterpretations of
Southern history.

Although the cotton industry, as we saw, has been the subject
of many investigations, other phases of the economic history of
the New South warrant investigation.   The rapid growth of
Southern industry during and after the Second World War should
lead to a revival of interest in the development and effects of manufacturing.   There are competent studies of many industries but,
as Clement Eaton has suggested,[49] there is a need for monographs
on Southern distilling, lumbering, mining, and banking.

Our knowledge of the political history of the New South has
been expanded by recent studies, but the subject is by no means
exhausted.   The historian of the New South would have an im-
measurably easier job if all states had received the careful and
competent study made of Mississippi; as before indicated, the
books of Wharton and Kirwan necessitate a reassessment of the
politics not only of that state but of the entire South.   Their
work suggests the desirability of a reexamination of the political
history of other Southern states.   Valid generalizations can only
be based on many such studies.

As a plethora of books and monographs reveals, the history of
the Negro in the South has not been neglected during recent
years.   But it is unfortunate that some scholars consider the

Negro as isolated from other Southerners as the most provincial historian considers the South isolated from the rest of the country. If the work of those who write on the Negro occasionally fails to show that it was as much the interaction of the two races as the actions of one that made the Negroes' history, the writings of others leave the impression that there were no Negroes in the South. H. C. Nixon, reflecting on fifteen presidential addresses before the Southern Historical Association, concluded that the typical presidential speaker "has sought to conceal the southern Negro in a woodpile of constitutional abstractions, ignoring him statistically and spiritually. . . . He writes very profusely of the South as a minority and of sins against that minority but very skimpily of the South's minority and the sins against that minority." [50]

Historians of the New South, finally, have failed to account for its uniqueness or to justify sectional history. That they have been unnecessarily obscure may be due, of course, to nothing more than the difficulties of defining that which everyone takes for granted. Many of those characteristics which make a section unique, Donald Davidson has written, "are imponderable and almost indeterminate; they are sectional attitudes, and have to do with the way in which people live and feel and think. They are, in the broadest and best sense, folkways." [51] Howard Odum and other sociologists of the University of North Carolina have attempted both to define precisely the nature of regionalism and to describe these folkways. Historians would profit from a study not only of the work of these and other sociologists but from anthropological and psychological studies of the South.[52] The culture concept as employed by anthropologists and the techniques of personality study as employed by psychologists might be useful tools in explaining, with some precision, the South's uniqueness. The behavioral sciences, of course, deal with the present, but by using those techniques and insights discovered by other social scientists which are applicable to the past, historians might better elucidate it.

NOTES

1. Philip A. Bruce, *The Rise of the New South* (Philadelphia, 1905), p. 472.

2. David M. Potter, "An Appraisal of Fifteen Years of the Journal of Southern History, 1935–1949," *Journal of Southern History,* XVI (February, 1950), 28.

3. C. Vann Woodward, *Origins of the New South, 1877–1913* (Baton Rouge, La., 1951), p. 22.

4. Quoted in Joel Chandler Harris, *Life of Henry W. Grady* (New York, 1890), p. 93.

5. Holland Thompson, *The New South: a Chronicle of Social and Industrial Evolution* (New Haven, 1921), p. 2.

6. Robert S. Cotterill, "The Old South to the New," *Journal of Southern History,* XV (February, 1949), 5.

7. Wilbur Cash, *The Mind of the South* (New York, 1941).

8. William B. Hesseltine, *The South in American History* (New York, 1943), pp. 539–42, 584.

9. Woodward, *Origins of the New South,* pp. ix, x, 174.

10. The difficulty of adequately explaining Southern uniqueness is, of course, a facet of the larger problem of defining and explaining sections and regions in the United States. For an able discussion of the regional concept in American history see Merrill Jensen, ed., *Regionalism in America* (Madison, Wis., 1951).

11. Julian A. C. Chandler and others, *The South in the Building of the Nation* (13 vols., Richmond, 1909–13), VI, xxv.

12. Albert Bushnell Hart, *The Southern South* (New York, 1912), pp. 2–3, 67, 68.

13. "The Central Theme of Southern History," in U. B. Phillips, *The Course of the South to Secession* (New York, 1939), p. 152.

14. More recent historians have continued to assert that the South is sufficiently different from the rest of the country to merit special treatment. See, for example, Francis B. Simkins, "The Everlasting South," *Journal of Southern History,* XIII (August, 1947), 307–22.

15. See Henry W. Grady, *The New South* (New York, 1890); Richard H. Edmonds, *Facts about the South* (Baltimore, 1902).

16. Edgar Gardner Murphy, *Problems of the Present South* (New York, 1904), p. 141.

17. George W. Cable, *The Negro Question* (New York, 1890), pp. 52–53.

18. Broadus Mitchell, *The Rise of Cotton Mills in the South* (Johns Hopkins University Studies in Historical and Political Science, XXIX, No. 2; Baltimore, 1921), pp. 77, 28, 85, 88.

19. Broadus Mitchell and George S. Mitchell, *The Industrial*

Revolution in the South (Baltimore, 1930), p. 95. See also Bruce, *The Rise of the New South;* Holland Thompson, *From Cotton Field to Cotton Mill* (New York, 1906); August Kohn, *The Cotton Mills of South Carolina* (Charleston, 1907); George T. Winston, *A Builder of the New South: Being the Story of the Life and Work of Daniel Augustus Tompkins* (Garden City, N.Y., 1920); Eugene C. Brooks, *The Story of Cotton and the Development of the Cotton States* (New York, 1911). For a single work which expresses many of the ideas of these historians see Chandler and others, *The South in the Building of the Nation,* VI.

20. For a succinct statement on the benefits of industrialization to the poor whites by a prominent New South promoter see David A. Tompkins, "The Mountain Whites as an Industrial Labor Factor in the South," in Chandler and others, *The South in the Building of the Nation,* VI, 58–61.

21. *I'll Take My Stand: the South and the Agrarian Tradition* (New York, 1930), pp. xv, 6, 59, 194.

22. Woodward questions the validity of dating cotton-mill growth in the South from 1880, challenges the view of those who view Southern industrial growth in the eighties as a form of civic piety motivated by "moral excitement," and refutes the assertion that the chief source of initial capital was local. He also qualifies the accepted interpretation of labor by doubting the sense of *noblesse oblige* and philanthropic incentives with which cotton mill employers have been credited. *Origins of the New South,* pp. 131–35, 292, 224–26.

23. Willie D. Halsell, "The Bourbon Period in Mississippi Politics, 1875–1890," *Journal of Southern History,* XI (November, 1945), 521.

24. Bruce, *The Rise of the New South,* pp. 439–40.

25. For a more severe arraignment of Bourbon government see William H. Skaggs, *The Southern Oligarchy; an Appeal in Behalf of the Silent Masses of Our Country against the Despotic Rule of the Few* (New York, 1924).

26. Woodward, *Origins of the New South,* Chap. III, *passim.*

27. John D. Hicks, *The Populist Revolt* (Minneapolis, 1931), pp. 404–5, 411–12.

28. Benjamin B. Kendrick and Alex M. Arnett, *The South Looks at Its Past* (Chapel Hill, 1935), pp. 139–42.

29. Francis Butler Simkins, *The South Old and New; a History, 1820–1947* (New York, 1953), pp. 355–56. For an interesting reinterpretation of Negro disfranchisement and the legalization of white supremacy in the years following the defeat of the Populists see William G. Carleton's introduction to H. D. Price, *The Negro and Southern Politics; a Chapter of Florida History* (New York, 1957), pp. xi, xii. Carleton argues that the disfranchisement of the Negro is not

to be explained in terms of either Southern or national politics; it was related to Western imperialism. Southerners were expressing the "mystique of Imperialism"—the racial superiority of the white man. A significant reinterpretation of Populism is given by Richard Hofstadter in *The Age of Reform; from Bryan to F. D. R.* (New York, 1955), Chaps. I–III, a work which, however, does not emphasize the uniqueness of Southern Populism.

30. Albert D. Kirwan, *Revolt of the Rednecks* (Lexington, 1951), pp. 310–13. Some historians have argued that the defeat of the Bourbons was more apparent than real. They reject the thesis that Populism meant the triumph of a democracy of white men or that the Southern demagogues were the representatives of the Southern lower classes. Such is the opinion of E. Franklin Frazier, *The Negro in the United States* (New York, 1949), p. 156, as well as Skaggs, *The Southern Oligarchy;* Paul Lewinson, *Race, Class and Party* (New York, 1932); and Hesseltine, *The South in American History,* p. 581.

31. Arthur S. Link, "The Progressive Movement in the South, 1870–1914," *North Carolina Historical Review,* XXIII (April, 1946), 172–97. Herbert J. Doherty, Jr., "Voices of Protest from the New South, 1875–1910," *Mississippi Valley Historical Review,* XLII (June, 1955), 45–66.

32. Gunnar Myrdal, *An American Dilemma; the Negro Problem and Modern Democracy* (New York, 1944), pp. 103–4.

33. The Negrophobes expressed the extreme bias of perhaps a majority of Southerners, the moderates attracted a much smaller following, but the dissenters from Southern policy were isolated. George W. Cable was almost alone in his radical indictment of Southern racial policy. See his *The Silent South* (New York, 1885), and *The Negro Question* (New York, 1890).

34. For an excellent discussion of the literature on Negrophobia see Guion Griffis Johnson, "The Ideology of White Supremacy, 1876–1910," in Fletcher M. Green, ed., *Essays in Southern History* (Chapel Hill, 1949).

35. Murphy, *Problems of the Present South,* p. 183.

36. *Ibid.,* p. 190.

37. Murphy, *The Basis of Ascendancy* (New York, 1909), p. xviii.

38. By many of his contemporaries John Spencer Bassett, professor of History at Trinity College, was considered a "radical." Although his historical works concerned American history before the Civil War, as editor of the *South Atlantic Quarterly* he wrote several articles on the Negro. In one of these, as is well known, he referred to Booker T. Washington as "the greatest man, save General Lee, born in the South in a hundred years." The article was widely printed and called forth ebullient tirades in many Southern news-

papers. A boycott of Trinity College was proposed by some irate parents and the college and its entire faculty came under attack. Soon after his article appeared, however, Bassett published an explanation. "Between the races," he wrote, "is a wide gulf and I should be the last man to try to bridge it. I had no thought of social equality in mind. I was thinking only of the industrial and civic outlook of the Negro race." Quoted in Wendell H. Stephenson, "The Negro in the Thinking and Writing of John Spencer Bassett," *North Carolina Historical Review,* XXV (October, 1948), 435–36.

39. Philip A. Bruce, *The Plantation Negro as a Freeman* (New York, 1889), pp. 243–45, 246.

40. Thompson, *The New South,* p. 71.

41. It should be borne in mind that the difficulties encountered by historians in the South were often insuperable. Any attempt to achieve impartiality was likely to offend upholders of local traditions or myths. It was not merely fortuituous that many of them left the South to teach in Northern and Western universities. For an able discussion of the difficulties of one prominent Southern historian of the time see Wendell H. Stephenson, "John Spencer Bassett as a Historian of the South," *North Carolina Historical Review,* XXV (July, 1948), 289–317.

42. Hart, *The Southern South,* p. 105.

43. Charles Francis Adams, Jr., *"The Solid South" and the Afro-American Race Problem* (Boston, 1908), pp. 18, 16.

44. George W. Williams, *History of the Negro Race in America* (2 vols., New York, 1882); William A. Sinclair, *The Aftermath of Slavery* (Boston, 1905); Kelly Miller, *Race Adjustment; Essays on the Negro in America* (New York, 1908), p. 85.

45. Quoted in John Hope Franklin, *From Slavery to Freedom* (New York, 1947), p. 388.

46. "The New Negro History," *Journal of Negro History,* XLIII (April, 1957), 93.

47. Vernon Wharton, *The Negro in Mississippi, 1865–1890* (James Sprunt Studies in History and Political Science, XXVIII; Chapel Hill, N.C., 1947).

48. George B. Tindall, *South Carolina Negroes, 1877–1900* (Columbia, S.C., 1952).

49. "Recent Trends in the Writing of Southern History," *Louisiana Historical Quarterly,* XXXVIII (April, 1955), 39.

50. "Paths to the Past; the Presidential Addresses of the Southern Historical Association," *Journal of Southern History,* XVI (February, 1950), 33–39.

51. Donald Davidson, *The Attack on Leviathan; Regionalism and Nationalism in the United States* (Chapel Hill, N.C., 1938), p. 22.

52. See, for example, the anthropological studies of Melville J. Herskovits, *The Myth of the Negro Past* (New York, 1941), and Hortense Powdermaker, *After Freedom; a Cultural Study in the Deep South* (New York, 1939), and the psychological studies of Abram K. Kardiner and Lionel Ovesey, *The Mark of Oppression* (New York, 1951), and John Dollard, *Caste and Class in a Southern Town* (New York, 1937).

AMERICAN HISTORIANS AND NATIONAL POLITICS FROM THE CIVIL WAR TO THE FIRST WORLD WAR [1]

by *James A. Rawley*
SWEET BRIAR COLLEGE
SWEET BRIAR, VIRGINIA

THE SOUTHERN HISTORIAN Douglas Southall Freeman recalled that his father, who served under General Lee, had never become reconciled to the outcome of the Civil War until the First World War. It was then that the old soldier saw the strength held by a united country, tightly federalized and powerfully industrialized.

The half century that it took to reconstruct the mind of a sturdy Confederate is an era in the political history of the United States. What gives unity to the politics of the era is industrialism—dynamic, formative, and pervasive; industrial advance colors, impels, shapes the lesser themes of the long interwar period. Political history, as we understand it, comprises in its major ingredients political parties, elections, issues, public policy, legislation, and political leaders. In the course of this paper we shall see how historical conceptions of these ingredients have undergone change and how political history itself has fared.

By political interpreters our period is often divided into two segments; from Appomattox to the first Bryan campaign (1865–96); and from the silver excitement to American intervention in the First World War (1896–1917). Within this framework sub-themes dominate: the formation of industrial capitalism and the integration of the nation characterized the first epoch. The rise of the general-welfare state and the widening activity of the nation in world affairs offer the key to the last two decades. With these changes in economy, society, and scope of government the political historian must deal, for without them politics is an uprooted tree whose very trunk on examination will prove hollow. As Arthur M. Schlesinger, Jr., has written: "Political history is a record and analysis of man's effort to resolve the problems of change within the social framework. . . . Cross-fertilization with intellectual history, biography, cultural history, social history, economic history will yield highly fruitful results for political studies. Otherwise political history will perish." [2]

A far different view of history and politics colored the writing of the first political history of the epoch. Out of the three great graduate centers of Johns Hopkins, Columbia, and Harvard universities came the impulse to write scholarly political history. Written history, as understood by the innovators at these institutions, was a science, not art or propaganda. As science it could be objectively recorded and was governed by the biological law of evolutionary growth. The beginning of the evolutionary process was found among Teutonic tribes, from whom American political institutions derived. The conscientious historian-scientist, by critical use of contemporary documents, by divesting himself of the present, and by avoiding interpretation of the facts of history, could attain Ranke's goal: transcribing history as it actually was. Political history was concerned with constitutions, political structure, legal origins, and the growth of institutions. Politics was the dominant concern of the scientific school, which flourished from the 1880s to about 1913.

Columbia University's great exemplar of scientific history was John W. Burgess, who through his German training became imbued with the Hegelian philosophy of history, stressing nationalism, constitutionalism, and the state at the cost of individualism and democracy.[3] From the pen of this master of social science, who like others of the scientific school emphasized the interdependence of history and political science, came two works on the political history of our period, *Reconstruction and the Constitution, 1866–1876,* and *The Administration of President Hayes.*

Burgess wrote on the Reconstruction decade with an open declaration of his desire "to foster the spirit of reconciliation between North and South, through an impartial adducement of the facts and a candid admission of errors." [4]   In similar fashion, *The Administration of President Hayes* was designed to emphasize "the re-establishment of constitutional normality in the United States" by the executive.[5]   It is apparent that Burgess, though an exponent of the scientific school, forsook some of its vaunted objectivity in favor of interpretive didacticism.

At Hopkins, in one of the first studies of contemporary American politics, Woodrow Wilson in *Congressional Government* (1885) struck out in new directions.   He confided to his future wife: "I want to contribute to our literature what no American has ever contributed, studies in the philosophy of our institutions, not the abstract and occult, but the practical and suggestive, philosophy which is at the core of our governmental methods; their use, their meaning, 'the spirit that makes them workable.' " This durable dissertation examined the workings of government and boldly essayed an interpretation of the American system. Inquiry into government as a process and rejection of objectivity in favor of criticism and prescription departed from the Hopkins spirit and looked to the twentieth century.[6]

A second classic description of American politics was written by James Bryce.   Following a method largely sociological, he produced *The American Commonwealth* (1888).   "There are three main things that one wishes to know about a national commonwealth," he wrote, "viz. its framework, and constitutional machinery, the methods by which it is worked, the forces which move it and direct its course." [7]   His study of public opinion blazed a trail which has widened and whose engineering has become more precise in the twentieth century.   His demonstration of inductive and sociological methods was a contribution to the attack on nineteenth-century abstractionism that dominated social thought in the United States.

The tendency of the writing of political history to move away from the scientific school gained impetus from the work of another Hopkins student—Frederick Jackson Turner.   Though Turner wrote little about the political history of the period, he wielded inestimable influence on those who have. Three emphases stand out in his attitude toward history. First is his belief that environment, not the heredity of the Teutonic "germ theory," is a major force in historical development. The frontier and the section, he urged, were native factors long overlooked in the quest for Teutonic origins. This urging suggests a second Turnerian emphasis: his willingness to interpret the past. And finally this open-mindedness toward hypothesis made room for discovery of uniqueness in historical development, in contrast to the unilinear evolution as posited by the comparative method of the scientific school.

Turner published in the eleventh edition of the *Encyclopaedia Britannica* an admirable essay on the United States from 1865 to 1910, brilliantly demonstrating his historical principles. Following a pluralistic interpretation of the period, he gave abundant notice to economic factors and the West. Sectional development within the national framework is a recurring topic, but attention to social forces is not at the expense of "the importance of personality in history." [8]

The scientific school had as its exemplar at Harvard Albert Bushnell Hart, who edited the American Nation series—the first comprehensive history of the nation to be written by the scientific school. Hart thus announced the aim of the series: "For this is not intended to be simply a political or constitutional history: it must include the social life of the people, their religion, their literature and their schools. It must include their economic life, occupation, labor systems, and organization of capital." [9]   The editor's statement of 1904 discloses a vast broadening of the conception of history in the generation that had elapsed since establishment of the first seminars.

Five volumes in the series fall in the period of 1865–1917. It must be said at once that they suffer from being written close to the events and that they do not enjoy the prestige of volumes in earlier periods. An exception is William A. Dunning's *Reconstruction, Political and Economic, 1865–1877*, which, though obsolete in many respects, has not been superseded by a superior narrative from a national point of view. Dunning aimed to portray Reconstruction as national rather than Southern history: "We must regard the period as a step in the progress of the American nation." [10] Professing to be aware of the significance of economic and social forces, Dunning nonetheless skimped on their treatment; the reader does not find adequate notice of industrial growth and public opinion, not to speak of their interrelation with politics. Dunning in fact charted the course of legislative and constitutional history, with sympathy for the South.

The succeeding volume, Edwin E. Sparks's *National Development, 1877–1885,* among the weaker contributions to the series, is marked by a scrupulous concern for facts, barrenness of analysis or interpretation, and a paucity of attention to public opinion. Political chapters are interspersed among treatments of social and economic conditions; and politics is looked on largely as matters of party struggles. Though the editor noted that during this epoch the nation was compelled to "consider a new theory of the relation of government to private and corporate business," [11] one searches in vain for references to Henry George, Henry Carey, or David A. Wells.

This specific shortcoming is partially amended in Davis R. Dewey's *National Problems, 1885–1897.* Dewey devoted three pages to Henry George and two to Edward Bellamy, though in a chapter on "Organized Labor." His treatment of politics, largely shorn of economic factors, addressed itself to parties, platforms, and personalities. John H. Latané in *America as a World Power,* extending the narrative to 1907, was engrossed in foreign relations, and here he failed to project the conduct of foreign policy "against a domestic background, a background not only of political forces and economic factors but also of social prejudices and cultural heritages." [12]

A supplementary volume by Frederic A. Ogg, *National Progress, 1907–1917,* published in 1918, is better balanced than the Latané work, giving half its space to domestic events. Political history receives its due not merely in three chapters on the presidential elections of the decade, but also, probably thanks to the author's training in political science, in chapters concerned with "Administrative Expansion and Reorganization" and "Democracy and Responsibility in Government." Ogg had at last brought to the American Nation series the study of administration and political methods.

The Hart series looms as a landmark in the writing of United States history. The associated authors were conscious of the limitations of the older political history, and they strove to delineate economic and social forces. They altered their conception of history but not of political history. They saw that political history was not enough but failed to see that what they added changed the nature of political history through the interplay of the forces.

Outside academic halls James Ford Rhodes was producing his monumental *History of the United States*. Rhodes first set out to do a comprehensive narrative of the years from 1850 to 1885, but he revised his periodization on finding "a more natural close" with 1877—a terminal date which has been widely accepted. The seven volumes that made up his massive account provided a staple for all students of these twenty-seven years. Later he added two volumes covering the thirty-two years from Hayes through Theodore Roosevelt.[13]

Rhodes wrote political history. His early volumes had unity in the themes of slavery and Lincoln; his work on Reconstruction placed in the foreground political questions centering on the freedmen, but his volumes on the years after 1865 became growingly diffuse and partial. Rhodes saw political history as the story of legislation, parties, nominations, campaigns, and cabinet selection. Writing in a spirit next of kin to the scientific historians, he belonged to no school save that which strives for thoroughness, fairness, and accuracy.

The first decade of the twentieth century witnessed the emergence of "the New History," arising from the growth of the social sciences and the appearance of pragmatism. New discoveries in science, moreover, were turning men's thinking from biology to physics, from evolution to relativity. The appearance of the New History marked the beginning of the decline of political history. *The New History* became the title of a famous work written in 1912 by James Harvey Robinson, a professor of history at Columbia University, who explained that "the New History will come in time consciously to meet our daily needs; it will avail itself of all those discoveries that are being made about mankind by anthropologists, economists, psychologists, and sociologists—discoveries which during the past fifty years have served to revolutionize our ideas of the origin, progress, and prospect of our race." [14]

The leading spokesman for the New History in its implications for politics became Charles A. Beard, who began his academic life as a political scientist. A colleague at Columbia of both Robinson and Burgess, Beard collaborated with the one and reacted strenuously against the other. Influenced by the Fabian Socialists whom he knew at Oxford, Veblen, and Professor J. Allen Smith of the University of Washington, and expressly indebted to Turner, Beard rebelled against older conceptions of politics and political history. For him the state was not Hegel's "Divine Idea as it exists on earth," but a government actuated by realistic factors of economic and class interest. He renounced the mechanical theory of law and politics by which law was inevitably deduced from fixed premises, and he agreed with O. W. Holmes that law and politics were expressions of the personality and political opinions of judges and of social stress. He had equally little respect for "the Teutonic theory of our institutions," a theory of racial genius he found incompatible with democracy. He believed that traditional notions of individualism and laissez faire were a fetish to safeguard minority property rights.[15]

Beard's unconventional views, especially his faith in the economic basis of politics, found dramatic application in his *An Economic Interpretation of the Constitution of the United States*, published in 1913. An eminent student of party politics, W. E. Binkley, has described the book's impact:

For many a decade party history was interpreted in terms of ideologies, of "loose construction" and "strict construction," of "national sovereignty" and "state rights." . . . The romantic interpretation of the politics of the post Civil War period so indoctrinated two generations of Americans that it became almost sacrilegious to regard the statesmen of an earlier generation as human beings. The magic spell of party mythology seems to have been broken largely by Beard's presentation of hitherto neglected data revealing a correlation between economics and politics.[16]

The following year Beard, transferring his attention from the founding fathers to his own time, boldly essayed to interpret the recent past. A treatment of American politics from 1877 to 1913, *Contemporary American History* sought to illuminate present issues by examination of the past. The historian's faith in the interrelation of economic processes and the growth of political institutions highlighted the narrative.

Contemporary American History obviously could not have come out of the seminars of Herbert B. Adams, Albert B. Hart, and John W. Burgess. Asserting that material changes produce changes upon the structure of society, he went on to say: "It is this social transformation that changes the relation of the individual to the state and brings new forces into play in the struggle for political power." One student of social thought in America has remarked that the book "in its quiet way helped shape the historical imagination of the coming generation." [17]

At the end of this century's second decade, The Chronicles of America series, a full fifty volumes, was issued under the editorship of Allen Johnson of Yale University. Directed toward a popular audience, written gracefully by able scholars, the volumes excelled in narration and interpretation rather than in the presentation of new facts which preoccupied contributors to the American Nation series. Some titles indicate the advance of economic emphasis in interpreting the period and the decline of political history: *The Age of Big Business, The Railroad Builders, The Masters of Capital,* and *The Armies of Labor.* At the same time the tendency to study sectional history was forwarded by *The New South* and *The Agrarian Crusade. The Boss and the Machine* foreshadowed the urban interpretation of history and demonstrated the progressives' concern with the framework and administration of government. World politics was the theme of *Woodrow Wilson and the World War.*[18]

The last man to try writing a full history of our period was Ellis P. Oberholtzer, author of *A History of the United States since the Civil War,* spanning the years from 1865 to 1901. Though he published the first of five volumes in 1917 and continued publication to 1937, Oberholtzer proved impervious to the newer emphases in historical scholarship. His version of history was social and political, yet he avoided analysis of the economic and social forces that were transforming American society and opening a gulf between the major parties and the farmer and the laborer. The historian's social insight seemed myopic, and he failed to win the audience that his toil and grand design might otherwise have brought him.

With the twenties older currents of the writing of political history deepened and new tributaries fed the stream, which nevertheless dwindled in volume. Establishment of the Social Science Research Council in 1920 gave formal organization to the New History, and at the same time channeled the study of history away from politics. The economic interpretation surged forward, attaining its crest in the depression decade. Social history won recognition with the launching of a cooperative History of American Life series. Intellectual history started to trickle from sources heretofore ignored by historians.

It is not surprising that economic interpretation should have received further impetus from Beard who with his wife as collaborator produced a brilliant survey of *The Rise of American Civilization* in 1927. Economics is consciously subordinated from Beard's previous high estimate. Now we are told:

In reality the heritage, economics, politics, culture, and international filiations of any civilization are so closely woven by fate into one fabric that no human eye can discern the beginnings of its warp or woof. And any economic interpretation, any political theory, any literary criticism, any aesthetic appreciation, which ignores this perplexing fact, is of necessity superficial.[19]

If this view of history represents, in application at any rate, a shift in emphasis, a second shift is in greater attention to ideas. The Beards devoted two sweeping chapters to the politics of the

era. They entitled the chapter treating the last third of the
nineteenth century "The Politics of Acquisition and Enjoyment."
In these three decades we are informed:

the general cast of thought and scheme of political practice in the
United States corresponded for a long time to the requirements of the
substantial owners of industrial property who ruled the country with
the aid of the more fortunate farmers. The philosophy which they affected was Doric in its simplicity: the state and society were nothing;
the individual was everything. A political party was a private association of gentlemen and others who had leisure for public affairs; its
functional purpose was to get possession of the government in the
name of patriotism and public welfare as a matter of course and to
distribute the spoils of office among the commanders, the army, and
its camp followers. How the party managed its caucuses, conventions, and committees was none of the general public's business.[20]

Here, then, Beard continued to recognize the ascendancy of
property rights in politics and stressed the ideology of individualism and saw political parties not as formalistic organs of government but vehicles toward "the national spoils."

Progressive politics are dealt with under the chapter title "Towards Social Democracy." What distinguishes the epoch is an altered concept of the state and its acceptance by political parties.
"The idea that the power of the state belonged to the majority of
the people and that it could be avowedly employed to control,
within certain limits, the distribution of wealth among the masses
was inherent in all the projects for direct government and in the
legislation . . . which occupied the attention of statesmen in the
new century." [21]   A good part of the chapter describes the transformation of political parties at the hands of progressive forces
and leaders. Untrammeled individualism grudgingly gave way
to the philosophy of the golden mean.

In 1927 also was published the first volume of Vernon L. Parrington's *Main Currents of American Thought*. Parrington's
third volume, incomplete and posthumously published, spans the
years from 1860 to the 1920s. A Jeffersonian dedicated to agrarian economics as well as eighteenth-century political liberalism,
Parrington discerned unity in the period since 1860: "The theme
of the present volume is the industrialization of America under

the leadership of the middle class, and the consequent rise of a critical attitude towards the ideals and handiwork of that class." [22] The brilliant fragment abounds in suggestions of how thought and politics intertwined in the generations of *The Beginnings of Critical Realism in America.*

The confluence of economic and intellectual emphases upon the interpretation of politics stands out conspicuously in the twenties. But the real growth of intellectual history lay in future decades; and it was economic emphasis that seized the imagination of political historians in the twenties and thirties. The high point, perhaps, of economic interpretation of the politics of our period was reached in the writings of Mathew Josephson, who treated the years 1865–96 in *The Politicos* and the years 1896–1919 in *The President Makers.*

Josephson, though influenced by the Beards' *Rise of American Civilization,* subordinated ideas to his own theory of politics. "For historical actions do not seem to arise from the ideas of men; but rather seem to be conditioned by the social being of political men, by their relation to the larger social movements in which the destinies of whole peoples and classes are embraced." [23] As for the epoch of *The Politicos:* "However, the true *style* character of the historical period pictured here arises from forces stronger than, and overlying the party institution itself. It is fixed by the absolute triumph of a single group or class, the industrial capitalists, over the landholders and proletarians." [24] For all his stress in theory on forces stronger than men, Josephson entitled his two books in terms of men and gave spacious treatment of personalities. His very title *The President Makers* suggests the impact of men upon history rather than the conditioning of political men by the social being.

The writing of political history through the medium of biography got a fresh stimulus with the launching of the American Political Leaders series in 1930. New trends in the writing of popular biography had emerged in the preceding decade and a half, the Englishman Lytton Strachey being the most influential innovator. Biography à la Strachey seemed to Allan Nevins, editor of the American Political Leaders series, "a stripped, spare

type, concentrating on essential traits, omitting detail, and pay-
ing but slight attention to background.   Without denying Strachey's consummate craftsmanship, I thought his method opened
the way to a selective manipulation of evidence which might
easily amount to falsification." [25]

The new series proposed not merely to counter these trends,
but also to supersede the American Statesmen series of the last
two decades of the nineteenth century.   That set was in general
not written from the sources, "and most of the biographies were
sadly second-hand."   Nevins stated:

My ideal was a biography written from the sources, and exhausting
those sources, with the object of presenting a full account of the interaction of the man and his times.   I tried to make plain my belief that
personality could be exhibited only in a full use of detail, from letters,
newspapers, speeches, anecdotes, and impressions by contemporaries;
and that the study of history could be served only by a careful dis-
section of critical situations in which the central figure had a role.
In short, I wanted a full biography of the life-and-times order, not a
mere study in personality or biographical sketch.[26]

The series promised "a thorough, scholarly, and interesting
biographical treatment of all the prominent political leaders from
1860 to the present day." [27]   The political leaders comprised in
the main presidents and their unsuccessful opponents, secretaries
of state, and lesser cabinet officials.   Contributors to the series
presented new knowledge and enriched the history of the times.
Philip Jessup's *Root,* J. G. Randall's *Lincoln,* L. B. Richardson's
Chandler, and Nevins's *Fish* and *Cleveland* all exploited heretofore unused sources.   On the other hand writers of the lives of
Arthur, Blaine, Carlisle, and Reed were handicapped by the
sparseness of personal papers.

Considering the low estate of political history, the series represented the principal medium of writing in the thirties on the
politics of our period.   But among many historians economic interpretation and social history were the vogue.   Louis Hacker
scathingly greeted Eckenrode's claim that Hayes was the "statesman of reunion," and asserted: "I submit that Morgan and Harriman, to take but two examples, accomplished a thousand times

as much. . . . The penetration of Northern capital into the South and the standardization of taste and the ordinary round of daily living—these, and not political gestures, healed the wounds of war." [28]

Two distinguished biographies, which were not in the American Political Leaders series, were written by Henry Pringle in the thirties. *Theodore Roosevelt* sharply reevaluated the glamorous figure, relying heavily on the exuberant Roosevelt's self-revelations. The book went to the farther extreme from J. B. Bishop's eulogy and descended in scholarly merit from the sparkling opening chapters on the prepresidential years, through the presidency, to the period after 1909 when the Roosevelt papers were closed to the biographer. The chief fault of the book lay in a lack of depth—in portraying Roosevelt as "the most adolescent of men" [29] and in failing to provide the historical milieu in which he moved. Subsequent studies by John Blum and George Mowry expertly delineated Roosevelt's role in Republican politics and the progressive movement.

The Life and Times of William Howard Taft offered a greater challenge to Pringle, because of the long and diverse career for which extensive manuscript sources were available. The second book, following the same method of the first in use of quotation and stress on personalities, revealed a surer hand in appraising the subject and narrating history. Pringle's *Taft* added to the stature of the beleaguered President and took a further cubit from that of Theodore Roosevelt.

At the same time that historians were turning away from politics, political scientists were turning away from the historical method. The two movements complemented one another in lowering the prestige of political history. Emphasis by historians upon economics, society, and to a smaller degree psychology marked the depression years of the thirties. With the forties new currents surged into the stream of political history. Three tendencies may be noted: the rise of intellectual history; the promulgation of the cultural approach to history; and the toppling of economic history from its eminence. Each of these served to divert the attention of historians from writing on the politics of our period; at the same time each made its contribution, or promised one, to the field.

The course of American intellectual history has been traced
elsewhere,[30] and it will suffice here to note something of its relevancy to our theme.   The role of the doctrines of the fundamental law, the free individual, and the mission of America was illustrated in Ralph Gabriel's *The Course of American Democratic
Thought*.   Merle Curti's *The Growth of American Thought* was
studded with suggestions of themes impinging upon politics: loyalty, patriotism, nationalism, conservatism, and liberalism—to
name but a few.   How *Social Darwinism in American Thought*
affected the idea of the state was a main theme in Richard Hofstadter's study.   All three of these books stressed the influence of
pragmatism upon politics, and the first two the influence of religious thought.   Religious and humanitarian forces, with political bearings on the social gospel, Christian socialism, and the progressive movement, were delineated in books by James Dombrowski, Charles H. Hopkins, and Aaron I. Abell.[31]   While much
remains to be said respecting the role of ideas in politics, these
works sowed broadcast seed for a future harvest.

The cultural approach to history bid for recognition in the
program of the American Historical Association in 1939.   It
served further to depress political history, as in its quest to find
"the total structure of society," it moved in the directions of anthropology, sociology, and psychology.   The papers subsequently
published did not seek to interrelate politics with the total culture, despite the premise of the editor that "no part is to be understood without reference to its place in the whole." [32]

What the cultural approach implied for the place of politics
in historical interpretation became more plain in the writings of
one of the contributors to the 1939 program.   In a paper entitled
"The 'Presidential Synthesis' in American History," Thomas C.
Cochran attacked the traditional organization and content of
American history.   Writers of history, he charged, had not caught
up with a half century of rapid growth in the social sciences.
They had failed to take into account "the importance and complexity of the elements in modern society that are but faintly re-

flected in national politics. . . . The precise social effect of the
rapid rise of the corporation from 1850 to 1873, for example, cannot be measured, but the social scientist is reasonably sure that it
is of more importance than the presidential aspirations of Horatio
Seymour." Declaring that one of the major misconceptions in
synthesis had been the idea of the primary role of the central
government in our historical development, Cochran recommended
a social science synthesis. What would this be like? "At the
center of any social science synthesis," we are told, "determining
its topical and chronological divisions, should be the changes,
whether material or psychological, that have most affected, or
threatened most to affect, such human conditioning factors as family life, physical living conditions, choice of occupations, sources
of prestige, and social beliefs." After removing the president
from the center of the synthesis in American history, Cochran
nominated his own candidates. "For the period since the middle
of the nineteenth century . . . my personal bias leads me to believe that business and economic changes should be recognized as
the most dynamic elements." [33]

Recognition of these dynamic elements was made in *The Age
of Enterprise* by Cochran and William Miller. Subtitled *A Social History of Industrial America,* this work in its synthesis drew
together not alone business and economic change but also the
philosophy of industrial progress, urbanism and industry, and
politics. The politics of the years 1865 to 1890 are interpreted
in a chapter headed "The Business of Politics," in which the argument is advanced that in the fifteen years after Appomattox politics was a business managed by the politicians. Political piracy
held sway, as the politicians in power treated the business men
as customers, "selling political support at the highest price the
traffic would bear." [34] In the 1880s businessmen took over politics, gaining control over the major parties. Never a solid front,
business men formed in cliques through which they prevented
the real issues from being incorporated in party platforms and
defended national business. From time to time the ruling cliques
ostensibly yielded to popular pressures: the Interstate Commerce
Act "was a sop to the malcontents in American political society." [35]

The politics of the years 1890 to 1916 are covered in a chapter, "Pressure Politics in an Age of Reform." In the score of years after 1890 investment bankers came into control of American politics and industrial labor sought strength through organization. Escape from subservience to these two groups was the *raison d'être* of the progressive movement, formed from the urban middle class and the yeomen farmers of the West. The progressives organized in countless associations as a means of playing pressure politics. After 1900 they were opposed by counter associations of businessmen. Without much leadership from Presidents Roosevelt and Taft, but with the vigorous leadership of Wilson, the progressives pressed on. Between 1910 and 1914 "Congress and the state legislatures . . . enacted a large part of the Progressive program." [36]

Cochran and Miller's underscoring of the business and economic forces underlying politics was meant as a departure from both the presidential synthesis and the economic interpretation of history. The collaborators wrote:

America has been settled mainly by enterprising immigrants seeking economic opportunities and freedom. That this quest has been most powerful in determining the nature of our culture, historians acknowledge when they write *economic* interpretations of our politics, our literature, our philosophy, our religion. They fail to do it justice when they make these and not business itself the kernel of their discussions.[37]

The triple impact of the rise of intellectual history, the advocacy of a cultural synthesis, and the waning of economic emphasis left the fate of interpretation of national politics uncertain in the renewal of historical activity following the Second World War. A committee appointed by the Mississippi Valley Historical Association in 1943 "to propose and formulate in detail a series of projects in American history and culture," gave short shrift to political history, disposing of it in one brief paragraph and making no specific suggestions about projects to be undertaken in this field.[38]

The neglect by this committee to reorient political history was compensated for by the Conference on American History held early in 1948 on the question, "Do We Need a 'New History' of American Political Democracy?" The consensus in the affirmative served several ends. It pointed to the need for the revival of political history. It urged the cross-fertilization of the newer emphases in historical research, particularly intellectual and cultural approaches, with political history. It advertised the continuing decline of materialistic interpretation, Louis Hacker decrying it as deterministic, monistic, and dialectical.[39]

In the years after the Second World War historians were sensitive to the summons to reappraise the past. No one, however, responded to the challenge to write anew the history of national politics in the era between the Civil War and the First World War. But in isolated works promise of a renaissance of political history could be perceived. Vigorous stirrings of a new spirit were seen in Richard Hofstadter's *The American Political Tradition and the Men Who Made It* (1948). Through the careers of political leaders Hofstadter searched for our major political traditions, which he found "have shared a belief in the rights of property, the philosophy of economic individualism, the value of competition." [40] Hofstadter's study of political tradition doubtless lost something in his recourse to biography; yet what was notable was his awareness of the complexity of political history. He drew upon intellectual history and political and economic theory; he gained dimension by use of psychology and sociology. His treatment of Bryan illustrates the approach. The "Cross of Gold" speech, the campaign of 1896 with Bryan touring the nation and McKinley sitting on his front porch in a rocking chair, Hanna's shock tactics—the customary trappings of political history—are minimized or ignored. Bryan's political leadership (described as the embodiment of popular feelings), his social philosophy (described as Jeffersonian-Jacksonian), and his psychology (described as his need for an audience, not success) round out the lineaments of Bryan and his part in the American political tradition.[41]

Various trends in the writing of political history exemplified in this book renewed their course in a subsequent volume of the same writer, *The Age of Reform*. Dropping the biographical medium he turned to analysis of the reform aspect of the American political tradition in the years from the 1890s through the New Deal. "The center of attention in these pages," the author announces, "is neither the political campaigns, the enactments of legislatures, the decisions of the courts, nor the work of regulatory commissions, but the ideas of the participants." [42]

Populism and progressivism in particular undergo reevaluation "from the perspective of our time." Populism is placed in perspective against a background of "the agrarian myth" opposed to the realities of the farmer's commercial role. "Populism can best be understood . . . not as a product of the frontier inheritance, but as another episode in the well-established tradition of American entrepreneurial radicalism, which goes back at least to the Jacksonian era." [43]

Progressivism is explained in terms of mass psychology. With the growth of corporate wealth after 1870 a "status revolution" brought about a decline in power and prestige of persons of local eminence—small merchants, lawyers, editors, and preachers. "It is my thesis that men of this sort . . . were Progressives not because of economic deprivations but primarily because they were victims of an upheaval in status that took place in the United States during the closing decades of the nineteenth and the early years of the twentieth century." [44]

Throughout Hofstadter's writings run certain emphases and themes that are hallmarks of the newer interpretation of national politics in our period: the role of ideas in history, psychological speculation, a cultural approach, and themes of government and the economy, urbanism, nativism, and international perspective. Similar trends may be found in the work of Eric F. Goldman, who wrote *Rendezvous with Destiny* in 1953. Spanning the years from the late 1860s through the Fair Deal, the book stood on the premise of an interplay between social change and ideas. "The reform movements that culminated in the New Deal and the Fair deal . . . are most directly a reaction to a rapidly urbanizing, industrializing America." [45] The departure from traditional interpretation of politics may be seen in laying the defeat of anti-Grantism in 1872 to Americans' desire to "get ahead" in prefer-

ence to reform, and in ascribing William Jennings Bryan's defeat
in 1896 to the fact that "reform associated with shaggy agrarianism could not carry a swiftly industrializing, swiftly urbanising
nation." [46]

Not far behind Hofstadter and Goldman marched other historians, whose eyes, if less intent on finding future pathways, perhaps had a broader view of the horizon.   In 1950 a sympathetic
analysis of party government in the United States came from the
pen of Herbert Agar.   Breaking away from older interpretations
Agar declared: "The meaning and the purpose of the national
parties cannot be sought in traditional alignments or old animosi-
ties, and still less in economic or political creeds.   They can only
be understood in the light of the regional problem created by
America's size, and the constitutional problem created by the separation of powers." [47]   Political parties help find the grounds for
compromise—the price of union; they give resiliency and adapt-
ability to our form of government.   Cleveland sowed the wind in
the 1890s when he resisted the new demands from the West and
trade unions; in doing so he destroyed the machinery of his party.
"Taft suffered . . . the fate of Presidents who treat Congress
meekly." [48]   Professing a distaste for party politics, he failed to
hold together the Republican coalition.   Agar's *The Price of
Union* was not based on the role of ideas or culture but was concerned with politics in a sense comprehending economic forces
and actual political practice.

Arthur Link's *Woodrow Wilson and the Progressive Era* was
issued in 1954 as one of the first volumes in the New American
Nation series.   Intended to supersede F. A. Ogg's *National Progress*, it invited comparison with the older work.   The perspective
had changed; it was not merely that three and half decades had
lent disenchantment to the years of "national progress," but the
New Deal and Fair Deal and the Second World War had inter-
vened.   Placed against this background the New Freedom of
1913–14 stood in bolder relief, capable of being distinguished
from the New Nationalism which, Link argued, Wilson had embraced after 1914.   And mid-century concerns prompted devotion
of a whole chapter to "The Preparedness Controversy."   Link thus

enriched the political history of the era by his attention to ideology and sensitivity to such issues as preparedness and segregation of Negroes in federal employment, as well as by his detached concentration on a short span of years.

A biographer of Wilson who had evinced a certain animus toward his subject in *Wilson: The Road to the White House* (1947), Link revealed a reluctant admiration in the New American Nation volume. By this time his *Wilson: The New Freedom* (1956) appeared, he had confessed to "the mellowing of his judgment of Wilson." [49]

The reader of the foregoing survey may be convinced of the need for a thorough, fresh history of national politics in the half century from the Civil War to the First World War. To be satisfactory, a comprehensive history of national politics must be multivolumed in length and doubtless cooperative in execution. A massive body of biographies, monographs, and periodical articles lies at hand awaiting synthesis. But more than synthesis is required; there are many specific fields of research to be explored, new views to be emphasized, and techniques to be tested.

For a basic political history there is wanting a probing analysis of democracy and what it has meant to successive generations of voters. There is wanting a thoroughgoing history of the operation of party government in the United States. A definitive exposition of political theory awaits some skilled hand. So obvious a factor in democratic politics as a comprehensive history of the suffrage needs to be freshly and adequately done. Areas of political behavior on election day, nonvoting, and nominating devices remain to be explored. The history of national and state interrelationships in politics, vital and patent in a federal system, has been insufficiently recorded. Similarly sectional and intrasectional history has been neglected.[50]

Apart from such basic matters many specific needs exist. Large lacunae appear in the field of biography, where studies in a modern manner of Hayes, McKinley, Bryan, La Follette, John Sherman, and Ignatius Donnelly—to suggest a few—form a void. The kind of biography that will be serviceable is a full-scale, life-in-the-round type, patterned on the American Political Leaders series better than upon the brief, eclectic portraits with a theme found in various series sponsored by present-day publishers.

A major task is the history of parties, especially our major parties, undertaken by impartial historians.[51]   The curse of party histories has been partisanship and the proneness to publish in campaign year markets.   The political history of Reconstruction, viewed as a national process and drawing on revisionist studies, is a clamorous need.   A sympathetic account of the radicals, not written from a doctrinaire point of view, is overdue.   The story of the Negro in politics, his impact upon practice and theory, requires narration for the whole of the period.

A proper evaluation of politics will be possible only when, if ever, the dust of controversy settles about the robber barons.   A consensus on the significance of the so-called one-party period or the generation of Republican rule might stem from intense analysis of the politics of the period; and possibly it will be found in general public approval of the great economic expansion of the epoch.

The political history of the West since the 1890s, when Turner prematurely hailed the passing of the frontier, is a relatively untilled field.   John W. Caughey's analysis of articles published in professional journals on the history of the western half of continental United States revealed that "it would appear that historians are not attempting a real account or explanation of the growth that has occurred since 1890." [52]   The role of the Supreme Court in politics has been inadequately noted by historians, who have heretofore concentrated on constitutional issues.

The immigrant in politics has been only suggestively treated, if brilliantly so, by Marcus L. Hansen and Oscar Handlin.   A full-length history of ethnic behavior in politics, such as has been undertaken for the Irish in individual cities, wants being done. The role of the boss, the contrasting behavior of first and second generation Americans, immigrant attitudes toward reform are themes already suggested by these historians, yet insufficiently exploited.

The related line of inquiry, how foreign influences have affected national politics, needs pursuing.   Foreign influences working through such individuals as Carl Schurz, E. L. Godkin, and Charles Beard have been studied; other biographical analyses will fill out present outlines.   The debt of American political theory to Europe needs assessment in these years after the waning of Locke's impact.   Foreign contributions to such specific practices as civil service and machine politics represent profitable fields of study.   Along this line may be mentioned the topic of the influence of religious groups, the Catholic Church particularly, on elections, choice of candidates, and like subjects.   Fragmentary work indicates that a systematic analysis of corruption as a factor in national politics would prove fruitful.

The role of public opinion in politics, while certainly not overlooked, has not been exploited to its fullest extent.   Thomas A. Bailey, author of a work in diplomatic history with a major emphasis upon public opinion, has stated: "In a democracy like the United States, where public opinion determines fundamental policies, it is necessary to consider what the people thought about what was happening, and to discover what pressure they brought to bear upon the government to change its course." [53]

The large-scale history envisioned here must include in its canvas the details mentioned above; it must also make use of the new techniques of research.   The foremost prerequisite is to employ the interdisciplinary approach; historians until recent years have been laggard in interrelating economic, social, and cultural forces with political history.   Historians have permitted these emphases to overwhelm the writing of history; political historians may find new dimensions for their work if they will push beyond the traditional limits of political history.   Recent studies of economic thought by Joseph Dorfman and Sidney Fine, for example, are indispensable to our theme; and a commentator on American political historiography has judged Harold Faulkner's *The Decline of Laissez-Faire,* "as far as it concerns economic implications and the effect of government policy thereon . . . one of the best treatments of the Progressive movement." [54]

During the decades of doldrums that becalmed political history, the historical profession allowed the initiative in devising and utilizing new concepts to pass into the hands of political scientists. The work of V. O. Key, W. E. Binkley, Pendleton Herring, and Leonard White exploited American politics with great insight and experimental techniques. Quantitative and precision methods, approaches to politics through "clusters of interest" rather than political parties alone, the conception of political science as the study of political power, analysis of administration both as a means of organization and of politics, stress on presidential leadership—all these are illustrative of what political scientists have done. Unfortunately so much of the research by political scientists is not historical in method—despite the chiding of them by Arthur Holcombe and Charles Beard—that its value to political historians is diminished.

To be sure, historians have not altogether neglected new techniques and related disciplines; William Diamond and George Mowry have applied statistical methods to the politics of our period; Hofstadter and Goldman have exploited mass psychology; and Harvey Wish has made forays into sociology. John Blum has treated *The Republican Roosevelt* from political science approaches as a conservative, pragmatic president.

However, the historical guild has not always asked itself the right questions in setting up political problems. Richard L. Watson, Jr., probingly wrote:

Given the fact that an American political party is a coalition of local organizations, which unite every four years to elect a President, obvious first questions are How does this coalition take form? How are its candidates chosen? and How is the coalition maintained? Related to these questions is the problem of congressmen: How are they chosen? How does Congressional leadership develop? How is a Congress organized? What is its relationship to the executive? Finally, How is the party program formulated and put into effect? What influences shape policy—ideas and principles, lobbies and the force of public opinion, economic and social conditions, or simply the search for what is politically possible? [55]

Yet at the same time a prudent word about the interdisciplinary approach needs to be said.[56] With its sometimes elaborate analysis of forces in history, this approach tends to crowd men and action off the stage.   Humanity and narration can be lost in description and interpretation.   Without men in motion there is no history.   A further pitfall is that both depth and art can be sacrificed in pursuit of breadth.

If a measured interdisciplinary view, with full appreciation of the contributions in particular of political scientists and a wider recognition of the nature of politics, is in order for a new history of national politics, acceptance of lines of inquiry sketched out by contemporary concerns is a last prescription.

Awareness of the relatedness of the United States to the world has been promoted by the Second World War and its sequel. That the United States has borrowed from abroad has earlier been said; that American political life may be characterized more accurately by comparison with foreign experience is a corollary. The influence of international politics upon domestic and that coin turned over present quizzical faces to researchers.   A truly cosmopolitan point of view will alter the provincial interpretation of United States politics that flourished in the days of isolation.

The current of conservatism that has surged through mid-century United States ought also to be recognized not merely as a phenomenon of the present but as a perennial part of our politics.   Just as Samuel E. Morison called in 1951 for a "sanely conservative" interpretation of our national history, so may we now call for such an interpretation of our national politics.   The day of the debunker and doctrinaire seems past; the liberal we shall always have with us; the tory is just venturing to raise his cautious head.   Russell Kirk and Clinton Rossiter have made useful studies of conservatism; Richard Leopold has reexamined Elihu Root to relate him to the conservative tradition; Arthur Mann and George Mowry have pointed to the role of the elite in our politics.   But these studies are inconsecutive guideposts, and the full length of the road that forks to the right is yet to be traveled by a perceptive recorder of the journey.

Roy Nichols ended his introductory editorial to the papers of the Conference on American History: "The history of American political democracy is still very much the historian's unfinished business." [57] The segment connecting the Civil War with the First World War is markedly "still very much the historian's unfinished business."

NOTES

1. Lord Acton in his review of Bryce's *The American Common-wealth* recalled Scaliger's statement amplified by Bacon: "*Nec ego nec alius doctus possumus scribere in politicis.*" The following essay is abundant proof of this warning against writing about politics. But I have been emboldened in this attempt by the encouragement and aid of President Anne Gary Pannell, Ralph Purcell, Walter Bennett, John Glaser, Bernard Mayo, David Donald, Harold Syrett, and my wife, Ann Rawley.

2. "The Need for a Cultural Comprehension of Political Behavior," *The Pennsylvania Magazine of History and Biography*, LXXII (April, 1948), 188, 195.

3. Bert J. Loewenberg, "John William Burgess, the Scientific Method, and the Hegelian Philosophy of History," *Mississippi Valley Historical Review*, XLII (December, 1955).

4. *Reconstruction and the Constitution* (New York, 1902), quoted by William R. Shepherd in Howard W. Odum, ed., *American Masters of Social Science* (New York, 1927), p. 51.

5. *The Administration of President Hayes* (New York, 1915), quoted by Shepherd in Odum, ed., *American Masters of Social Science*, pp. 52–53.

6. Arthur S. Link, *Wilson: The Road to the White House* (Princeton, 1947), pp. 12–13; *Congressional Government* originally appeared in 1885 and has gone through many editions; it is presently available in a paper binding with an introduction by Walter Lippmann.

7. Bryce's book originally appeared in 1888, and it too went through many editions; the quotation is from the new and revised edition (New York, 1912), p. 5.

8. Frederick Jackson Turner, *The Frontier in American History* (New York, 1920); and his "United States [History, 1865–1910]," *Encyclopaedia Britannica* (11th ed., Cambridge, Eng., 1910), XXVII, 711–35.

9. Albert Bushnell Hart, ed., *The American Nation; a History* (26 vols., New York, 1904–08), I, xvii.

10. William A. Dunning, *Reconstruction, Political and Economic, 1865–1877* (New York, 1907), p. xv.

11. Edwin E. Sparks, *National Development, 1877–1885* (New York, 1907), p. xvii.

12. A standard suggested by R. W. Leopold, "The Mississippi Valley and American Foreign Policy, 1890–1941: an Assessment and an Appeal," *The Mississippi Valley Historical Review,* XXXVII (March, 1951), 625.

13. James Ford Rhodes, *History of the United States from the Compromise of 1850* (7 vols., New York, 1893–1906), *History of the United States from Hayes to McKinley* (New York, 1919), and *The McKinley and Roosevelt Administrations* (New York, 1922).

14. James Harvey Robinson, *The New History* (New York, 1912), p. 24.

15. Max Lerner, "Charles Beard's Political Theory," in Howard K. Beale, ed., *Charles A. Beard* (Lexington, Ky., 1954).

16. W. E. Binkley, *American Political Parties; Their Natural History* (New York, 1945), p. ix.

17. Morton G. White, *Social Thought in America; the Revolt against Formalism* (New York, 1949), p. 32.

18. Allen Johnson, ed., *The Chronicles of America Series* (50 vols., New Haven, 1918–21).

19. Charles A. Beard and Mary R. Beard, *The Rise of American Civilization* (New ed., 2 vols. in 1, New York, 1933), I, 124.

20. *Ibid.,* II, 539.

21. *Ibid.,* II, 577.

22. Vernon L. Parrington, *Main Currents in American Thought* (3 vols. in 1, New York, 1939), III, xxvi.

23. Matthew Josephson, *The Politicos, 1865–1896* (New York, 1938), p. ix.

24. *Ibid.,* p. viii.

25. Private communication from Allan Nevins to James A. Rawley, July 27, 1956; see also Allan Nevins, "Washington à la Strachey," *Saturday Review of Literature,* VI (February 22, 1930), 749ff.

26. Private communication from Allan Nevins to James A. Rawley, July 27, 1956; see also Allan Nevins, *The Gateway to History* (New York, 1938), Chap. XII.

27. *Book Review Digest, 1930* (New York, 1931), p. 312.

28. Louis Hacker, "How to Become President: [review of] Rutherford B. Hayes, by H. J. Eckenrode," *The Nation,* CXXX (June 4, 1930), 655.

29. Henry F. Pringle, *Theodore Roosevelt* (New York, 1931), p. 4.

30. John S. Higham, "The Rise of American Intellectual History," *American Historical Review*, LVI (April, 1951), 453–71.

31. James Dombrowski, *The Early Days of Christian Socialism in America* (New York, 1936); Charles H. Hopkins, *The Rise of the Social Gospel in American Protestantism, 1865–1915* (New Haven, 1940); Aaron I. Abell, *The Urban Impact on American Protestantism, 1865–1900* (Cambridge, Mass., 1943).

32. Caroline F. Ware, ed., *The Cultural Approach to History* (New York, 1940), p. 11; see review by Charles A. Beard in *American Historical Review*, XLVI (July, 1941), 844–46.

33. Thomas C. Cochran, "The 'Presidential Synthesis' in American History," *American Historical Review*, LIII (July, 1949), 748–59.

34. Thomas C. Cochran and William Miller, *The Age of Enterprise* (New York, 1943), p. 154.

35. *Ibid.*, p. 171.   36. *Ibid.*, p. 295.   37. *Ibid.*, p. 2.

38. Louis Pelzer and others, " Projects in American History and Culture," *Mississippi Valley Historical Review*, XXXI (March, 1945).

39. Richard P. McCormick and others, "Conference on American History," *The Pennsylvania Magazine of History and Biography*, LXXII (April, 1948).

40. Richard Hofstadter, *The American Political Tradition and the Men Who Made It* (New York, 1948), p. viii.

41. *Ibid.*, pp. 183–202.

42. Richard Hofstadter, *The Age of Reform* (New York, 1955), pp. 5–6.

43. *Ibid.*, p. 58.   44. *Ibid.*, p. 135.

45. Eric Goldman, *Rendezvous with Destiny* (New York, 1953), p. viii.

46. *Ibid.*, pp. 24–28, 68.

47. Herbert Agar, *The Price of Union* (Boston, 1950), p. xvii.

48. *Ibid.*, pp. 577, 657.   For an interesting anticipation of Agar's thesis see Allan Nevins, "The Strength of Our Political System," New York *Times Magazine*, July 18, 1948.

49. Em Bowles Alsop, *The Greatness of Woodrow Wilson* (New York, 1956), p. xii.

50. Hannah Grace Roach, "Sectionalism in Congress (1870 to 1890)," *American Political Science Review*, XIX (August, 1925), 500–26, is an admirable pioneer study.

51. Malcolm Moos, *The Republicans; a History of Their Party* (New York, 1956) and Eugene H. Roseboom, *A History of Presidential Elections* (New York, 1957) make virtually no use of primary sources.

52. John Walton Caughey, "The Mosaic of Western History," *Mississippi Valley Historical Review*, XXXIII (March, 1947), 599.

53. Thomas A. Bailey, *A Diplomatic History of the American People* (5th ed., New York, 1955), p. xi.

54. Richard L. Watson, Jr., "American Political History, 1900–1920," *South Atlantic Quarterly*, LIV (January, 1955), p. 109.

55. *Ibid.*

56. Harold T. Parker, "A Tentative Reflection on the Inter-disciplinary Approach and the Historian," *South Atlantic Quarterly*, LVI (January, 1957), 105–11.

57. McCormick and others, "Conference on American History," p. 115.

REFLECTIONS ON URBAN HISTORY
AND URBAN REFORM, 1865-1915[1]

by Mark D. Hirsch

BRONX COMMUNITY COLLEGE

NEW YORK

AMONG the manifold results of the Civil War, the one most frequently neglected or belittled in the usual historical cataloguing and made the mote in the new national eye has been the swiftly expanding city, so multiplied over the land as to constitute an urban movement if not a wave. This urban march was in turn productive of an age of reform in the cities so significant and influential as probably to prove the major force behind the progressive movement. It is heartening to observe, therefore, that historians have become increasingly attentive to urban history and its ramifications, and it is to this development that this study will seek to address itself.

Our cities were of course no new phenomenon—their origins can be traced back to earliest colonial times—but their amazingly accelerating growth, beginning with the 1840s and 1850s, was. Carl Bridenbaugh earlier and Richard C. Wade recently have already illuminated the growth and importance of cities in the colonial period and the young, transmontane Midwest, respectively, and done urban history a great service.[2] Our concept of an early rural America without an urban counterpart will have to undergo modification. Franklin Pierce's biographer, for example, has noted that basic to all of the President's difficulties "was a great social and political transformation which few, if any, of his contemporaries understood in all its ramifications," revolving around westward expansion, and *urban industrialization,* which were soon to threaten the eclipse of the Southern politicians.[3] In 1830, only

New York City and Philadelphia had populations of over 100,000; in 1880, there were twenty cities of that size. By 1900, there were 545 cities of 8,000 or more population. Of the decade 1890–1900, Harold U. Faulkner has written that "the growth of cities remains the most arresting demographical development of the period." [4] In 1926, Thomas H. Reed could survey the urban march and conclude: "This is the age of the city." [5]

The two main causes of urban population growth were, of course, immigration, which had resumed dramatically after the war and furnished a phenomenally burgeoning industrialism with a rich labor reservoir, and the continuing *landflucht* of native American farmers. The immigrants came increasingly from the south, central, and southeastern areas of Europe, beginning with the 1880s, and allegedly were creating an urban political and sociological problem by becoming ballot fodder for city bosses and by breaking down the homogeneity of our population with a less assimilable people whose culture and religions, and frequently their peasant economy, were "alien." Matching them, came the countless farmboys deserting their heritage for an urban mess of pottage; "they sang the praises of agriculture but eschewed farming as a vocation and sought their careers in the towns and cities." [6] Indeed, Fred A. Shannon raised the likelihood that the city, not the frontier, had been labor's safety valve.[7] This was part of a world-wide phenomenon: farmers faced competition from their brethren all over the earth and needed capital and machines to survive. The drabness, loneliness, and isolation in widely scattered homesteads decided others—and particularly their women-folk—to abandon the rural way of life.

The dean of our urban historians, Arthur Meier Schlesinger —Gene M. Gressley has aptly termed him "an apostle of urbanism"—opened our eyes a quarter century ago to the urban side of the ledger, to "the lure of the city," of urbanization in the 1880s becoming "a controlling factor in national life," and to the superior opportunities that helped to make the city

the supreme achievement of the new industrialism. In its confines were focused all the new economic forces: the vast accumulations of capital, the business and financial institutions, the spreading railway yards, the gaunt smoky mills, the white-collar middle classes, the motley wage-earning population. By the same token the city inevitably became the generating center for social and intellectual progress. . . . In a populous urban community like could find like; the person of ability, starved in his rural isolation, might by going there find sympathy, encouragement and that criticism which often refines talent into genius.

The refinements and pleasures of city living additionally sharpened the desire to come: professional fire and police protection; street lighting and paved streets; an unfailing water supply; rapid transit; a sewerage system; garbage disposal (although New York's Mayor Mitchel was years later to find himself in an unhappy imbroglio because of Staten Island's objection to having a garbage disposal plant there, proving that mundane considerations can have deadly consequences at election time); growing mass education; an increasing emancipation of women; medical, hospital, and public health facilities; and cultural, literary, sports, and recreational resources that were awesome compared to the countryside.[8]

Our cities had played no such vital role in the major movements of history as had the cities of Europe, but what the great English historian Sir Lewis Namier has written of the latter, two decades after Schlesinger's *The Rise of the City,* applies with but little diminution to ours.

It was the agrarian movement that rendered invincible the French Revolution and the Russian of 1917, but it was the cities which supplied these two revolutions with their ideology and their striking force; and a metropolitan population is the common denominator of the nation detached from its lands.

Is it not possible to draw some analogy in the case of the Civil War? It was these urban communities, "with their strong educated class and their new proletariat, which were now coming to the fore," Namier continued. "The uprooted individual becomes conscious of his personal rights, rational rather than traditional; and so does the crowd detached from the soil." [9]

The history of cities, however, is far from an idyllic account. The historian knows of their faults and shortcomings, of their slums and what they breed, and of their staggering administrative

and functional problems. Related disciplines have been fruit-
fully at work in this realm. The Committee on Historiography
of the Social Science Research Council has observed that urban
industrialism was "the chief external pressure that upset existing
family patterns"; and, "in all this confusing historic picture of
shifting ideas, folkways, and mores, of new family relationships
and of growing urban problems, the massive physical force producing change has been industrialism." [10]   Even those who bestow with the right hand the accolades, take away with the left
hand the problems.   William Anderson calls cities "the very centers of the new life of man" and describes their importance as productive agencies, but two pages later speaks of the problems of city
life which did not "force themselves insistently upon the American people until the 70's.   Then the rapid growth of city populations and expenditures, and the exposure of a most shocking
state of corruption in the government of New York City, compelled the people to give some attention to the new situation." [11]

Reed declares: "The city is the most marvelous material manifestation of man.   Nothing else he has done can equal the magnitude and complexity of even a modest city, while the modern
metropolis outruns imagination"; without it, "civilization was in-
achievable . . . one must respect the city as the cradle of progress"
and honor it as the custodian of twentieth century life—and then
he provides a fine analysis of "The Triumph of the Machine." [12]
Schlesinger quotes Josiah Strong's phrase of the city being "the
mighty heart of the body politic, sending its streams of life pul-
sating to the very finger-tips of the whole land"; he warns on the
next page, however: "But this was not the whole story"!

The most recent probing into the problem of an impersonal
industrialism and its impact upon American life is by Samuel P.
Hays, who incisively shows how the new factory techniques and
the revolutions in transportation and communications destroyed
localism and separatism "and linked more tightly every group and
section into one interdependent nation."   He explains that "businessmen, farmers, and workers individually could not cope with
the impersonal price-and-market network, but they soon discovered that as organized groups they could wield considerable

power," and thus through the corporation (and, later, more advanced forms of combination), farmers' cooperatives, and "business unionism" these groups answered the challenge of "organize or perish." His basic contribution is his contention that during the thirty years between 1885 and 1914, the social, economic, and political movements

comprised a reaction not against the corporation alone but also against industrialism and the many ways in which it affected the lives of Americans. The people of that era sought to do much more than simply to control corporations; they attempted to cope with industrial change in all its ramifications. True, they centered their fire on the business leader, but he was a symbol of change which they could conveniently attack, rather than the essence of change itself. A simple interpretation of the discontented poor struggling against the happy rich does violence to the complexity of industrial innovation and to the variety of human striving that occurred in response to it.

This approach permits a highly suggestive treatment of the Populist-progressive era. Regardless of their goals, different kinds of people "had to come to terms with the vastly new society brought about by industrialism." [14]

One of the gravest charges brought against that new urban society was its materialism. "In industrial America material success became the predominant measure of human achievement; the very term 'success' implied material prosperity." Men of talent and ability were encouraged to enter the business world rather than politics; their worldly gains only meant the impoverishment of the latter sphere, but their consciences were salved since so many of the churches of the time "justified the creation and acquisition of wealth, thus keeping in tune with the materialistic temper of America." [15] Elihu Root, one of Clinton Rossiter's true conservative statesmen, was able to compromise with this trammel, doing much useful public service in mid-career. Henry L. Stimson, one of Richard Hofstadter's mugwump type, rose above it; in 1908, he stated that he had never found the legal profession

thoroughly satisfactory . . . simply because the life of the ordinary New York lawyer is primarily and essentially devoted to the making of money—and not always successfully so.[16] . . . It has always seemed to me, in the law from what I have seen of it, that wherever the public interest has come into conflict with private interests, private interest was more adequately represented than the public interest.

When he did turn to federal service, he found it rewarding because of its ethical side and for getting closer to the problems of life. "And one always feels better when he feels that he is working in a good cause." [17]

What is disconcerting, then, is to find a letter from young Willard Straight—brilliant, balanced, idealistic—while consul-general at Mukden, China, to his intimate friend Henry Schoellkopf in 1907: "I many times think that it would have been much better to get well out of it [the diplomatic service] and mix up with a good business instead—money being the great thing in the world." [18] He did go on to make his fortune in banking, syndicate, and promotional activities. In 1916, seeing a dear, familiar world already toppled two years by the First World War, a wiser but still youthful Straight groped back after traditional values. He wrote to another good friend, Edwin V. Morgan, American ambassador to Brazil:

My dear Excellency, if you had lived as long in New York as I have, you would realize that there are darned few statesmen in industry, and that while questions of policy may form interesting subjects for after-dinner conversations, there are very few who care about and less who know about them. I have heard the situation summed up many times, "We are out to make money, not history." Some day perhaps we will learn better.[19]

It took a quarter century and another world war to make us learn better.

One clue to our materialistic bent may well have been the new, fluid, and hopeful urban middle class arising within the urban shell. Their enthusiasms seemed about equally divided between rising economically and socially and increasingly hoping for the reform of evils they observed during the progressive era—an attitude which tended to make them become progressives.[20] Arthur N. Holcombe has devoted himself to the story of their rise to status and importance in American politics and of their increasing consciousness of their special interests and their great opportunities in politics.[21]   About a society still so amorphous, Schlesinger admits candidly:

Americans had developed their political institutions under simple rural conditions; they had yet to learn how to govern cramped populations.   Preyed upon by unscrupulous men eager to exploit the expanding public utilities, municipal politics became a byword for venality.   [Elsewhere he adds:] Fortunately . . . this failure did not prevent cities from exerting a fructifying influence on cultural life.[22]

And Henry S. Commager makes the pithy observation that

few who knew the conditions of life in the large cities would contend that Americans had come to terms with their cities as their grandparents had come to terms with the countryside: American civilization was urban, but it was not yet an urbane civilization.[23]

Withal, cities could still develop and acquire, or retain, a personality indelibly associated with them.   For New York City, Bayrd Still has singled out four long-term characteristics: "its business-mindedness, its conviviality, its cosmopolitanism, and its constant change." [24]

Helping us to thread our way through this maze of urbanism's complexities with greater ease and perspicacity have been some important and stimulating contributions to our knowledge of this neglected field.   Schlesinger expanded his vital thesis in an article, "The City in American History," in 1940;[25] and further amplified upon it in 1949 in an essay called "The City in American Civilization," one of a collection in *Paths to the Present*.[26]   He declared that Turner, in his zeal to correct older notions,

overlooked another order of society which, rivaling the frontier even in the earliest days, eventually became the major force.   The city marched westward with the outposts of settlement, always injecting exotic elements into pioneer existence, while in the older sections it steadily extended its dominion over politics, economics and all the other interests of life.   The time came, in 1925, when Turner himself confessed the need of "an urban reinterpretation of our history." A true understanding of America's past demands this balanced view— an appreciation of the significance of both frontier and city.

For the period under consideration, in his discussion of urban influences and contributions, he then stated:

In the generation following the Civil War the city took supreme command. Between 1860 and 1900 the urban population again quadrupled while the rural merely doubled. With one out of every six people inhabiting communities of eight thousand or over in the earlier year, the proportion rose to nearly one out of four in 1880 and to one out of three in 1900. Considerably more than half of the urban-moving throng gravitated to places of twenty-five thousand and upwards.

He noted that the city imposed its will upon less developed regions and that "the rift between country and town widened portentously"; as a result, this rural inferiority and frustration erupted politically against "urban imperialism" through the Granger, Farmers' Alliance, and Populist movements.[27] "The Republicans in this county and many Democrats supported you on election day," Bert Lord commiserated with Theodore Roosevelt, Jr., who had just been defeated by Alfred E. Smith in the gubernatorial election of 1924, "but we did not have enough of them to compare with the city." [28]

Schlesinger soon found that pioneers may have a difficult time of it! Hard upon the appearance of his basic essay of 1940, a Festschrift in honor of Professor W. Stull Holt was published;[29] among the essays in American history was a distinguished effort by William Diamond, "On The Dangers of an Urban Interpretation of History," which posited urban interpretation from the rather jealous point of view of the urban sociologist. After a top-notch bibliographical survey of the field, in which the problems approach heavily predominated, Diamond declared:

This brief sketch of the development of sociological interest in the American city should make evident the fact that the historian of the American city has already at his disposal a wealth of literature on almost every phase of urban development. Unfortunately the great bulk of that material, since it has been produced by the sociologist, relates to the recent history of the American city. . . . Nevertheless, not much of modern urban life has been neglected, though little effort has been devoted to the development of a comprehensive theory of urbanism.

He then noted in a strange admission that "it is the history of the total city which the historian wishes to distil from the frequently formless, fluid mass of material available to him." [30]

But the historian may not want to be directed to study and gather together the leaves of disparate plants; it would seem that his temperament and training incline him to get down to the roots and then relate the history of the entire growth. For Diamond, therefore, to have been critical of the labors of Constance M. Green, Thomas J. Wertenbaker, Sidney I. Pomerantz, Robert G. Albion, and Ralph Foster Weld because they stemmed instead "from the growing interest in economic and social history, are not closely related to the thoughts and efforts of urban sociology, and do not attempt to integrate all aspects of the history of the city" [31] was excessively severe. The one book that Diamond definitely praised as "a synthesis of all aspects of the life of a great American city" is Bessie L. Pierce's monumental *A History of Chicago,* whose excellence, I believe, would have been increased by a little more attention to political history.

Diamond then took Schlesinger to task—in what became an amiable game of parry and riposte between them—for failing to define the terms "city" and "urbanization" according to four pages of criteria adduced by sociologists and for some conceptual suggestions. No one can quibble with the desire for precise terminology or pellucid analysis, but a certain amount of latitude might reasonably have been conceded in a philosophical interpretation of a general theme couched in a polished literary style. One might compare Diamond's treatment with the urbane one by the distinguished Committee on Historiography of the Social Science Research Council, also seeking improved sociological interpretations, which declared: "Even A. M. Schlesinger, Sr., who did much to start study of urbanism by historians and whose general synthesis in the latter half of *Land of the Free* is one of the best, keeps the city in a relatively subordinate position." [32] What Schlesinger, I believe, had done so ably was to point an inspirational finger down a new, roughly hewn path, after surveying for the route, and to plead for the laying down of a concrete highway by the craft.

In 1952, our historiographic knowledge of urbanism was further enhanced by the appearance of an important and useful "survey of urban historical writings since 1930" by Blake McKelvey,[33]
from whom we also have a notable history of Rochester, New
York.   He remarked upon "the awakening of scholarly interest
which soon occurred in this field" after Schlesinger, two decades
earlier, had "first revealed the dominant role played by urban developments in late nineteenth-century America"—some forty volumes since 1930 of what might be called "urban biography."   He
observed that the urban period from 1835 to 1870

might be characterized as one of Yankee cities—if that adjective may
be used in its broadest sense.   The enterprise and ingenuity and
capital of old Americans developed more efficient trade facilities,
transformed earlier handicrafts into factory industries and exploited
the labor of hundreds of thousands of newcomers from across the
Atlantic.

When however, the need for municipal improvements and services developed in the seventies, and "the street car, telephone, gas,
and electric utility corporations, with large favors to ask and to
offer, reached monopoly proportions in the eighties and nineties
. . . the old Yankee pattern of municipal democracy suffered a
breakdown in most large cities." [34]

Urbanism is a national and unifying phenomenon.   No section has been invulnerable to its coming.   Even typically agrarian
areas—East and West—were not untouched by its impact.   Lee
Benson has significantly described [35] for us the efforts and cooperation in the 1870s and early 1880s of farmers, and merchants and
manufacturers of New York State—but particularly the merchants
of New York City—against their common foes, the Erie and New
York Central Railroads, whose management and lobbies sought to
perpetuate high discriminatory freight rates at the shippers' expense but in favor of through, long-haul shipments from farther
states to New York City.   Laissez-faire railroad competition had
become so intense as to get out of control and was therefore abandoned by the roads in their Trunk Line Pool in 1877 with other
major carriers elsewhere, despite the injury and threat it would
pose to New York City's commercial interests and position as an

entrepôt. The business community, allying with farmers equally injured, consequently struck back against this effort at monopoly, inspiring the State Assembly's Hepburn Investigation and the restrictive railway legislation adopted by the state in 1879 that saw the repudiation of the free interplay of competition and the end of a perfect example of laissez faire that had become irrational and lethal. After this success, New York's merchants, Benson believes, "played the leading role in the campaign to achieve national regulation of railroads," which culminated in the passage of the Interstate Commerce Act of 1887.[36]

Benson made some additional important points. One was that "the impress of urban thought patterns, urban interests, and urban influences was much more pervasive in New York agrarian areas than in other regions. Agriculture was subordinate in the East." Another of Benson's points was that, in the West, the power of the Grangers "sharply and permanently declined" in the later seventies, whereas "the New York Grange became more militant and influential." Later, when Westerners again joined an agrarian order, "they turned to the Farmers' Alliance, which was born in New York and spread out from that state." And, finally, when the National Anti-Monopoly League was organized in 1881, it was in a restaurant on Sixth Avenue in New York City! Started by merchant reformers (of the kind who had been injured by the railroad abuses), Jeffersonian democrats, labor leaders, Greenbackers, "and socially conscious ministers" to resist corporate monopoly, "the heart of the movement was in Manhattan, and the National Executive Committee located there maintained a tight rein on the entire apparatus."[37] It is noteworthy that this League, seeking the reform of monopolistic abuses, should have been founded at exactly the same time as a political organization that was to prove the most potent foe of Tammany Hall within the Democratic party in the city, the New York County Democracy. Abuses and evils might be abroad in the land, but reform was also in the air.

Benson's findings for the East reflected in part the contributions of two earlier articles on the West and urbanism. In 1941, Bayrd Still's "Patterns of Mid-Nineteenth Century Urbanization in the Middle West" appeared in the *Mississippi Valley Histori-cal Review*,[38] and provided us with a significant concept:

Until recently a persistent preoccupation with the agrarian aspects of the westward march of American settlement has to some extent ob-scured the fact that the prospect of future towns and cities as well as the promise of broad and fertile acres lured settlers to the "sunset regions." On many a frontier the town builder was as conspicuous as the farmer pioneers; the western city, through the efforts of its founders to extend its economic hinterland, actually facilitated the agrarian development of the West; and the opportunities attending city growth as well as those afforded by cheap farm lands contributed to the dynamic sense of economic abundance felt by Americans of the mid-nineteenth century.

As a result, by the 1870s, "the Middle West showed a spectacular urban growth. It could then boast seven cities of more than a hundred thousand people, whereas thirty years before only New Orleans had achieved that size." A comparative analysis of five Great Lakes cities—Buffalo, Cleveland, Detroit, Chicago, and Mil-waukee—showed that "they all responded to the democratic move-ment by extending popular participation in municipal govern-ment and then by broadening the authority of the executive or administrative commission."

As in their eastern counterparts, "a predominant concern for trade and commerce gave way in the middle sixties to the encour-agement of manufacturing," and within a few years more they too were bedeviled by the problems of size. Still concluded that these Midwestern cities had both a frontier and an urban heritage.

As they grew, their concern for popular management and their em-phasis upon the intrinsic role of the individual in the promotion of the physical and cultural growth of the city reveal attitudes often ob-served by students of the agrarian frontier. At the same time, they showed a willing dependence upon eastern sources in the transmis-sion of culture, a studied imitation of tested forms of municipal prac-tice and urban service, and an expanding assumption of community responsibility.

Next, Chester M. Destler, in his "study of western radicalism in terms of ideological interchange and conflict between western agrarians and urban radicals," had "uncovered urban origins of a number of supposedly rural stereotypes and remedial proposals

that Turnerians have regarded as peculiarly western." [39]   He felt
that the existence of a system of democratic thought in the upper
Mississippi Valley after the Civil War, "derived from an earlier
integration of urban radicalism with the coonskin democracy of
the hardwood frontier, suggests that subsequent intercourse between urban and agrarian radicals occurred within a conceptual
pattern common to both."   Destler traced "non-agrarian elements" in the liberal Republican movement; saw a similar "dual
character" in Greenbackism; maintained that "the co-operative
movement is another example of the alacrity with which western
agrarians borrowed urban formulas ready-made in their attempts
to solve agricultural problems"; and noted, in reverse, the *Western* urban impact of the thinking and writings of Henry Demarest
Lloyd and Henry George upon the radical movements of the rural
West and urban East.

This approach suggested to him "that in Populism may be
found the system of radical thought that emerged in the West
from three decades of recurring unrest, agitation, and intercourse
with radical and reform movements in the urban world."   Populism's central principle was antimonopolism, but it also advocated
"a program of economic collectivism," was sympathetic to cooperatives, borrowed the "labor-cost theory of value" from earlier labor
and agrarian movements—all with some urban root or foundation
—and eagerly sought a coalition with urban labor, although in
vain.   Destler, incidentally, paid full tribute to the importance
of a transplanted working-class Loco-Focoism of Jacksonian and
Eastern urban origins.   The cycle full round again!

Thus, even in militant agrarian movements aiming at redress,
seek out the urban hand!   The leadership, the educational resources, the stimulation of systematic thinking and derivative
principles, the organizing ability and managerial talent, the media
of public information, the legislative connections, the moneyed
strength, and the greater loyalty and devotion of urban followers
to their particular organizations or movements made urbanism
on all economic levels a force of compelling influence.   Could
these factors become sinister?   They did in the hands of Horace
Samuel Merrill, who like Still had also turned his attention to
growing Midwestern urbanism but had conjured up such a malev-

olent picture of an Eastern "big-business imperialism" acting through a subservient "Bourbon democracy" in the Midwest as to make his book read like a latter-day Populist tract! [40]   The "businessmen with bulging purses" were pitted against the "farmers with slim purses"; and, likened to something verminous, "with unprecedented speed and singleness of purpose, entrepreneurs swarmed out of the Civil War debris, carrying with them plans, inventions, and war-born fortunes to be used in turning the nation's natural resources and man power into instruments of unprecedented gain."   This Bourbon democracy "was a cabal of industrialist-financier entrepreneurs operating within the Democratic Party," a concept that must delight Republicans.   To end the cabal, all the voters need have done was to vote Republican! If we read some of the "Wall Street fever" out of the book, there is much of solid value, for it shows the march of urbanization and industrialization into the Midwest, the resulting political maturing of the area, and the interrelationship between this pattern and the agrarianism there.[41]

Aside from the excellent bibliographic surveys and resources called to our attention in the works of Schlesinger, Still, Diamond, Destler, McKelvey, and Benson, there is a common denominator running through most of them.   The first five call for further investigations and fresh efforts in this newly shaping area. It is a legitimate complaint.   So much must yet be added to the sum total of our knowledge.   We just simply need to know more about our cities and their histories in order that we may gain depth and perspective and synthesize the research in every related branch of the social sciences.   The Committee on Historiography declared in 1954:

In all this confusing historic picture of shifting ideas, folkways, and mores, of new family relationships and of growing urban problems, the massive physical force producing change has been industrialism. Yet, judging from the narrative synthesis, the obvious fact that it was industrialism that moved us from the world of George Washington to that of the present day apparently needs still more emphasis.[42]

A modern history of New York City, for example, would help us better to understand Tammany Hall, municipal administration, the evolution of a free, universal public education, and the impact of Puerto Rican immigration upon the life of the community. There never yet was a forest without the trees.

Just as the period of our history from the Civil War to the 1890s was chiefly "a period of industrial and continental expansion and political conservation, so the age that has just passed, running from about 1890 to the second World War, can be considered an age of reform," Richard Hofstadter has written in his scintillating *The Age of Reform*.[43] Eric F. Goldman has preferred to go back earlier, to "the years immediately after the Civil War," in his own excellent history of reform, *Rendezvous with Destiny*, believing that

the reform movements that culminated in the New Deal and the Fair Deal, in my opinion, are most directly a reaction to a rapidly urbanizing, industrializing America. I have therefore begun with the late 1860's of American history, when the factory and the city were swiftly taking over dominance of the United States.[44]

In either case, we shall no longer be able to explore further into Populism and the progressive movement without leaning heavily upon these two stimulating labors.

"'An age of reform' was under way, the anti-Grant Lyman Trumbull announced in 1871, and so it was," avers Goldman to sustain his view.[45] "Nevertheless," Harold U. Faulkner contends in turn, "if there was a decade in city affairs that could be called an 'age of reform,' it was the nineties." [46] Some ten years later, Woodrow Wilson in a speech before the City Club of Philadelphia on November 18, 1909, could declare: "The desire for reform is everywhere manifest enough, and many thoughtful and energetic persons are devoting themselves to it with ardor and seriousness." [47] And therein lies the essence and the miracle of reform: it is simply timeless. Whether against Grantism and Tweedism earlier or conservative Republicanism and corporate monopoly later, whether in the days of a calloused Spencerian social Darwinism or of an awakening social concern in the collective welfare, whether in behalf of limited single reforms and solitary objectives or towards vast and sweeping recasts of society, in

all the realms of man's interests, the reformer toils without end
to eradicate evils and abuses and to improve conditions. He cannot be pinned down to the 1890s or the 1900s; he can be found in
our early history and yet is with us today. He may strive independently or in reform organizations or through the established
parties; he may even oppose other reformers! He is difficult to
classify, but, by constantly endeavoring to leave society a little
bit better and by being solicitous of the status of the individual,
he comes close indeed to being our perennial liberal.

Basically, the urban reformer seeks to alleviate the corrosive
effects of excessive partisanship by being constantly alert to detect, challenge, and publicize; or he can seek to alter the forms of
that partisanship by planning for corrective change and convinc-
ing the public to support it. His devotion compensates for public apathy and indifference, and he gets us better government than
we deserve. As a gadfly to authority and as our nonpartisan
watchdog and our conscience both, the urban reformer contests
against the boss and his machine and seeks to educate the citizen
to his opportunities and his obligations.

The Citizens Union, for example, recently sued to prevent the
appointment of a candidate into the civil service on the ground of
not being properly qualified for the job. Its analyses of candidates' records permit a thoughtful appraisal before elections. The
League of Women Voters periodically distributes effective literature. Papers of the Civil Service Reform Association, also vigilant of civic welfare, reveal that their representatives have attended countless public hearings before the Municipal Civil Service Commission to challenge the fitness of candidates; they too
have brought legal action when necessary and have successfully
fought for legislation tightening "exemptions." Or, regard the
New York Committee of One Thousand which in 1932 drew up
a commanding program of legislation aimed at obtaining a new
city charter, amending the state constitution, and reforming the
county governments and the civil service; [48] and, that its chairman,
William Jay Schieffelin, on its behalf petitioned Governor Franklin D. Roosevelt for the removal from office of Mayor James J.
Walker after presenting fifteen grave charges in evidence.[49]

Over forty-five years ago, Ostrogorski paid tribute to such efforts as paving the way for a new method of political action in this country.   He wrote:

Its basis has been laid in the struggles for emancipation in the form of "committees of seventy," or of "one hundred," of the "citizens' movements," of the "mugwumps," of the "leagues" or "civic federations," all of which represented free associations of men brought together for a particular cause, completely setting aside, for the nonce, their views on other political questions.   By this method it has been possible to combine all the living forces of American society in the struggle against political corruption, and to win victories which enable us not to despair of American democracy and of the government of the people by the people.   In the sphere of great national questions, as well as in municipal life, everywhere the "leagues" have been the instigators of the civic awakening; all the great reforms which have been passed to purify political life, beginning with that of the civil service, are due to their initiative or to their efforts.[50]

It may be fashionable to deprecate the reformers, as Edward J. Flynn, late Democratic boss of the Bronx did,[51] hardly with disinterestedness, but this stout minority carries on despite sneers and ridicule, humiliations and defeats, and social ostracism by neighbors and associates.   The urban reformer is as preoccupied with life's daily concerns as we are, yet he takes the time to do what he proposes.   For a reformer is a man who is constantly, in a democracy, on the firing line in season and out, whom historians at some later time may treat as a transient phase and consign to the historical graveyard without appreciating that devoted men and women of this kind are in twenty dozen organizations, ever doing picket duty.   "As a constitutional anti-Tammany Democrat," wrote attorney John C. Mahon in 1935,

who watched at the polls for John Purroy Mitchel when he beat Tammany—and as one of the sympathizers with the work done by the Seabury Investigation and the Committee of One Thousand under William J. Shefflin [sic], I have taken it on the chin all these years without the slightest protest.   A good soldier is always prepared to be consigned to the scrap heap if it is necessary to further a cause.[52]

That great time of the reformer's ascendancy, the progressive era, has generally been regarded either as having arisen unilaterally out of the spate of agrarian movements that made their ap-

pearance in the years of bitter farm discontent between the Civil
War and the turn of the century and as being itself an evolving
way-stop on the road to the reformism of the New Deal; or, alter-
nately, as resulting from *two* converging forces in those germinal
years, the same farmers' movements *and* the unrelenting municipal reform movements against political graft and corruption operating within a general urban campaign against most of the de-
basing ills of an industrial society.[53]   Even the latter approach
understates the case for urban reform.

The progressive movement sought to restore representative
government and to shore up the small businessman, the farmer,
the self-employed and the professional, the middle class and the
white-collar worker against massive corporate organization through
the intercession of the federal government after all other ways
had come to naught.   It was the first national assault upon en-
trenched big business and corrupt machine politics.   Urban reformers took the lead and directed the strategy against railroads,
utilities, corporations, and rings, thus providing the preponderant
urban base for progressivism, whether under Wilson's version
evolving from Populism and urbanism, that aimed at restoring
and controlling competition, or Theodore Roosevelt's more ur-
ban-centered desire to regulate monopoly at the source.   This,
then, was the goal shared by Populism, and by a progressivism that
had been nurtured from the earlier, urban reform strain that for
thirty long years had sought to eliminate the boss, purify municipal politics, and revivify the participating political role of the
plain citizen in a democratic society.   This was progressivism's
great heritage, and its champions sought to continue the crusade
on all levels of government against the overbearing political machine.   As Hofstadter has pinpointed it:

Populism had been overwhelmingly rural and provincial.   The ferment of the Progressive era was urban, middle-class, and nationwide.
Above all, Progressivism differed from Populism in the fact that the
middle classes of the cities not only joined the trend toward protest
but took over its leadership.

Seen whole and in context, progressivism was infinitely more urban than agrarian.[54]

In any case, we have emphasized the agrarian crusade heritage and slighted or ignored the obverse side of the coin, the urban crusade. This is not meant to minimize the desperate plight of debtor farmers of major cash crops in an age of machines who were beset by increasing international competition and rising costs, trapped by the technical "closing" of the frontier and the exhaustion of free lands, and impelled by an impersonal price-and-cost system into belligerent combinations. Nor is it meant to deprecate the profound importance of the agrarian crusade in our history, a last-ditch political attempt to storm the urban citadel. All this is conceded. It is possible, however, that we have been so bemused at the disquieting prospect of bidding a nostalgic farewell to a fading yeomanry as to overlook urban reform's efforts for better government, merit civil service, municipal ownership and operation, social justice, slum clearance and industrial welfare legislation, and a host of kindred struggles. For in these years of growing imbalance in American life, the cities had had equal title with the countryside to discontent and reform necessity.

By failing to give proper weight to this thrusting surge of urban reform, we are in the anomalous position of analyzing the fruition before dissecting the seed. Actually, Populism was considerably antiurban, and the very conditions that farmers bitterly assailed and united to overcome were mainly unleashed by urbanization and the industrial state. Populists lashed out at the cities and their money lenders, currency and tariff policies, and mortgage foreclosings.[55] The farmer seemed to turn radical for survival rather than by conviction, for his spotty record—particularly in the South—in liberal and progressive movements since the turn of the century should give the scholar deep pause for reflection. That progressivism took over and effected most of Populism's program is no proof of lineal descent. Both were arrayed against the evils detailed, and, moreover, part of Populism's platform of 1892 was calculated to woo the labor vote and construct a farmer-labor alliance that never materialized. The urban headwaters are there: how flows the stream?

Kenneth W. Hechler sought to carve out a slightly different

river bed between agrarian protest and the progressive years by turning scholarly attention to "insurgency," the activities of "a group of dissentient Congressmen representing the more progressive wing of the Republican Party" that defied their House and Senate leaders, broke the power of Speaker Cannon, harassed Taft, and who were the Republican counterparts of the Populists to the Democratic party. Hechler maintains:

The hotbed of Insurgency was in the agrarian states of Kansas, Nebraska, Minnesota, Wisconsin and Iowa. The movement overflowed into the Dakotas and Indiana, and there were also traces of it in New England and on the Pacific Coast. But in large part it was a middle-western agrarian protest differing little from similar waves of discontent that had risen in this area during the last quarter of the nineteenth century.

Yet, the insurgents had to adopt "the Hamiltonian tool of a powerful government" in order to graft Jeffersonian principles onto a modern industrial economy. Hechler also admits that the muckrakers greatly shaped insurgent thinking; and, that while insurgency battled for agrarian interests, "the progressive movement enlisted social reformers, champions of the rights of labor, and scions of the business world advocating a greater sense of responsibility to the public"—truly an urban galaxy! While insurgents were on the attack in Washington, the progressives battled largely in "the city hall and the state capitol." [56]

Some dozen years later, Theodore Saloutos and John D. Hicks jointly authored an important study of the "long history of farm discontent" in the "western Middle West" that dug deeper the traditional channel of a direct connection "From Populism to Insurgency," and which, they contended, culminated ultimately in the Progressive party of 1912. Ironically, however, their work demonstrated that farmers, to survive, had to adopt the methods of businessmen, to improve their distribution and marketing techniques in their organizations and cooperatives, and to control production.[57]

That same year, 1951, Russell B. Nye's excellent work on progressive politics in the same area also held to the older interpretation that nineteenth-century agrarian revolt fathered twentieth-century progressivism. A considerable rivulet, however, drained off to merge with the newer stream of urban interpretation: investigating Midwestern *urban* reformism as well, he inevitably showed agrarian indebtedness to its educational resources and philosophy, to the social sciences, to theology through "the social gospel" and reformer-ministers, and to socialism—intellectual and spiritual forces that were decidedly non-Populistic but came out of the universities, the labor force, and the reawakening religious response to social needs.[58]

Most tantalizing of these double-edged swords, however, arose in the case of George E. Mowry, who observed that the progressive movement was not restricted to one party and was not the product of a single economic class.

Farmers and laborers were at its core, but they were soon joined by multitudes from the white collar and small business classes and even by some of the very rich. In fact, few reform movements in American history have had the support of more wealthy men.

And Mowry cites such a gallery of urban businessmen. After noting that the movement "was a way of thought that separated an old and a new America," and some of its contributions, he then declared very plainly:

But the real seedbed of progressivism was of course Populism. The progressive movement was cradled in the home of the Populists, the Middle West. The progressive program was grounded upon the Populist platform. As the historian of the Populist movement [John D. Hicks] has pointed out, almost every plank in that platform was written into law during the progressive years. Moreover, there was a direct political bloodline from Bryan to Wilson and on to a young assistant secretary of the navy, Franklin Delano Roosevelt. . . . The Populist center of gravity was, and remained, among the farmers.[59]

A few years later, Mowry did an illuminating study on *The California Progressives* in which progressivism was shown to be "not just a reformulation of an older radicalism. . . . On the whole its leaders were drawn from a different class than were those of the Grangers and the Populists. In its origins it was an urban rather than a rural movement." He also noted that "from Theodore Roosevelt and Woodrow Wilson down through all the

levels of local government, most progressive leaders had been vio-
lently opposed to the nineteenth-century agrarian radicalism of
William Jennings Bryan and the Populists"! His analysis of
forty-seven such leaders further indicated their "upper middle
class" status; they were mainly professional, but about a quarter
were smaller businessmen and a third, journalists; they averaged
under forty years of age and three quarters had a college education; they were equally opposed to organized labor or to corporate wealth grown too powerful and arrogant; and, paramount,
they had given "California honest and decent government." [60]

This dichotomy was resolved in 1958 when Mowry wrote a
pamphlet surveying the progressive movement for the American
Historical Association's new and indispensable Service Center for
Teachers, in which he stated:

Starting in Midwest cities and states, it spread geographically to both
the east and west coasts and by 1910 was nationwide. Its impulse was
felt in the farm communities of Iowa and Wisconsin, in the great
urban centers of New York, Cleveland, Chicago, and San Francisco.
. . . On the local municipal level the movement comprehended such
reform crusades as those of Mayor Seth Low of New York against
Tammany, of Tom Johnson and Golden Rule Jones in Cleveland
and Toledo, Ohio, the fight against the Union Labor Party machine
in San Francisco, and the struggle of the "good government" leagues
in Los Angeles.

Now his approach was urban orientated: he spoke of the direct
primary, nonpartisan tickets, and the city manager and commission plans and other aims of progressivism as devices for the overthrow of boss rule and franchise politics. Moreover, "but an
even more comprehensive aim of the municipal movement was to
make the twentieth-century city a decent, healthy, and enjoyable
place in which to live." Nationally, progressivism concerned itself with trusts and unions—hardly rural phenomena—and addressed itself to the general query: "How were the nation's historic values of individualism and equality to be preserved in the
new twentieth-century collective world of highly organized industry, highly organized labor, and the highly organized city." Finally, and most significant, Mowry, under a sectional heading,
"The Old Interpretations," relegated his own earlier thinking:
"Their conclusions were that the progressive movement was little

more than an extension of the Populist crusade of the 1880's and 1890's which reached its climax and failed in the defeat of William Jennings Bryan and the Democratic party in 1896"! [61]

Anticlimactic, therefore, is Mowry's 1958 volume, *The Era of Theodore Roosevelt: 1900–1912*, which, to this writer, is the ablest and most brilliant synthesis of the dozen years of Roosevelt's and Taft's administrations and which takes its place alongside the volumes of Hofstadter and Goldman for the period treated. In it he fastens down the hatches with swifter, briefer strokes. These years marked the birth and growth of the progressive movement which "attempted to find solutions for the amazing number of domestic and foreign problems spawned by the great industrial, urban, and population changes of the late nineteenth century." Why had the agrarian crusades of the previous century failed? Their main difficulty was that "they were essentially rural answers to urban problems, and thus they missed their mark by a little wider margin than is customary." Describing this "new and strange immigration" that had settled in our cities by 1900 and after, he notes:

Thus, just at the time that it was becoming the dominant force in American life, the city was being rapidly differentiated from the rest of the nation by the growing ethnic, religious, and cultural differences. . . . Perhaps at no other time was the line of demarcation between urban and rural America so sharp as it was in the first two decades of the twentieth century.

By 1900, too, the progressive politician had already made his appearance in city and state governments throughout the nation.

"Populism," Mowry declares, "arose from farmer distress in a period of acute depression. Its reforms were belly reforms." Progressivism, however, "arose in a period of relative prosperity. Its reforms were more the results of the heart and the head than of the stomach. Its leaders were largely recruited from the professional and business classes of the city." In this Republican phase of progressivism, from 1900 to 1912, Theodore Roosevelt obviously was the pivotal figure.

A twentieth-century urban man, Roosevelt was extremely sensitive and responsive to the new doctrines abroad in the United States and the world. He recognized the reactionary impulse of much of Midwest progressivism. It was really "a kind of rural toryism," he remarked. Being a good politician, he compromised with the agrarians, but his heart and head were elsewhere. An admirer of organization, a seeker of power, and a glorifier of strength, Roosevelt was really devoted to the New Nationalism.[62]

With impeccable integrity and scholarship, Mowry had modified some earlier thinking in a way inspiring and instructive to younger members of the profession.

Arthur S. Link belongs to the new generation of scholars that Mowry mentioned in his pamphlet. Link's claim is cemented by his outstanding books on Woodrow Wilson, with more to come. In his work on Wilson and progressivism, he also demonstrates the "new" or urban viewpoint; and, in mentioning that American humanitarianism was not entirely dead, has written: "This spirit manifested itself in an organized way mainly in the cities." Discussing the reform crusade in the years 1900 to 1917, he discerns some unity and chronological thread in it. "The first reform wave came in the cities, with a great drive to overturn the politicians allied with corporations, railroads, and utilities." Next, the reformers campaigned to capture the state governments and thenceafter welled on upwards to affect the national parties.[63] But the chain reaction of reform had exploded initially in the cities.

During these years, urban reformers, in varying numbers, pressed for a staggering array of reforms: for short ballot (the New York reformer, Richard S. Childs, founded the Short Ballot Organization in 1909, with Woodrow Wilson as president), direct primary, and civil service reform; for the simplification of municipal government, the concentration of power and responsibility in executive hands, and the separation of state and local elections; for the strong mayor or the city commission or the city manager plans; and, very definitely, for nonpartisanship in municipal politics. They agitated for voting machines, for proper administrative and police supervision of primary and polling places, for corrupt practices legislation, for governmental provisions for campaign financing; and, many of them were impressed with the initiative and referendum (which were Western in origin), and with the recall, which had first been introduced in the Los Angeles city charter in 1903. They favored absent-voters legislation, the Australian ballot, and some form of proportional representation or of preferential voting.

Their story was repeated in our major cities. Reform organizations either distributed political information (the Municipal Voters League of Chicago, or the Citizens Union), endorsed slates drawn from all parties (the Library Hall Association of Cambridge, Massachusetts), presented their own parties (Fusion, in New York), studied problems and published information but took no sides (the City Club of New York), or undertook specialized functions (the Citizens Budget Commission, or the Charity Organization Society of New York). Finally, one could not fail to mention the Bureau of Municipal Research, formed in New York in 1906, a model for many similar bureaus elsewhere, which provided expert studies and undertook research projects to give governmental agencies the facts they needed for efficient administration and sound action.

Thus, the urban crusade, followed by a quarter century of progressivism, has proved a constantly significant and frequently vital force in American life. That story is now being increasingly told, and the time may not prove too distant when Turner's later thoughts about the need of "an urban reinterpretation of our history" will achieve full fruition.

NOTES

1. This paper is part of a study done under the auspices of the Institute of New York Area Studies at the City College of New York, 1958.

2. See Carl Bridenbaugh, *Cities in the Wilderness: the First Century of Urban Life in America, 1625–1742* (New York, 1955); his *Cities in Revolt: Urban Life in America, 1743–1776* (New York, 1955); his *Rebels and Gentlemen: Philadelphia in the Age of Franklin* (New York, 1942); his *Seat of Empire: the Political Role of Eighteenth-Century Williamsburg* (Williamsburg, Va., 1950); and Richard C. Wade, *The Urban Frontier: the Rise of Western Cities, 1790–1830* (Cambridge, Mass., 1959).

3. Roy F. Nichols, *Franklin Pierce: Young Hickory of the Granite Hills* (Philadelphia, 1958), pp. 542, 543.

4. Harold U. Faulkner, *Politics, Reform and Expansion, 1890–1900* (New York, 1959), p. 10.

5. Thomas H. Reed, *Municipal Government in the United States* (New York, 1926), p. 6. Cf. Faulkner, *Politics, Reform and Expansion*, pp. 1, 10–12, Chap. 3, *passim*.

6. Richard Hofstadter, *The Age of Reform: from Bryan to F.D.R.* (New York, 1956), pp. 8, 32. For a general survey and review of the basic economic history of the post-Civil War period, from among the voluminous literature in the field, see Fred A. Shannon, *America's Economic Growth* (New York, 1940), Part III, pp. 339–543, *passim;* Edward C. Kirkland, *A History of American Economic Life* (New York, 1951), pp. 379–571, *passim;* and Harold U. Faulkner, *American Economic History* (New York, 1954), pp. 365–552, *passim*.

7. See Gene M. Gressley, "The Turner Thesis—A Problem in Historiography," *Agricultural History*, XXXII (October, 1958), 235. See also Shannon, *America's Economic Growth,* pp. 369–70, 373.

8. Arthur Meier Schlesinger, *The Rise of the City, 1878–1898* (New York, 1933), Chaps. III and IV, especially pp. 78 ff. See also, Gressley, "The Turner Thesis," p. 236; and Homer C. Hockett and Arthur M. Schlesinger, *Land of the Free: a Short History of the American People* (New York, 1944), pp. 368–71. Professor Faulkner has summarized this transformation thus: "It was inevitable that cities should become centers of culture at the expense of the country, for wealth and leisure were increasingly concentrated there." (*Politics, Reform and Expansion,* p. 43.)

9. Sir Lewis B. Namier, *Avenues of History* (London, 1952), pp. 25–28.

10. *The Social Sciences in Historical Study: a Report of the Committee on Historiography* (Social Science Research Council, Bulletin 64; New York, 1954), pp. 166, 167.

11. William Anderson, *American City Government* (New York, 1932), pp. 3, 5. Cf. Chap. II: "The Growth of Cities in the United States," pp. 18–37.

12. Reed, *Municipal Government in the United States,* pp. 3, 14, 15, Chap. VI, *passim*.

13. Hockett and Schlesinger, *Land of the Free,* pp. 370, 371.

14. Samuel P. Hays, *The Response to Industrialism: 1885–1914* (Chicago, 1957), pp. 2, 7, Chap. III, and pp. 188–90, especially. See also Hofstadter, *The Age of Reform,* Chap. VI: "The Struggle over Organization," pp. 213 ff.

15. Hays, *The Response to Industrialism,* pp. 2, 22–27. Cf. Sidney Fine. *Laissez Faire and the General-Welfare State: a Study of Con-*

flict in American Thought, 1865–1901 (Ann Arbor, 1957), pp. 117–25, *passim.*

16. In this connection, it is interesting to compare the advice given by ex-President Grover Cleveland to young Fred C. Bacon, of Toledo, Ohio, in a letter dated August 14, 1889 (quoted in *Library of Congress Information Bulletin,* June 30, 1958, from one of three new Cleveland letters recently acquired).

17. Quoted in Hofstadter, *The Age of Reform,* pp. 162, 163.

18. Willard Straight Papers, Cornell University Library, Box 38, "Far East, 1907" Folder, from Mukden, February 3, 1907.

19. *Ibid.,* Box 5, Folder 92, to Rio de Janeiro, October 31, 1916.

20. Hays, *The Response to Industrialism,* pp. 73, 74; Hofstadter, *The Age of Reform,* pp. 5, 210, 215–217.

21. Arthur N. Holcombe, *The Middle Classes in American Politics* (Cambridge, 1940); see also his *The New Party Politics* (New York, 1933). Cf. Samuel Lubell, *The Future of American Politics* (New York, 1952), pp. 28, 29. Lubell stresses the consciousness of "the climbing urban masses."

22. Arthur M. Schlesinger, *Paths to the Present* (New York, 1949), p. 226; Hockett and Schlesinger, *Land of the Free,* p. 371.

23. Henry S. Commager, *The American Mind: an Interpretation of American Thought and Character since the 1880's* (New Haven, 1950), p. 406.

24. Bayrd Still, "The Personality of New York City," *New York Folklore,* XIV (Summer, 1958), 83–91. In this connection, "Changing New York," *Newsweek,* LII, No. 2 (July 14, 1958), 75–77, may be of interest.

25. *Mississippi Valley Historical Review,* XXVII (June, 1940), 43–66.

26. Schlesinger, *Paths to the Present,* Chap. XI, pp. 210–33.

27. *Ibid.,* pp. 210, 223–25, 228, 229, especially. See also Gressley, "The Turner Thesis," pp. 238, 239, for his account of Henry Nash Smith's contention that the frontier had nourished an "agrarian myth" and the unfortunate distrust of the city.

28. Bert Lord Papers, Cornell University Library; Albany to Oyster Bay, N.Y., November 5, 1924.

29. Eric F. Goldman, ed., *Historiography and Urbanization: Essays in American History in Honor of W. Stull Holt* (Baltimore, 1941). William Diamond's essay is on pp. 67–108.

30. *Ibid.,* pp. 89–91.   31. *Ibid.,* p. 92.

32. *The Social Sciences in Historical Study,* p. 166.

33. Blake McKelvey, "American Urban History Today," *American Historical Review,* LVII (July, 1952), 919–29.

34. *Ibid.,* esp. pp. 919, 923, 926.

35. Lee Benson, *Merchants, Farmers and Railroads: Railroad Regulation and New York Politics, 1850–1887* (Cambridge, Mass., 1955).

36. *Ibid.*, pp. vii, 30, 36–53, *passim.* Fine adds in support, that "merchants and shippers played the crucial role in the framing of the so-called Granger laws in Illinois, Iowa, Wisconsin, and Minnesota." (*Laissez Faire and the General-Welfare State,* p. 107.)

37. Benson, *Merchants, Farmers and Railroads,* pp. 87, 150–173, *passim.*

38. XXVIII (September, 1941), 187–206.

39. Chester M. Destler, *American Radicalism, 1865–1901: Essays and Documents* (New London, Conn., 1946). Chap. I, "Western Radicalism, 1865–1901: Concepts and Origins," appeared in the *Mississippi Valley Historical Review,* XXXI (December, 1944), 335–68.

40. Horace Samuel Merrill, *Bourbon Democracy of the Middle West, 1865–1896* (Baton Rouge, La., 1953).

41. *Ibid.*, esp. pp. 1–3, 98, 99, 140, 141, 158, 159, 272, 273.

42. *The Social Sciences in Historical Study,* pp. 166, 167.

43. Hofstadter, *The Age of Reform,* p. 3.

44. Goldman, *Rendezvous with Destiny,* p. viii.

45. *Ibid.*, p. 19.

46. Faulkner, *Politics, Reform and Expansion,* p. 44. See Chap. 2, *passim,* for an excellent summary of reform, among other developments, owing to "The Revolt of the Cities."

47. Woodrow Wilson, *College and State: Educational, Literary and Political Papers* (1875–1913), ed. by Ray Stannard Baker and William E. Dodd (New York, 1925), II, 188.

48. Civil Service Reform Association Papers, Cornell University Library, Folder 549 XIII, 00 b 9. H. Eliot Kaplan to Judge Samuel H. Ordway, October 26, 1932, enclosing copy of letter from Committee.

49. New York Committee of One Thousand, *Text of Charges against Mayor Walker,* No. 14 (June, 1932).

50. M. Ostrogorski, *Democracy and the Party System in America* (New York, 1912), p. 443.

51. Edward J. Flynn, *You're the Boss* (New York, 1947), pp. x, 8, 13, 14, 16, 222, 223.

52. William Sulzer Papers, Cornell University. Mahon to Sulzer, New York City, February 18, 1935.

53. Cf. Hofstadter, *The Age of Reform,* pp. 131–33; Goldman, *Rendezvous with Destiny,* pp. 82, 83.

54. Hofstadter, *The Age of Reform,* p. 131, and Chap. VI, *passim;* Goldman, *Rendezvous with Destiny,* pp. 75–83; and Thomas C. Cochran and William Miller, *The Age of Enterprise; a Social History*

of Industrial America (New York, 1942), pp. 164, 202, 203, 276, 277, 354.

55. See, for example, Washington Gladden, "The Embattled Farmers," and Daniel R. Goodloe, "Western Farm Mortgages," *The Forum,* X (November, 1890), 315–22 and 346–55.

56. Kenneth W. Hechler, *Insurgency: Personalities and Politics of the Taft Era* (New York, 1940), esp. pp. 12, 16, 20–26, 220–226.

57. Theodore Saloutos and John D. Hicks, *Agricultural Discontent in the Middle West, 1900–1939* (Madison, Wis., 1951), Chaps. I, II, V, VII, VIII, and p. 56.

58. Russell B. Nye, *Midwestern Progressive Politics: a Historical Study of Its Origins and Development, 1870–1950* (East Lansing, Mich., 1951), pp. 9–27, Chaps. II, III, esp. IV: "The Capture of the Ivory Tower," and V.

59. George E. Mowry, *Theodore Roosevelt and the Progressive Movement* (Madison, Wis., 1947), pp. 10, 11.

60. George E. Mowry, *The California Progressives* (Berkeley, Calif., 1951), p. ix, Chaps. IV and V, *passim,* pp. 295–99, and 303–5.

61. George E. Mowry, *The Progressive Movement, 1900–1920: Recent Ideas and New Literature* (Washington, D.C., 1958), pp. 1–3.

62. George E. Mowry, *The Era of Theodore Roosevelt: 1900–1912* (New York, 1958), pp. xv, 13, 14, 58, 66, 67, 87, 88, 294, 295.

63. Arthur S. Link, *Woodrow Wilson and the Progressive Era, 1910 to 1917* (New York, 1954), pp. 1, 2.

THE IDEA OF THE ROBBER BARONS
IN AMERICAN HISTORY

by Hal Bridges

UNIVERSITY OF COLORADO

BOULDER, COLORADO

WIDESPREAD in American historical writing is the idea that business leaders in the United States from about 1865 to 1900 were, on the whole, a set of avaricious rascals who habitually cheated and robbed investors and consumers, corrupted government, fought ruthlessly among themselves, and in general carried on predatory activities comparable to those of the robber barons of medieval Europe. Such at any rate appears to be the content of the idea when put into plain language. As actually used by historians, the concept tends to become more suggestive than precise. In this essay it will be referred to as the idea of the robber barons, and an effort will be made to trace the broad outlines of its historical development after the Civil War, to point out historical interpretations at variance with it, and to appraise its value for present-day historians.

In the post-Civil War era, some relatively early expressions of the idea of the robber barons can be found. In 1869 E. L. Godkin in *The Nation* denounced Cornelius Vanderbilt's extortionate ways and called the Commodore "a lineal successor of the mediaeval baron that we read about." [1] In the early seventies the Grangers adopted resolutions comparing American railroad corporations to oppressive "feudal barons of the Middle Ages." [2] In the eighties and nineties cries of robbery came from Greenbackers and Populists. Matthew Josephson states that he drew the title of his book *The Robber Barons* from "the folklore of the Kansas Green-backers and Populists of the 1880's." [3]

With the publication in 1894 of Henry Demarest Lloyd's *Wealth against Commonwealth,* the idea of the robber barons gained new importance for American intellectuals. Lloyd, an independently wealthy journalist, was an Emersonian religious thinker and a social reformer who almost but never quite joined the Socialist party.[4] The impassioned rhetoric of his book was aimed not only at the Standard Oil monopoly but at an even bigger target—business, the capitalistic system as it then existed. "Business," he wrote, "colors the modern world as war reddened the ancient world." And, anticipating somewhat a later theme of Thorstein Veblen, he declared that if civilization was destroyed it would not be by Macaulay's "barbarians from below" but by "barbarians . . . from above," the "great money-makers" who now exercised "power kings do not know." Among these moneyed barbarians were the rulers of Standard Oil. The record of the Standard corporation, which Lloyd set forth in detail, illustrated his thesis that "Monopoly is Business at the end of its journey." [5]

Allan Nevins has called *Wealth against Commonwealth* propaganda rather than history; Chester M. Destler has defended the book as essentially accurate; and the most recent study of the rise of the Standard monopoly supports Nevins's judgment.[6] But if there is controversy over Lloyd's accuracy, there is general agreement that his book strongly influenced public opinion. More, probably, than *Chapters of Erie, and Other Essays,* or *Progress and Poverty,* or such relatively mild novels as *The Gilded Age, Looking Backward,* and *A Traveler from Altruria,* it served to fasten a robber baron portrait of the postwar businessman into the American mind.

This portrait was etched more deeply as the century waned and Populism broadened into progressivism. The intellectual preoccupations of the progressive era—the national debate over controlling the trusts, the muckrakers' revelations, socialist agitation, and the novels of big business by naturalists like Frank Norris and Theodore Dreiser—created a climate of suspicion and hostility toward American business leaders. Business chicane was held up to the public by a host of writers, including Lincoln Steffens, whose *Shame of the Cities* exposed corrupt politics and corporate privilege more fully than had James Bryce's *American Commonwealth;* Gustavus Myers, whose socialist *History of the Great American Fortunes* was to become a source book of future writers of robber-baron history; Thorstein Veblen, who began in the *Theory of the Leisure Class* and the *Theory of Business Enterprise* a series of attacks on predatory businessmen; E. A. Ross, whose *Sin and Society* denounced corporate amorality; and Ida Tarbell, who retraced Lloyd's steps more thoroughly and objectively in her *History of the Standard Oil Company.*

Two eminent American historians whose work reflected the progressive ideology were Vernon Louis Parrington and Charles A. Beard. Both made zestful use of the idea of the robber barons. Parrington, whose progressive cast of mind was reinforced by a Jeffersonian agrarian bias against businessmen, seems to have accepted the idea with little reservation, though he expressed it in maritime metaphors. When in the last volume of his *Main Currents in American Thought* he presents his "Figures of Earth," the outstanding personages of the Gilded Age, he discusses "ruthless, predatory" business leaders, "the raw materials of a race of capitalistic buccaneers." Within the space of three more sentences he remarks that "pirate and priest issued from the common source," and again in the next sentence, "the romantic age of Captain Kidd was come again." Plainly this master of metaphors loved to take his figures of earth to sea aboard a pirate ship; and it is perhaps not unfair to say that few if any of his metaphors, either in his description of the Gilded Age or in his artistic narrative of the progressive era, convey other than a predatory image of the American businessman.[7]

To the mind of Charles Beard, historical patterns were not so clear-cut. His analysis of post-Civil War business leaders in *The Rise of American Civilization,* written with Mary Beard, emphasized the historical importance of the businessman in successive civilizations from ancient times to modern America. The Beards not only pointed out the creative results of American business expansion but held Ida Tarbell "partly responsible for the distorted view" of the Standard Oil Company to be found "in the popular mind." Her history they dismissed as "a drama with heroes and villains, rather than a cold and disinterested summary by an impartial student." And yet, for all their interest in objectivity, the Beards made extended use of the idea of the robber barons. Phrases like "barons of business" and "the new capitalist baronage" run through a narrative that presents a generally negative analysis of the methods and motives of business consolidation. The following passage is typical:

If the barons of capitalism did not themselves put on armor and vanquish the possessors of desirable goods in mortal combat . . . they did sometimes hire strong-arm men. . . . Usually, however, they employed less stereotyped means to attain their ends; namely, stock manipulation, injunctions, intimidation, rate cutting, rebates, secret agreements, and similar pacific measures.[8]

Why did Beard and Parrington so freely employ the idea of the robber barons? The answer to this question, to the extent that it can be provided, would seem also to help us understand the meaning and uses of the idea for progressive writers in general and for the many latter-day historians who have been influenced by Beard and Parrington.[9] A number of factors must be considered.

First, it seems proper to place both Beard and Parrington within the general category of Richard Hofstadter's discontented professoriat of the progressive era, those members of a rising academic profession who were critical of American business civilization, resentful of being controlled by boards of trustees dominated by conservative businessmen, and troubled by academic-freedom cases.[10] Parrington and Beard knew from personal experience how conservative pressure could affect college faculties. In 1908 Parrington lost his position as professor of English at the University of Oklahoma during the controversy that arose when President David R. Boyd of that university was replaced by a political supporter of Governor C. N. Haskell, who was soon to be accused of improper affiliations with the Standard Oil Company.[11] In 1917 Beard resigned from Columbia University after he became convinced that conservative trustees were trying to purge the faculty of liberals on the pretext that they were disloyal Americans.   Max Lerner has described this resignation as basically "a protest against business control of university educational policy." Such unpleasant experiences may well have influenced Parrington and Beard toward a readier acceptance of what Hofstadter and Walter Metzger call the "potent academic stereotype" of "the businessman as a malefactor." [12]

Another probable influence upon Beard and Parrington is the progressive concept of reality.   The progressives, according to Hofstadter, conceived of reality as something akin to what the muckrackers revealed.   Basically it was "rough and sordid . . . hidden, neglected, and . . . off-stage . . . essentially a stream of external and material events." [13]   The relation of the robber baron idea to this kind of reality is obvious.   When Beard and Parrington wrote of the rough, sordid, hidden and off-stage methods by which a Jay Gould manipulated railroads, they could sincerely feel that they were describing the basic reality of business in Gould's time.   Parrington also reflects the fascination with brute strength that Alfred Kazin has emphasized as a facet of the progressive mind.   His business leaders of the seventies were vital, "primitive souls . . . never feeble . . . never given to puling or whining," men of the bold buccaneer or robber baron breed.[14]

Also pertinent to this inquiry is the Marxian economic approach to history that has influenced Beard and Parrington and other progressive writers,[15] and indeed the entire American historical profession, which has made much fruitful use of economic interpretation while rejecting other aspects of Marxism.   The idea of the robber barons fits nicely into economic interpretation; the very imagery of it tends to exclude noneconomic analysis. Moreover, the idea affords a convenient means of classifying a lot of individualistic businessmen, plus an opportunity for interesting, colorful writing.   The business buccaneers though wicked, were "picturesque in their rascality." [16]   Nor, finally, should it be forgotten that at the time *Main Currents* and *The Rise of American Civilization* were written historians knew relatively little about post-Civil War business expansion, aside from the more sensational and sordid events.   The Beards, in fact, carefully pointed out that the methods that brought about this expansion had "never been subjected to scientific analysis." [17]

Readily available to other writers, then, in the history of Parrington and Beard, the idea of the robber barons flourished in the debunking twenties and took on fresh vitality in the thirties. During the great depression, businessmen were more suspect than ever. Intellectuals quoted the Brookings Institution on America's wasted capacity to produce, Keynes on the "secular stagnation" of capitalism, and Berle and Means on the future dangers of corporate growth. Businessmen were blamed for America's entry into the First World War, and also, after a brief NRA honeymoon, for the continuing depression. Some former progressives, and young intellectuals who might once have been progressive, embraced communism.[18]

The nation was in a mood receptive to a number of new books that embodied the idea of the robber barons, such as Lewis Corey's *The House of Morgan,* Frederick Lewis Allen's *The Lords of Creation,* and Josephson's *The Robber Barons.* Josephson, who dedicated his book to Charles and Mary Beard, traveled further down the road of Marxian determinism than the Beards had gone. His barons, though touched with an aura of glamor, were essentially grim, amoral figures, furthering the Marxian process of expropriation and consolidation of property. Their activities were making the masses of workers dissatisfied with the old business system and "the fearful sabotage practiced by capital upon the energy and intelligence of human society." [19] In the stricken nation of the thirties, epitomized in John Dos Passos's *U. S. A.,* Josephson's book read convincingly enough. Perhaps more than any other single volume it served to disseminate the phrase, "the robber barons," through American historical writing. It was, in a sense, the culmination of the idea expressed in its title.

Now let us consider some views of American business leaders that, taken all together, might be termed the revisionist approach to the idea of the robber barons. Edward C. Kirkland has called attention to Charles Francis Adams, Jr., E. L. Godkin, and Andrew Carnegie as conservatives of the Gilded Age whose "conclusions that the business order of their day was not all evil, loss, and hypocrisy should contribute to a more balanced judgment of the era." [20]   Adams considered the robber-baron metaphor, as applied by the Grangers to railroad corporations, "a grotesque absurdity." [21]   However it should be noted that in 1869, the year he wrote *Chapters of Erie,* Adams remarked in a private letter that Daniel Drew, Cornelius Vanderbilt, and Jay Gould made "the old robber barons" appear like "children in the art of thieving." [22]   Actually Adams seems to have entertained toward the American business world ambivalent attitudes that reflect his personal aspirations and experiences as railroad reformer, railroad president, and victim of Jay Gould.[23]

If Adams did not wholly accept the idea of the robber barons, neither did a major American historian, Frederick Jackson Turner.   Turner was certainly no apologist for industrial wrongdoing, yet his complex approach to the past led him to see aspects of American industrial expansion that did not fit into the robber-baron mold.   In an essay first published in 1926 he distinguished Western builders of new industry from Eastern speculative investors in old enterprises and characterized John D. Rockefeller, Cyrus McCormick, J. O. Armour, and Jay Cooke, among others, as creative sons of Middle-Western pioneers.[24]   Earlier, at a time when trust-busting ideas were in the air, he had stressed the complexities involved in historical analysis of the two decades of industrial expansion from 1890 to 1910.   The occasion was his presidential address of 1910 to the American Historical Association.   He noted that the two decades in question were "peculiarly the era when competitive individualism" in America changed into monopoly, but quoted E. H. Harriman to the effect that industrial combination and expansion were in keeping with the speculative pioneer spirit that had developed the nation.   He then pointed out that American ideals and moral standards were changing. The squatter ideal of "individual freedom to compete unrestrictedly for the resources of a continent" was yielding to an increasing use of government in order that Americans might preserve another ideal—democracy.   Violations of land laws that were formerly condoned by the public and defended in Congress now resulted in jail sentences.   "That our great industrial enterprises

developed in the midst of these changing ideals," Turner concluded, "is important to recall when we write the history of their
activity." [25]

In this same address Turner reminded his fellow historians
that among the "complex of forces" molding the past were individual leaders, who in turn were shaped by their own creative
genius, and by the psychology, moral tendencies, and ideals of
their time and place.[26]   His words, which thirty-nine years later
would be echoed by historians seeking greater understanding of
American business leaders,[27] might well serve as a general criterion for biographical writing, and biographers who have studied
American businessmen in this spirit have produced works that
seriously challenge the idea of the robber barons.   A number of
non-robber-baron biographies appeared in the antibusiness thirties, contrasting markedly with the general tenor of popular
thought.   Among these were works by John T. Flynn, Burton J.
Hendrick, William T. Hutchinson, Allan Nevins, and Henriettta
M. Larson.[28]   All wrote with varying degrees of sympathy, and
recreated business leaders too multisided to be dismissed simply
as predatory money seekers.   In each business career examined,
negative and positive means and ends seemed inseparably bound
together.   With this duality in mind, N. S. B. Gras in his introduction to Larson's *Jay Cooke* declared that businessmen are generally "above the average in creative work" and complained that a
"recent national pastime" had been to judge them without studying them.[29]

The dual nature of business careers was one of several theses
advanced in Allan Nevins's *John D. Rockefeller,* which appeared
in 1940.   Nevins as early as 1927 had published a balanced account of post-Civil War business, and in 1934 had demurred at
Josephson's sweeping use of the robber-baron metaphor.[30]   In the
Rockefeller biography, he followed the English economist Alfred
Marshall in ascribing the Standard Oil Trust to "a combination
of exceptional constructive ability and astute destructive strategy."   He held that Rockefeller and his associates had often used
methods that were morally wrong as well as unlawful, but like
Charles R. Van Hise he argued that the kind of monopoly control

they effected was a natural and even inevitable response to the cut-throat competition of the times, in Europe as well as in the United States. Like Turner, he stressed the changing business ethics of Rockefeller's era. And like Joseph Schumpeter he drew attention to the complexity of the motives of entrepreneurs. The chief motive of leaders like Rockefeller, Nevins asserted, was not greed but "competitive achievement, self-expression, and the imposition of their wills on a given environment." Schumpeter had distinguished entrepreneurial activities in which financial gain was secondary and "economic action becomes akin to sport." Nevins wrote: "In business . . . Americans of the nineteenth century found the Great Game." This analysis contrasts somewhat with that of Werner Sombart, who conceded that entrepreneurs have nonacquisitive motives but argued that since profit is the measure of capitalistic success all other motives in capitalistic enterprise become "subordinate to profit making." [31]

When Nevins in 1953 published a second biography of Rockefeller, he adhered essentially to his earlier interpretation but advanced a more elaborate hypothesis of business leadership after the Civil War. The constructive aspects of this leadership were in the long run, he declared, more important than the destructive. American historians should follow the English example and correct their national industrial history—too long based mainly on legislative investigations of business chicane—to show the constructive side. America's industrial revolution had "cost less than Germany's, much less than England's, and infinitely less than Russia's." Further, and most important, the rapid expansion of American industry after the Civil War had come just in time to insure victory for "the free world" in the two world wars. But had better ways been available for building national industrial strength? Nevins did not inquire. His broad hypothesis, which of course did not escape challenge, probably represents the culmination to date of the revisionist approach to the idea of the robber barons. [32]

Yet business history of all types, biographical and otherwise, offers numerous other studies of a non-robber-baron nature, some of them quite recent. James Blaine Hedges, Richard C. Overton, Edward C. Kirkland, and Thomas C. Cochran, among others, have emphasized the constructive work of certain railroad leaders of the Gilded Age.[33]   Fritz Redlich has redefined Schumpeter's "entrepreneur" as "creative entrepreneur" and analyzed the creative achievement of American business leaders in banking and the iron and steel industry.[34]   Ralph and Muriel Hidy, restudying the rise of the Standard Oil monopoly, have portrayed Rockefeller as only one member of a business team that mistakenly tried to apply previously learned small business mores to giant industry, and responded somewhat involuntarily to the "prods and pressures" of a changing political and legal climate.[35]   Other writers have produced biographies of secondary business leaders who were not robber barons,[36] while statistical studies have thrown new light on the American business elite.[37]

The American business mind is a fruitful field of present-day investigation for entrepreneurial historians who utilize the concepts of social role, social sanctions, and cultural codes of conduct. Notably, Thomas Cochran has demonstrated that social Darwinism and the gospel of wealth are, though certainly important, not the whole story of the business mind, and that certain American railroad leaders of the period 1845–90 could be influenced quite as often by their view of their proper social role in a given situation as by predatory motives.[38]

Thus, although some historians continued vigorously to defend the idea of the robber barons,[39] the current trend in American historiography is away from this concept.   Michael Kraus has written that the idea is fading; the 1954 report of the Committee on Historiography of the Social Science Research Council views it skeptically; Thomas Cochran calls it legend.[40]   All this may be in part a manifestation of present-day conservatism, but this writer regards it primarily as the logical reaction of historians to the cumulative evidence contained in the studies that have been designated here as the revisionist approach to the idea of the robber barons.   Of course the revisionist views are not flawless. As a summary critique of them it can be said that the naturalness or inevitability of monopoly at any time in the United States is a moot question;[41] that both Turner and Nevins have been accused of ignoring important aspects of the American economy;[42] that all biographers are open to the charge of being too sympathetic toward their subjects; and that the company records with which business historians work make it difficult for them to avoid a board-of-directors bias. Yet when all discounts have been made for possible error, there does seem to be enough truth left in the revisionist views to reveal the inadequacy of the idea of the robber barons. In an emotional, romanticized way, this concept sums up the business activities of Jay Gould and his kind and expresses the predatory side of the careers of many other business leaders of the post-Civil War era. But it grants insufficient recognition to the creative aspects of such careers or to business leaders of habitually high moral standards. It tends to deny to business leaders through thirty-five years of American life that basic capacity for doing good as well as evil which historians freely concede to other members of the human race. Born apparently of a desire for denunciation rather than objective analysis, the idea of the robber barons seems destined to fall into increasing disuse, as historians seek to apply ever more precise thinking to the complex American past.

NOTES

This paper appeared in Harvard University's *Business History Review,* Spring, 1958, under the title "The Robber Baron Concept in American History."

1. "The Vanderbilt Memorial," *The Nation,* IX (November 18, 1869), 431–32; quoted in Edward C. Kirkland, *Business in the Gilded Age; the Conservatives' Balance Sheet* (Madison, Wis., 1952), p. 37.

2. Charles Francis Adams, Jr., *Railroads: Their Origin and Problems* (New York, 1893), pp. 128–29.

3. Allan Nevins and Matthew Josephson, "Should American History Be Rewritten?" *The Saturday Review,* XXXVII (February 6, 1954), 10. H. D. Lloyd in "The Political Economy of Seventy-Three Million Dollars," *The Atlantic Monthly,* L (1882), 69–81, compared Jay Gould to an assassin. Inspired by this article, Carl Schurz referred to contemporary business leaders as "the robber barons" in a Phi Beta Kappa oration at Harvard University. Also, in *The Chicago Tribune* "of the early eighties" Lloyd's editorials "made repeated com-

parisons between the great railroad magnates and the nobility of the Medieval Rhine." See Chester M. Destler, "Entrepreneurial Leadership among the 'Robber Barons': a Trial Balance," *The Journal of Economic History*, VI (1946), Sup., p. 28, *n*. 1.

4. Daniel Aaron, *Men of Good Hope; a Story of American Progressives* (New York, 1951), pp. 150, 158, 169.

5. Henry Demarest Lloyd, *Wealth against Commonwealth* (New York, 1902 ed.), pp. 509, 510, 6.

6. For the Nevins-Destler debate over Lloyd's accuracy see Chester M. Destler, "Wealth against Commonwealth, 1894 and 1944," *American Historical Review*, L (October, 1944), 49–69, and Allan Nevins, letter to the editor, *American Historical Review*, L (April, 1945), 676–89. Ralph W. Hidy and Muriel E. Hidy, *Pioneering in Big Business, 1882–1911* (New York, 1955), p. 644, supports Nevins's judgment.

7. Vernon Louis Parrington, *Main Currents in American Thought* (New York, 1930), III, 10–12, 405–13.

8. Charles A. Beard and Mary R. Beard, *The Rise of American Civilization* (New York, 1934), II, 166–210; for quoted portions see pp. 187, 201.

9. Richard Hofstadter has called attention to the progressive bent of Beard and Parrington and their wide appeal to other writers. See his "Charles Beard and the Constitution," in Howard K. Beale, ed., *Charles A. Beard: an Appraisal* (Lexington, Ky., 1954), p. 88. That there is high professional regard for *Main Currents* and *The Rise of American Civilization* is clearly shown in John Walton Caughey, "Historians' Choice: Results of a Poll on Recently Published American History and Biography," *Mississippi Valley Historical Review*, XXXIX (September, 1952), 299.

10. Richard Hofstadter, *The Age of Reform; from Bryan to F. D. R.* (New York, 1955), pp. 154–55.

11. Parrington called this controversy a "political cyclone." George Harvey Genzmer, "Vernon Louis Parrington," *Dictionary of American Biography*, Vol. XIV (New York, 1934), p. 253. Along with President Boyd, some dozen members of the Oklahoma faculty were fired. The controversy arising from these dismissals and the accusations of improper relationships with Standard Oil that led in the fall of 1908 to Governor Haskell's resignation as treasurer of the Democratic National Committee can be followed in a series of unsigned editorial articles in *The Outlook*, XC (1908), September 5, pp. 15–17, October 3, pp. 233, 235–37, 242–44, 249–51, October 17, pp. 325–26. It might also be noted that Parrington's good friend and colleague at the University of Washington, J. Allen Smith, was fired from Marietta College for publishing liberal monetary views and supporting William Jennings Bryan in the election of 1896. Richard Hofstadter and

Walter P. Metzger, *The Development of Academic Freedom in the United States* (New York, 1955), pp. 423–24.

12. Investigations by the trustees and summary dismissals of faculty members preceded Beard's resignation. See Charles A. Beard, "A Statement," *The New Republic,* XIII (December 29, 1917), 249–50. Lerner's interpretation can be found in his *Ideas Are Weapons; the History and Uses of Ideas* (New York, 1939), p. 158. Additional details are given in Hofstadter and Metzger, *Academic Freedom,* pp. 501–2.

The reference to the academic stereotype of the businessman is on page 420 of this work; in Chapter IX, "Academic Freedom and Big Business," Hofstadter and Metzger show how the stereotype developed in the Populist and progressive eras and how it does not always fit the facts of academic-freedom cases prior to the first World War.

13. Hofstadter "Charles Beard and the Constitution," p. 87.

14. Alfred Kazin, *On Native Grounds; an Interpretation of Modern American Prose Literature* (New York, 1942), p. 93; Parrington, *Main Currents,* III, 12.

15. Hofstadter, "Charles Beard and the Constitution," pp. 81–82.

16. Parrington, *Main Currents,* III, 12.

17. C. A. and Mary Beard, *The Rise of American Civilization,* II, 198.

18. A. D. H. Kaplan, *Big Enterprise in a Competitive System* (Washington, D. C., 1954), pp. 27–29; Eric F. Goldman, *Rendezvous with Destiny* (New York, 1953), pp. 353–67; Aaron, *Men of Good Hope,* pp. 295–97.

19. Matthew Josephson, *The Robber Barons: the Great American Capitalists, 1861–1901* (New York, 1934). The quoted portion is from p. 453.

20. Kirkland, *Business in the Gilded Age,* p. 59.

21. Adams, *Railroads,* pp. 128–29; Kirkland, *Business in the Gilded Age,* p. 12.

22. Joseph Dorfman, *The Economic Mind in American Civilization, Vol. III: 1865–1918* (New York, 1949), p. 23.

23. In his autobiography, Adams set forth his often quoted view of American big businessmen as "mere money-getters . . . essentially unattractive and uninteresting," but also confessed that as his life's achievement he "would like to have accumulated—and ample and frequent opportunity for so doing was offered me—one of those vast fortunes of the present day, rising up into the tens and scores of millions" so that he could have donated a fortune to Harvard. *Charles Francis Adams, 1835–1915: an Autobiography* (Boston, 1916), pp. 190, 210.

24. Frederick Jackson Turner, *The Significance of Sections in American History* (New York, 1932), pp. 262–64. Compare the strong

emphasis on the creative achievement of post-Civil War industrial capitalists in Louis M. Hacker, *The Triumph of American Capitalism* (New York, 1940), pp. 427–35.

25. Frederick Jackson Turner, *The Frontier in American History* (New York, 1920), pp. 317–21, 328.

26. *Ibid.*, p. 322.

27. There is a striking similarity between the approach to the past advocated here by Turner and the modern methods for understanding business leaders that are set forth, much more fully, of course, and in more technical language, in *Change and the Entrepreneur: Postulates and Patterns for Entrepreneurial History* (Cambridge, Mass., 1949), pp. 108–75.

28. John T. Flynn, *God's Gold; the Story of Rockefeller and His Times* (New York, 1932); Burton J. Hendrick, *The Life of Andrew Carnegie* (2 vols., Garden City, New York, 1932); William T. Hutchinson, *Cyrus Hall McCormick: Harvest, 1856–1884* (New York, 1935); Allan Nevins, *Abram S. Hewitt; with Some Account of Peter Cooper* (New York, 1935); Henrietta M. Larson, *Jay Cooke: Private Banker* (Cambridge, Mass., 1936).

29. Larson, *Jay Cooke*, p. xiv.

30. *The Emergence of Modern America, 1865–1878* (New York, 1927), pp. 42, 397–400; review of *The Robber Barons* in *The Saturday Review of Literature*, X (March 3, 1934), 522. But in *Grover Cleveland; a Study in Courage* (New York, 1933), p. 607, Nevins in summarizing the social unrest of the nineties mentioned only the sordid side of the Standard Oil record and favorably described Lloyd's *Wealth against Commonwealth* as a "searching exposure" and the parent of later muckraking literature.

31. Allan Nevins, *John D. Rockefeller; the Heroic Age of American Enterprise* (New York, 1940), I, 603–22, II, 707–14; Charles R. Van Hise, *Concentration and Control; a Solution of the Trust Problem in the United States* (New York, 1912); Joseph A. Schumpeter, *The Theory of Economic Development,* tr. Redvers Opie (Cambridge, Mass., 1934), p. 93; Werner Sombart, "Capitalism," *Encyclopedia of the Social Sciences,* III (New York, 1930), 200.

32. Allan Nevins, *Study in Power: John D. Rockefeller* (New York, 1953), I, viii, II, 426–36. See also Allan Nevins, "New Lamps for Old in History," *The American Archivist,* XVII (January, 1954), 3–12. Josephson opposes this hypothesis in Nevins and Josephson, "Should American History be Rewritten?", pp. 9–10, 44–46.

33. James Blaine Hedges, *Henry Villard and the Railways of the Northwest* (New Haven, 1930); Richard C. Overton, *Burlington West; a Colonization History of the Burlington Railroad* (Cambridge, Mass., 1941); Edward Chase Kirkland, *Men Cities and Transportation; a Study in New England History, 1820–1900* (2 vols., Cambridge, Mass.,

1948); Thomas C. Cochran, *Railroad Leaders, 1845–1890; the Business Mind in Action* (Cambridge, Mass., 1953).

34. Fritz Redlich, *History of American Business Leaders: a Series of Studies,* Vol. I: Theory, Iron and Steel, Iron Ore Mining (Ann Arbor, Michigan, 1940), Vol. II: The Molding of American Banking: Men and Ideas, Pt. I: 1781–1840 (New York, 1947), Pt. II: 1840–1910 (New York, 1951).

35. Hidy and Hidy, *Pioneering in Big Business,* pp. xxviii, 3–8, 201–32, 715–17.

36. For example, Hal Bridges, *Iron Millionaire: Life of Charlemagne Tower* (Philadelphia, 1952); Philip Dorf, *The Builder: a Biography of Ezra Cornell* (New York, 1952).

37. For example, Francis W. Gregory and Irene D. Neu, "The American Industrial Elite in the 1870's: Their Social Origins," in William Miller, ed., *Men in Business: Essays in the History of Entrepreneurship* (Cambridge, Mass., 1952), pp. 193–211. See also Sidney Ratner, ed., *New Light on the History of Great American Fortunes: American Millionaires of 1892 and 1902* (New York, 1953), in which Ratner in his introduction criticizes various statistical studies of American business leaders.

38. Cochran, *Railroad Leaders,* pp. 1–16, 92–93, 172, 182–83, 200–28. For another interesting approach to the business mind of the Gilded Age see Edward C. Kirkland, "Divide and Ruin," *Mississippi Valley Historical Review,* XLIII (June, 1956), 3–17, and his *Dream and Thought in the Business Community, 1860–1900* (Ithaca, N.Y., 1956).

39. Josephson, "Should American History Be Rewritten?," pp. 9–10, 44–46; Destler, "Entrepreneurial Leadership," pp. 28, 38, and "The Opposition of American Businessmen to Social Control during the 'Gilded Age,'" *The Mississippi Valley Historical Review,* XXXIX (March, 1953), 641–72.

40. Michael Kraus, *The Writing of American History* (Norman, Okla., 1953), p. 337; *The Social Sciences in Historical Study: a Report of the Committee on Historiography* (Bulletin 64; New York, 1954), p. 154; Thomas C. Cochran, "The Legend of the Robber Barons," *Pennsylvania Magazine of History and Biography,* LXXIV (July, 1950), 307–21.

41. Vigorous arguments against the inevitability of monopoly are presented in Walter Adams and Horace M. Gray, *Monopoly in America; the Government as Promoter* (New York, 1955).

42. On Turner see for example Louis M. Hacker, "Sections—or Classes?" *The Nation,* CXXXVII (July 26, 1933), 108–10. On Nevins see for example Lewis Galantière, "John D.: an Academy Portrait," *The New Republic,* CIII (December 9, 1940), 795–97.

SOME ASPECTS OF EUROPEAN MIGRATION TO THE UNITED STATES

by Carlton C. Qualey

CARLETON COLLEGE

NORTHFIELD, MINNESOTA

THE HISTORY of American immigration is more than the sum of the histories of the national group migrations. It is in a larger sense the history of America. Apart from the American aborigines, who were themselves probably immigrant-descended, the American continents were occupied and developed by Europeans, Africans, and Asiatics. It was in large measure the interaction of American regional environments and immigrant group backgrounds that determined the character of the evolving American civilizations.

In the history of continental United States, the nearly two centuries of English control established the legal-constitutional ideas and traditions that were combined with colonial experience to form the constitutional system that has endured to the present. The coming of large numbers of non-English during the colonial period—Germans, Scotch-Irish, Scots, Huguenot French, Swedes, Dutch, Jews, Africans, and others—did not significantly alter the basic institutional framework of the American governments, but these groups had important secondary influences that persisted far beyond the colonial period, most notably perhaps in the case of the Pennsylvania Germans. By the end of the colonial period, the population of the territory that was to become the United States was already a cosmopolitan one.[1]

In the forty years after 1775, only about a quarter-million persons came to the United States—a trickle of Irish coming as return

cargo on lumber ships plying between the Canadian Maritime
Provinces and the British Isles, seamen off ships docking at American ports, refugees from European revolutions and wars, displaced persons from the agricultural and early industrial changes
in England, and many others, all imperfectly recorded.   This
period has been aptly called the time of the "first Americaniza-
tion," an interlude between the colonial migrations and the huge
folk migrations of the century after 1815.[2]   This period of relatively light immigration coincided with the establishment and
consolidation of governmental institutions, the acquisition of territories that made possible a continental United States, and the
beginnings of emancipation from Europe.   It was the period of
the beginning of large scale migration into the trans-Appalachian
West and the opening of new transportation systems on inland
waterways.   Within a decade of 1815 and especially with the
opening of the Erie Canal, the floodgates were opened to the
great streams of migrants and immigrants who occupied with as-
tonishing rapidity the American heartland.

    Although the immigrants of the century after 1815 came into
a society of established institutions, these were changing, and the
American story from this point is in important respects the merg-
ing of peoples and institutions and customs.   While Americans of
older stocks were discovering America anew, millions of Europeans and some Asiatics were discovering America as well.   It is
in the context of this intermingling of peoples that the history of
European migration to the United States must be studied.

    European migration to the United States after 1815 was a part
of a vast movement of peoples within and out of Europe.   It has
been estimated that some fifty million people left Europe in the
century after Waterloo, and that about thirty-seven million of
these came to the United States.   About eleven million are estimated to have returned, most of them since 1900, making a net
gain over all of about twenty-six million people for the United
States.[3]

    The significance of this huge emigration *for Europe* is almost
incalculable. Despite phenomenal population growth, the drain

from certain areas such as Ireland and Norway was so heavy that emigration exceeded real population increase during the periods of heaviest emigration.[4] The huge exodus, largely from rural areas, undoubtedly relieved serious problems of overpopulation in some regions, such as Ireland and Italy, but it represented nevertheless a great loss of labor power. In another sense, the migration represented a significant transfer of capital from the Old World to the New, not so much in the way of actual movement of monetary capital as in the sense of productivity.[5] To compensate in some measure for this outflow from Europe, there was the very large volume of remittances by emigrants to families and creditors back in the old country. No accurate statistics are available as to the total of remittances, but those that are available indicate that the amount for certain countries runs into the millions of dollars for each. For the period between 1885 and 1937, remittances by postal money order alone to Sweden amounted to about one hundred million dollars, and it is estimated that the annual remittances between 1906 and 1930 to Sweden amounted to eight to ten million dollars.[6] This huge volume of remittances to Europe from the Americas is comparable to the influx of American treasure through Spain in the sixteenth and seventeenth centuries. No adequate studies have been made of the impact of this capital increment upon European economies.

Not only were the exodus of labor-capital and the remittances of importance for each European nation, but the emigration of vast numbers of agricultural people represented a net loss of skilled farmers. Along with this loss there was the departure of large numbers of skilled laborers, chiefly handicraft workers, displaced by the coming of the factory system.[7] Among the emigrants were men trained in European technical schools who took their place in the upper ranks of American technologists, and this at a time when few technicians were being trained in America.[8]

As American consuls reported on the growing stream of common folk embarking at Atlantic ports—Liverpool, Le Havre, Hamburg, Bremen, Naples, Genoa, Trieste, and others—it became apparent that this human freight would become a major source of

profit to Atlantic shipping interests.   There was little effective
regulation, and the field was wide open to enterprise.   Liverpool
became a great port in the emigrant trade, serving not only the
British Isles but the continent as well, with travelers coming via
east coast English ports.   Le Havre enjoyed an early success,
which stimulated the north German ports to improve their facilities.   To overcome Hamburg's advantages, Bremen created Bre-
merhaven and became an important competitor.[9]   The old Mediterranean ports took a new lease on life as the mass migration
from Italy and the Balkans got under way.   Steamship lines pro-
liferated to compete for the new business.   As the age of white
sails was succeeded by the age of steam power, larger and more
powerful ships came into service, and the new "middle passage"
came into being, analogous to the colonial slave trade.   To millions of emigrants the holds and steerages of the trans-Atlantic
ships were remembered as ordeals in the transit from Europe to
America.[10]   To the shipowners, however, the profits were large.
Not until conditions became intolerable did reforms find their
way to the statute books, and then only after millions had suffered their way across the Atlantic.[11]   The trans-Atlantic emigrant
traffic is a neglected chapter of immigration history, but it is of
genuine significance in the economic histories of the nations of
western Europe.

Not only was emigration significant in the economic history
of Europe to an extent inadequately studied by European historians, but it was of significance in the political, religious, and
intellectual histories of almost all the nations of Europe.   The
degree to which American democratic political ideas infiltrated
Europe's agricultural and working classes by way of the emigrant
letters ("America letters") and the returned emigrant has only
begun to be explored.[12]   The genuine significance of the prosely-
tizing of the Mormons is receiving belated attention.[13]   From
these instances, which could be multiplied, it should be apparent
that one of the more neglected fields of immigration history is the
emigration to America as a chapter of the history of Europe.[14]

It has been almost commonplace for writers on American immigration, and, in their turn, for textbook writers, to treat the subject as composed of two types of immigrants: the "old" or northern European, and the "new" or southern and eastern European and Oriental.   The terms were born of the immigration restriction controversy that raged from the 1880s to the 1920s, and they have therefore invidious connotations of better and inferior stocks, reflecting the racist thinking that was so characteristic of the nativist movement.[15]   As greater perspective is given the historians of immigration, it becomes increasingly apparent that the terms serve no good purpose.   The similarities of the migrations of the early nineteenth century to those of the later period are greater than the differences.

Rather than writing about the "old" and the "new," it seems far more accurate to describe emigration from Europe as a vast movement of peoples from western Eurasia, starting at the western most fringes of that land mass and gradually spreading over much of what is called Europe.   This movement of peoples started with the close of the Napoleonic wars and it ended with the aftermath of the First World War.   To use the 1880s as a point of change in the immigration story is inaccurate, for the migration of northern Europeans actually mounted after that decade, while the movement from southern and eastern Europe and Asia began before then.   All that happened was that the movement spread to all of Europe rather than being largely from the northern regions.   To arguments that there were real differences between the movements from northern and from southern and eastern Europe, it can be demonstrated that the differences were those of institutional background rather than of aptitude for the "American way of life."   Even as to contract labor, a recent study has shown that large numbers of immigrants were recruited in northern Europe for the American labor force: Irish laborers, Welsh, Cornish, and Scandinavian miners, and the like.[16]   As one delves more deeply into the history of this vast folk movement, the similarities between the patterns of migration seem striking and the differences seem to be those of time and place.   In fact, this similarity of patterns extends back to the colonial period, and, without much straining, one could treat the story of American immigration as a more or less continuous process from the early seventeenth century to the present.

The arrival of immigrants in American ports and their reception constitute a lively chapter of the story.   What is emerging is the story of the struggle of large numbers of impecunious immigrants to secure a foothold in an evolving American society.   Coming in usually at the bottom of the economic heap, the Irish became the workers who built American cities, canals, and railroads. Their Catholicism and convivial habits offended Protestant Americans until their usefulness and political aptitude won for them a grudging acceptance.   Better supplied with capital and skills, the Germans took off for western lands and the cities sprouting along the midwestern rivers, and the Germans flourished.   In like manner the Scandinavians and the Dutch flocked with seemingly unslakable land-hunger to the western regions.   Because the Germans, Scandinavians, and Dutch "succeeded" more rapidly, they were deemed more desirable as recruits for the American population.   The purgatory of the Civil War enabled those early groups to prove their worthiness, and they became accepted.

The economic status of the immigrants from the Mediterranean and eastern Europe was more like that of the Irish, and they too were mostly Catholic, either Roman or Greek-Orthodox, and Protestant nativism was thereby revived.   Physically they seemed different, and they spoke "outlandish languages."   In like manner, the Orientals were even lower in economic status, and the matter of race was added to complicate acceptance.   Thus, on a much larger scale, there occurred a repetition of the Irish story: the cluttered tenements, the social problems attendant upon low standards of living and economic exploitation, the conflict of interest between the vast army of unskilled immigrants and the American labor movement, the bigotry and discrimination, and all the uglinesses attendant thereunto.   Again it took the purgatory of war to erase the prejudices of the generations of "Americans" from the 1880s to the 1920s, and even the great holocaust of the Second World War failed to accomplish this completely.   In the foxholes of the greatest of all wars, the differences between an

Eliet, an Olson, a Grabowski, a Lopez, and a Hayashi seemed un-important, and there was hope that in time even Congress might catch up with the infantry.

In an earlier publication I have written:

The word "immigrant" has been somewhat indiscriminately used as applied to the settlement of foreign stocks in the United States. After having established a first place of residence, the immigrant ceases to be an immigrant, properly speaking. He becomes a part of the American population, subject to all the influences to which that population is subjected. If he makes further moves within the United States after his first period of residence, he must be denominated a migrant, not an immigrant. The manuscript population schedules of the United States census, which give the nativities of individuals and families, as well as other sources, indicate clearly that most Norwegian settlements in the United States came into being and spread as a result of domestic migration—migration from older to newer areas of settlement—rather than as a result of direct immigration to new areas from Norway. In place of thinking of Norwegian settlement as a part of the process of emigration from Norway to the American shore and thence inland, one may regard it as a separate process—an integral part of the westward movement of the American population. The conclusion becomes inescapable when the later stages of settlement are studied, for large numbers of Norwegian pioneers who pushed out upon the frontier in the late nineteenth and early twentieth centuries had never seen Norway. A similar generalization holds true of all those immigrant groups who participated in the settlement and development of the West." [17]

It is unfortunate that few students have been willing to tackle the manuscript census schedules. In none of the printed schedules before 1930 is the nativity of the second generation in the United States indicated. The first census to indicate the ancestry of the native-born of foreign descent was that of 1880, but these statistics were not given fully in the printed reports. Most of the census schedules for 1890 were destroyed by fire in Washington years ago, leaving a gap in the sources except as state copies were preserved. Only by direct examination of these invaluable sources can an accurate conception be gained of the extent of distribution of any given immigrant stock in the United States. Except for my volume on the Norwegians and limited studies on the Germans, little use has been made of this vital material.

The theme of interaction of the immigrants and the west-ward-moving frontier presents one of the more fruitful approaches to the study of the immigrant. This approach was mentioned by Frederick Jackson Turner, but he did not develop it.[18] Students from his seminars, such as George M. Stephenson and Marcus L. Hansen, followed up the theme, but they likewise did not de-scribe the process in any detail. In some respects, the most fruit-ful method of study of the combination of immigration and the westward movement is by detailed analysis of small areas, such as townships or, at most, counties. Such detailed studies were started by the State Historical Society of Wisconsin some years ago on old Dane County, and a study has been completed by a University of Wisconsin group on Trempeleau County, Wisconsin.[19] This involves minute examination of geographic conditions, land acqui-sitions, family histories, group frictions, evolving religious and social institutions, political organization, the coming of transpor-tation services, the achievement of stable community life, and the formation of habitual patterns of custom and behavior. The neglect of such local history has deprived historians of vitally im-portant monographic studies of the evolution of American ideas and institutions.

Historians were slow to understand the significance of the great folk migrations to America. Preoccupation with political and constitutional history is an obvious explanation. More con-vincing as an explanation is the fact that it took a long time for the immigrant groups to become sufficiently history-conscious to begin to assemble materials. Even more important was the language obstacle, for few historians seemed able or willing to tackle the mass of foreign language material. The increased productivity in the field of immigration history in the past gen-eration may in large part be attributed to the entry into the ranks of professional historians of a number of bilingual scholars who themselves grew up in immigrant-American families which pre-served the use of the old country language. More such historians are needed.

Much of the significant publication in the field of immigrant-American history has occurred since the First World War. Before then the writing was either part of the literature of the restriction controversy and heavily sociological, or it was scattered through the writings of general historians of the United States. The former writings are well summarized in John Higham's *Strangers in the Land*, while both in his volume and that of Edward N. Saveth on *American Historians and European Immigrants, 1875–1925*,[20] there are good accounts of how American historians approached the subject of immigration.

It is perhaps symptomatic of the lack of adequate monographic studies in the field of immigration that no satisfactory general synthesis of writing on American immigration has yet appeared.[21] The best of the early syntheses was that by George M. Stephenson who made no pretense of writing a definitive or comprehensive history of American immigration but whose volume continues to be useful.[22]   The book was written in response to the need for a scholarly historical approach to the history of immigration at the time of the restriction controversy.   The influence of the volume was considerable in bringing order into a heterogeneous field and in focussing the attention of historians upon the necessity to do basic research work on the European background of the great migrations.   Stephenson's book provided a convenient and well-written account of the coming of the principal immigrant groups and some of the problems created by the influx of millions of immigrants.   It included a long bibliographical essay which became a manual for further studies.

In the same category with Stephenson is Carl Wittke whose *We Who Built America* continues to be the only fairly comprehensive history of American immigration of recent date.   Despite omission of nineteenth-century English immigration, Wittke's volume is filled with useful information.   It represents a faithful digest of available monographic literature in the field at the time of publication.   In addition to accounts of the background factors and the migration process for each of the principal national groups, Wittke endeavors to show the contributions that each group made to American life.

One of the tragedies of the historical profession occurred in 1938 with the death at the age of fifty of Marcus Lee Hansen.

Unfinished at the time of his death were three manuscripts, one in an advanced stage of preparation on Canadian-American population movements,[23] another scheduled for extensive revision,[24] and a third comprising lectures delivered in 1935 at the University of London.[25]   Devoted friends edited and brought out all three in 1940.   Any criticism of Hansen's volumes must take into account that they were published posthumously.   Only the lectures and some essays had been previously issued to the public. In many respects, Hansen's reputation rests most happily on the volume on Canadian-American migrations but less so on *The Great Migration*.   The attempt in the latter volume to include some account of colonial immigration resulted in inadequate treatment of that field, but from Chapter IV the book is based on use of materials gathered in England, Ireland, Germany, and Denmark.[26]   From examination of his papers, one can say that Hansen faithfully reported on his findings in the European depositories visited, but he did not deal fully with his subject nor did he cover more than some features of the movement of peoples in America in the period covered, 1815–60.   The German and Irish movements are the most satisfactorily covered, but even these are incomplete.   Desiring as he did to synthesize in a field with inadequate monographic literature, Hansen was forced to generalize. In his lectures, by imaginative and often moving prose, he evoked a series of impressions of northern European migration across the Atlantic to the farms and cities of America.   This is perhaps best shown in the lecture entitled "The Odyssey of the Emigrant." Hansen's essay on "Immigration as a Field of Research"[27] is still worth reading, but the field has been broadened so much since 1927 that the essay is no longer truly challenging.

Because students of general American history tend to seek a short cut to the field of immigration by reading only the writings of the generalists, they miss some of the most significant writing yet published in the field.   These writings are to be found in the publications concerning certain of the immigrant groups.   One may brush aside the large amount of filio-pietistic writings that seek to prove the distinctive role played by each nationality group in the making of America.   Yet one finds a surprisingly large amount of solid historical research and writing on these groups. The best work done to date, both qualitatively and quantitatively, has been on the Norwegians. Equally good work though not in such quantity has been done on the Swedes, Germans, Irish, Italians, Poles, English, Netherlanders, and Jews.

In writings about an immigrant group, few can equal the record of Theodore C. Blegen. Under his skillful editorship since 1925, the Norwegian-American Historical Association has published forty volumes of histories, journals, travel accounts, and articles, and the work continues. Not only has he inspired dozens of scholars to produce for these volumes, but he has led the way with what is by common consent the model study of a single immigrant group, his *Norwegian Migration to America, 1825–1860,* and its sequel *Norwegian Migration to America; the American Transition.*[28] His recently published *Land of Their Choice* presents one of the rare compilations of "America letters," letters written home by emigrants in America and invaluable as sources for the immigration story.[29] Blegen's conception of immigration is that of a dynamic, individualistic process of transition of almost countless persons from Old World villages to New World farms and factories and mines. He has written:

There has been all too often an air of impersonality in accounts of American immigration. The coming of thirty millions of people was a movement of such magnitude that, to many, it seemed futile to try to disengage personalities from the mass. Many writers have forgotten the individual man in the surging complex of international circumstances. World forces pushed people out of their accustomed environment; world forces pulled them westward with magnetic power. But the pivot of action is individual life. Migration was a simple individual act—a decision that led to consequences—and the "America letters" were a dynamic factor, perhaps the most effective single factor, in bringing discontent to a focus and into action.[30]

In appraising the work of the Norwegian-American Historical Association, Franklin D. Scott has written:

Its publications are gradually creating a mosaic. . . . Each colorful piece is small and distinct; placed in a pattern by the artistic choice and the precise workmanship of scholarly planning, these studies are becoming a true historical mosaic. . . . Here is a prototype for other groups who would search the past to gain understanding of themselves, and of the America they have helped to build.[31]

Briefer comments may be made on the work of scholars of other immigrant groups. George M. Stephenson's work on Swedish immigration is similar to that of Blegen on the Norwegians. His *Religious Aspects of Swedish Immigration* is a definitive work in its field.[32] In the field of German studies, H. A. Pochmann's monumental and impressive volume, *German Culture in America: Philosophical and Literary Influences* [33] and his highly useful *Bibliography of German Culture in America to 1940* [34] are outstanding. The older work of William F. Adams on the Irish remains a classic,[35] while Oscar Handlin's *Boston's Immigrants, 1790–1865,* is excellent,[36] and Carl Wittke's recent volume has brought the Irish story up to date.[37] Robert F. Foerster's book on the Italians remains a model study,[38] while the great sociological treatise by Thomas and Znaniecki on the Poles will doubtless continue useful for generations.[39] The gap in studies of nineteenth-century English immigration has been filled by several first-rate volumes previously cited.[40] A distinguished medievalist, Henry S. Lucas, has improved his later years by producing not only an encyclopedic history of *The Netherlanders in America,* but he has turned out two large volumes of illustrative documents.[41] The Jewish tercentenary was fruitful of several volumes, two being worthy of special mention, a factual study by Rufus Learsi and a more interpretive one by Oscar Handlin.[42]

From Oscar Handlin, in addition to the solid study of immigrant acculturation in Boston, there has come a number of interpretive works. In *The Uprooted* [43] an attempt is made to evoke an impression of the experience of the emigrant in the frequently wrenching transition from old-world village patterns to new-world immigrant group life. He has drawn upon the experiences of the more recent immigrant groups and their life in eastern urban communities, and the volume is therefore somewhat limited for purposes of general interpretation of immigration. Limited documentation makes the volume useful primarily for suggestions as to interpretation of one aspect of the immigrant story.

Handlin's *The American People in the Twentieth Century* emphasizes group minority problems.[44]

Among the most useful of recent studies is Robert Ernst's *Immigrant Life in New York City, 1825–1863*.[45]   The hostility of Americans toward immigration in the pre-Civil War period has been studied commendably by Ray A. Billington in his *Protestant Crusade, 1800–1860*,[46] while nativism of the period since the 1880s has been treated excellently by John Higham in the previously cited *Strangers in the Land*.[47]

As has been indicated, a number of areas of the history of American immigration have been fairly adequately covered, but the gaps in the literature of the field are serious.   We need studies of more of the immigrant groups themselves, such as of the Danes, Czechs, Poles, Hungarians, Rumanians, Bulgarians, Yugoslavs, Greeks, Russians, and others.   We need new studies of the Chinese and Japanese migrations.   The field of acculturation of the immigrants in the United States offers an endless body of opportunities.[48]   Immigrant nationalism has not been studied, and the impact of such nationalisms on European nation-making has been only slightly indicated.[49]   The influence of immigrant groups on American politics has been examined to some extent but not systematically.[50]   The same can be said for immigrant influences on almost all aspects of American life and culture.   However, despite some demand that historians of immigration devote more attention to the influence of immigrant groups on American civilization, the requirements of the field for primary research on European backgrounds and on the transition of the groups to America seems to indicate that the preoccupation of historians since the 1920s with these subjects will continue for some time to come.

NOTES

1. For studies of the colonial population stocks see Evarts B. Greene and Virginia D. Harrington, *American Population before the Federal Census of 1790* (New York, 1932), and American Historical Association, *Annual Report 1931* (Washington, D.C., 1932), pp. 107 ff.

2. Marcus Lee Hansen, *The Atlantic Migration, 1607–1860* (Cambridge, Mass., 1940), Chap. III.

3. See *Historical Statistics of the United States, 1789–1945* (Washington, D.C., 1945), pp. 18 ff., and E. P. Hutchinson, *Immigrants and Their Children, 1850–1950* (New York, 1956), for discussion of statistical problems.

4. "The drain upon the population was so great that in the last quarter of the nineteenth century Norway retained only forty-six per cent of its natural increase—less than one-half." Carlton C. Qualey, *Norwegian Settlement in the United States* (Northfield, Minn., 1938), p. 4.

5. Brinley Thomas, *Migration and Economic Growth; a Study of Great Britain and the Atlantic Economy* (Cambridge, Eng., 1954).

6. Franklin D. Scott, "The Causes and Consequences of Emigration from Sweden," *The Chronicle,* Spring, 1955, p. 9.

7. See Rowland Tappan Berthoff, *British Immigrants in Industrial America, 1790–1950* (Cambridge, Mass., 1953).

8. Kenneth Bjork, *Saga in Steel and Concrete; Norwegian Engineers in America* (Northfield, Minn., 1947).

9. Ludwig Beutin, *Bremen und Amerika; zur Geschichte Der Weltwirtschaft und der Beziehung Deutschlands zu den Vereinigten Staaten* (Bremen, 1953).

10. Almost all accounts of group migrations carry descriptions of the Atlantic crossing.

11. Carl Wittke, *We Who Built America; The Saga of the Immigrant* (New York, 1939), Chap. VII; Robert Ernst, *Immigrant Life in New York City, 1825–1863* (New York, 1949).

12. G. D. Lillibridge, *Beacon of Freedom; the Impact of American Democracy upon Great Britain, 1830–1870* (Philadelphia, 1954); W. S. Shepperson, *British Emigration to North America; Projects and Opinions in the Early Victorian Period* (Minneapolis, 1957); Berthoff, *British Immigrants in Industrial America;* H. Koht, *The American Spirit in Europe* (Philadelphia, 1949); Arnold Schrier, *Ireland and the American Emigration, 1850–1900* (Minneapolis, 1958).

13. Two unpublished doctoral dissertations: P. A. M. Taylor, Mormon Emigration from Great Britain to the United States, 1840–70 (Cambridge University, 1950), and M. Hamlin Cannon, The Gathering of British Mormons to Western America; a Study in Religious Migration (American University, 1950). Two portions of Cannon's study appeared in the *American Historical Review,* LII (April, 1947) and LVII (July, 1952). Also William Mulder, *Homeward to Zion; the Mormon Migration from Scandinavia* (Minneapolis, 1957).

14. Little if any treatment of emigration has been given in textbooks on European history.

15. See John Higham, *Strangers in the Land; Patterns of American Nativism, 1860–1925* (New Brunswick, N.J., 1955).

16. Charlotte Erickson, *American Industry and the European Immigrant, 1860–1885* (Cambridge, Mass., 1957).

17. Qualey, *Norwegian Settlement in the United States,* pp. 14–15.

18. See his somewhat nativistic articles on immigrant groups in the Chicago *Record-Herald,* August 28, September 4, 11, 18, 25, October 16, 1901.

19. The Dane County study was directed by the late Joseph Schafer; Merle Curti, ed., *The Making of an American Community; a Case Study of Democracy in a Frontier County* (Stanford, Calif., 1959). See also Carlton C. Qualey, "A Typical Norwegian Settlement: Spring Grove, Minnesota," *Norwegian-American Studies and Records,* IX (1936), 54–66.

20. New York, 1948.

21. See *A Report on World Population Migrations as Related to the United States of America* (Washington, D.C., 1956). This compilation includes essays on needed research and writing on immigration. There is also an extensive annotated bibliography.

22. George M. Stephenson, *A History of American Immigration, 1820–1924* (Boston, 1926).

23. Marcus Lee Hansen, *The Mingling of the Canadian and American Peoples,* completed and prepared for publication by John Bartlett Brebner (New Haven, 1940).

24. Hansen, *The Atlantic Migration.*

25. Marcus Lee Hansen, *The Immigrant in American History* (Cambridge, Mass., 1940).

26. Now available in the Houghton Library, Harvard University.

27. Originally published in the *American Historical Review,* XXXII (April, 1927), 500–18.

28. Northfield, Minn., 1931, 1940.

29. Minneapolis, 1955.

30. *Ibid.,* p. 7.

31. "Controlled Scholarship and Productive Nationalism," *Norwegian-American Studies and Records,* XVII (1932), 147, 148.

32. Minneapolis, 1932.

33. Madison, Wis., 1957.

34. Madison, Wis., 1952. See also the older work by A. B. Faust, *The German Element in the United States* (Boston, 1909), and John A. Hawgood, *The Tragedy of German-America; the Germans in the United States of America during the Nineteenth Century* (New York, 1940). Carl Wittke's *Refugees of Revolution; the German Forty-Eighters in America* (Philadelphia, 1952) is excellent.

35. William F. Adams, *Ireland and Irish Emigration to the New World from 1815 to the Famine* (New Haven, 1932). Now available on microcard.

36. Cambridge, Mass., 1941.

37. Carl Wittke, *Irish in America* (Baton Rouge, La., 1956).

38. Robert F. Foerster, *The Italian Emigration of Our Times* (Cambridge, Mass., 1919).

39. William I. Thomas and Florian Znaniecki, *The Polish Peasant in Europe and America* (Chicago, 1918–20).

40. See notes 5, 7, and 12. See also Clifton K. Yearley, Jr., *Britons in American Labor: a History of the Influence of the United Kingdom Immigrants on American Labor, 1820–1914* (Baltimore, 1957).

41. Ann Arbor, Mich., 1955; *Dutch Immigrant Memoirs and Related Writings* (Assen, Netherlands, 1955, distributed by the University of Washington Press).

42. Rufus Learsi, *The Jews in America: a History* (Cleveland, 1954); Oscar Handlin, *Adventure in Freedom; Three Hundred Years of Jewish Life in America* (New York, 1954).

43. Boston, 1951.

44. Cambridge, Mass., 1954.

45. New York, 1949.

46. New York, 1938.

47. See also Robert A. Divine, *American Immigration Policy, 1924–1952* (New Haven, 1957).

48. Among the better studies of immigrant adjustment is William Carlson Smith, *Americans in the Making; the Natural History of the Assimilation of Immigrants* (New York, 1939). Edith Abbott, *Immigration: Select Documents and Case Records* (Chicago, 1924) remains very useful.

49. Louis L. Gerson, *Woodrow Wilson and the Rebirth of Poland, 1914–1920; a Study of the Influence on American Policy of Minority Groups of Foreign Origin* (New Haven, 1953).

50. See D. F. Bowers, ed., *Foreign Influences in American Life* (Princeton, N.J., 1944).

THE EVOLUTION CONTROVERSY

by Joseph A. Boromé
THE CITY COLLEGE
NEW YORK

CHARLES DARWIN, in 1859, did not spring the surprise of evolution on a totally unsuspecting world. The idea of evolution—whether called development, growth, change, or progress—had been mused upon by the Greeks and their cultural captives the Romans, by isolated thinkers of the later Middle Ages, and by the fascinating *philosophes* of the Age of Reason. As the eighteenth century merged into the nineteenth, the idea was increasingly advanced in scattered branches of knowledge, including science. Hegel's evolutionary metaphysics, Tennyson's Nature red in tooth and claw, and Comte's three evolutionary stages of society were fairly contemporaneous with the uniformitarianism of Lyell. Religion, the central pivot of Western culture, also admitted evolution into its presence, occasionally with hesitation but with no apparent ill effects.

Indeed, since the age of the *Principia,* it had been usual to regard science as a leading support of orthodoxy, and scientific problems, such as the origin of species, as having religious import. The universe was considered a permanent creation in which all that occurred followed a carefully planned design and fulfilled the purposes of the Creator. Change might exist, but it was always slight and superficial; and in no way did it alter the structure of the Newtonian world-machine or the divine *déroulement.* Natural theology permitted the scientific study of natural phenomena, for which it assigned supernatural causes. Given classical expression in Paley's simile of the watch, the watch-maker, and the watch-repairer, natural theology remained the dominant religious view as the nineteenth century progressed, though challenged first by materialism and Deism and, later, by transcendentalism.

The heightening activity of nineteenth-century naturalists had resulted in startling disclosures that posed the serious problem of reconciling science (naturalism) and religion (supernaturalism). By accenting the doctrine of design, it was possible to accommodate naturalism to supernaturalism, although heavy accenting was sometimes required, as when Lyell read the record of the rocks (1830–32).   Still, before 1859, the surface of the waters was calm. One work, dangerous in its notions, might have precipitated a storm and wrecked the accommodation: Chambers's anonymously published *Vestiges of the Natural History of Creation* (1844). But it was so loose in language and so replete with blunders in scientific details, that it was pitilessly shredded by both theologians and scientists.   Despite a rebuttal by the author, the label "vestigarian" became synonymous with absurd, sentimental, or "unscientific."

By 1859 the idea of evolution was in the air in diverse fields of learning; the natural sciences, in particular, were expanding with geology and paleontology in the lead; and religion, far from being antagonistic to science, was welcoming it as a bulwark of supernaturalism.

When first issued in England, Darwin's *Origin of Species* was not immediately greeted with general cries of alarm.   The London *Times* gave it a laudatory review (written, understandably, by Huxley); the *Saturday Review* and the *Guardian* were by no means unfavorably disposed; and the *Daily News* accepted it all rather as a rehash by Chambers's *Vestiges*.   Even the *English Churchman* granted an approving appraisal.   The preponderant approach of controverting Darwin was largely moderate in tone out of respect for his reputation and his twenty-odd years of labor. Severe criticism, to be sure, came from the *Athenaeum* and, via the pen of Bishop Samuel Wilberforce, from the *Quarterly Review;* while Richard Owen, then in the midst of a scientific quarrel with Huxley, delivered a savage attack in the *Edinburgh Review*.   (The

North British Review was alone in trumpeting the charge of atheism.) In fact, a number of leading journals hardly deigned to notice a volume whose first printing of 1,250 copies had been completely sold out on the day of publication. Nevertheless, the "wait and see" attitude expressed by the *Dublin Review* did not long prevail in the court of public opinion, being swept aside by the awareness of the wide implications of the Darwinian hypothesis that followed upon the almost legendary encounter between Wilberforce and Huxley.

Based on a comprehensive mastery of scientific evidence, the *Origin* was written, without due recourse to technical terms, in a style readily understandable to the intelligent reader. It urged that the major *modus operandi* of evolution was natural selection, which, through the ages, had gradually transformed species. (In all organisms, according to Darwin, small inheritable variations occur constantly. Meanwhile there is also a continuous struggle for existence between organisms, in which those having favorable variations will survive while those less endowed will perish.) This theory was simple enough on first glance. Its very simplicity was on second glance all the more shocking.

Many were the second glances given the work—already gone into several printings—after the June, 1860, conference of the British Association at Oxford. During one of its sessions Bishop Wilberforce, after having lambasted Darwin's suppositions somewhat superficially, turned towards Huxley and flippantly asked on which side of his family Huxley claimed descent from the monkey. Now "Soapy Sam," was not a stupid man; his sally was that of one momentarily too sure of his power of wit. And during his speech he had put his finger on the apparent clash between Darwinism and traditional religion that was soon largely to motivate public discussions. He had also hit hard upon its central issue, the demotion of man from his august position in the universe. Huxley's crushing rejoinder plus the excitement of the meeting—a few ladies fainted—generated a publicity that brought the entire matter unhesitatingly into the open.

Darwin himself, fearful of intemperateness in any form and unwilling to commit himself before exhaustive investigation, had carefully eschewed any extended exposition of man's origin and history. The implication that man, like other organic beings, had descended from an earlier and simpler form, was in the volume however. And this implication, which he might as well had printed on the title page, raised the main question of public controversy; to wit, is man the result of creative design or of natural forces operating on nature's variations.

The battle of words and ideas got under way, additional ammunition being supplied in 1863 by Huxley's *Lectures on the Origin of Species* and *Evidences as to Man's Place in Nature* and Lyell's *Geological Evidences of the Antiquity of Man*. The air became charged with every conceivable variety of pronouncement from Disraeli's dramatic declaration in 1864 that he stood with the angels and not the apes, to Tyndall's all out attack on religious orthodoxy in his 1874 Belfast address. The flood of literature and oratory, often polemical and impassioned, swirled not only about what Darwin had said, but about what it was thought he had said. The most arrant and platitudinous nonsense was uttered by those least qualified to speak. Critics who misunderstood Darwin were taken to task by Darwin's supporters who misunderstood the critics. Few stopped to define terms, so that many denouncing evolution meant Darwinism and many denouncing Darwinism meant evolution. Heavy smoke rose from very little fire as extremists assailed each other. Some scientists, restive under the yolk of religion, used Darwinism as a club with which to batter a way to independence, even to destroy the citadel of religion. Some religionists, fearful of the results, sought to pull down the columns of science that did not rest on the Scriptural foundation stone; they also set out to meet the dangers of civilization that lay in words now associated with Darwinism: whether chance, change, agnosticism, skepticism, atheism, relativism, free will, secularism, or modernism. The sky was further clouded as blows intended for Spencerianism were freely bestowed on Darwinism, and vice versa.

At the height of the din an exasperated gentleman exclaimed, "Leave me my ancestors in Paradise and I will allow you yours in the Zoological Gardens." [1] His was an accurate reflection of the public's chief concern in a land where a great religious revival had been experienced before 1860 and there was widespread belief in the plenary inspiration of the Bible (that it was of divine origin and all in it was substantially true)—a land where religious books annually topped the lists of new titles.

When Darwin finally released *The Descent of Man* (1871), it aroused nothing like the hue and cry that had followed upon the *Origin*. Its propounding of man's kinship to lower creation had been anticipated and exhaustively argued on both sides. After a brief flare-up of partisan belaborings, more and more individuals began to close their ears to depreciatory rumblings. They set out, under calmer counsel, to join those already seeking the middle path in the ill-named war between science and religion. If few accepted Darwinism (or evolution by natural selection), at least a greater number were now willing to accept evolutionism. By 1880 there would still be opposition to the Darwinian hypothesis and to evolution, but the opposition—based rather on scientific than religious grounds—would be, as Huxley put it, more respectable.

In America, where interest in the origin of species had been displayed as early as 1787—when the Reverend Samuel Stanhope Smith regaled the American Philosophical Society with an oration, "On the Causes of the Variety of Complexion and Figure in the Human Species"—sharp reaction to Darwin's first monumental opus was not delayed. At the time organized scientific activity centered in five cities. Washington had the National Institute for the Promotion of Science and the Smithsonian Institution; Philadelphia, the Academy of Natural Sciences and the American Philosophical Society; New York, the Lyceum of Natural History; New Haven, the Connecticut Academy; and Boston, the American Academy of Arts and Sciences and the Boston Society of Natural History. New England was the vineyard of the triumvirate then dominating the field: Agassiz, Dana, and Gray. All were teachers, evidence-gatherers, and writers. All were close to Darwin in age, but only one was close to him in ideas. Louis Agassiz, as a disciple of Georges Cuvier, had inherited a firm opposition to evolution. In 1850, however, he had enunciated his theory of the multiple origin of mankind and had been well cannonaded by the orthodox in religion for his pains. Still, he had managed to survive the uproar over his opinion that the human race, though a single species, was originally divided into "varieties"; and he was not prepared on the basis of his observations and deductions to admit that species since their original creation were mutable. James Dwight Dana's uncompromising position on species was well-known; if not before, certainly after 1855, when, having reviewed Tayler Lewis's *Six Days of Creation,* he identified the volume by Union College's professor of Greek with Chambers's *Vestiges* and solemnly termed it infidel. Asa Gray was otherwise disposed. His own researches had thrown doubts on the old views and convinced him of their shakiness. Then too, as far back as 1855, Darwin had initiated correspondence with him, and in a letter of September 5, 1857, had sent him a detailed account of his evolution theory. In December of the following year, five months after Darwin and Wallace first publicly stated their theory of evolution in papers read before the Linnean Society of London, Gray introduced the principal ideas at a discussion club of which he and Agassiz were members. Agassiz rose immediately to the occasion and further argued the matter with Gray during 1859 meetings of the American Academy of Arts and Sciences. Their earnest exchanges thus preceded the appearance of the *Origin.*

The announcement of the November London publication of the *Origin* excited interest in America. Dana, who might have reviewed it in the *American Journal of Science*—Benjamin Silliman, his father-in-law, was the editor—had suffered a nervous collapse and gone to Europe to recover. The task fell to Gray. His March review was not only a masterly evaluation of the strong and weak points of Darwinism, but an attempt to head off anticipated religious objections, by especially showing that Darwin had not destroyed the argument from design. Simultaneously, spirited debates ensued at meetings of both the American Academy of Arts and Sciences and the Boston Society of Natural History. Agassiz and Francis Bowen led the assaults, which by July, 1860, were buttressed by the elaborate critique of Darwinism that Agassiz included in the third volume of his *Contributions to the Natural History of the United States.* Gray took on all comers and was ably seconded as the year wore on by Theophilus Parsons and William Barton Rogers.

Outside of Boston, where the scientists soon lapsed into almost complete silence, leaving only Gray's pen busy in defense of Darwin, kindred societies were stirred to a bare mention of Darwinism, if that.

In the nonscientific press, for which scientists often wrote, as in England, there was an initial flurry over the *Origin.* The *Atlantic Monthly,* through Gray, naturally supported Darwin. In the *North American Review* Bowen breathed forth a fiery hostility. The *American Theological Review,* the *Christian Examiner,* and the *Methodist Quarterly Review* were equally unaccepting but controlled their temper. The *Princeton Review* completely ignored the volume, and when it got around to the mere mention of Darwin's name in 1863, it did so in articles critical of Agassiz, unforgiven since he had done away with Adam and Eve in 1850.

Just at the point where popular interest was being kindled by distribution of the *Origin*—5,000 copies had been sold before the end of January, 1860; 500 more were printed in February and in March; and a revised edition was issued that very summer—and by circulation of informed opinions for and against its affirmatives, the domestic crisis diverted attention. The mounting political tension that characterized the presidential election, the fateful November returns that induced the actuality of secession, the lengthening shadow of civil war, and the firing on Fort Sumter put a temporary end to the debate on Darwinism, which had been rejected almost outright. During the four years of armed conflict it was difficult for any but professional scientists, a few theologians, and a handful of intellectuals to keep *au courant* with the latest developments in scientific thought.

Save for Gray, no prominent scientist stood up repeatedly to be counted for the cause. Indeed, upon Dana's return from Europe, opposition was considerably strengthened, for in writing his 1863 *Manual of Geology* he firmly insisted apropos of the great issue, "Deus fecit." Religionists seized upon the phrase. By quoting Dana and his confreres of like mind against Darwin, who after all had addressed his lucubration to scientists, they could crush the mischievous sage of Down with resounding effect. During the same year of 1863 they were furnished with yet another cudgel in Huxley's and Lyell's volumes. If these two noted proponents were right in spelling out that man was a product of natural selection, at what point in the process did the Creator intervene to endow him with a soul? God's intervention in nature high-lighted the falsity of Darwinism for the religionists, who proceeded more righteously to reject it on theological and Biblical grounds.

With Appomattox the calm of rejection continued, and by 1867 the number of published articles on Darwinism sank almost to the vanishing point. But several forces were quietly preparing the way for a crescendo of controversy. The scientists, influenced by the natural theology tradition or awed by the formidable personality and antagonism of Agassiz, or both, had remained silent. They were not found refuting Darwin in the periodicals as were occasional religious writers. Nevertheless, a slow conversion in their ranks was under way.

For one thing the Civil War, the first modern war, lent an impetus and added prestige to science, both practical and theoretical. Caught up in a veritable technical revolution that embraced oil, coal and silver mining, railroad building and mechanized agriculture, the country would look to introduce and expand science teaching in the great universities that were rising under able presidential leadership aided by philanthropy and in the institutions sponsored by the Morrill Act. The inauguration of scientist Charles W. Eliot as president of Harvard in 1869 heralded the dawn of a new day. Young men sitting at the feet of teachers reared on Paleyean doctrines began, in the new climate, to accept less the old ideas and to consider more the new. A remarkable group, including Samuel Scudder, Alpheus Spring Packard, Alpheus Hyatt, and Nathaniel Shaler, was trained at Harvard by Agassiz, from whom they heard sufficient criticism of Darwinism but by whom they were encouraged to do research for themselves. One by one, testing the hypothesis for themselves, they moved more to Gray's point of view. Agassiz was almost in the position of Noah Porter of Yale who, having conducted a class to refute Spencer's *First Principles,* discovered that his students had become evolutionists. By 1873 many of Agassiz's pupils had slipped away from the theory of special creation, and others were on the verge of doing so. And gradually they would receive appointments in the expanding science departments of universities and colleges in the East and Midwest. By 1873, too, Agassiz himself had come to admit, as against his earlier contentions, that though Darwin's facts did not warrant his assumptions, he had employed scientific methods. All the while Agassiz's increasing tendency to become overbearing, to insist he was always right, and to utter rash statements had imperiled his reputation as an authority par excellence on evolution. At the 1873 meeting of the American Association of Science he was clearly swimming against the current, supported mainly by individuals of minor stature. His death before the close of the year removed an obstacle to the acceptance of evolution; it did not remove a road block.

Within the scientific community resistance to evolution was dying. Some scientists found peace of mind by ruling man out of the evolutionary process; others by adopting the attitude that Darwinism was really theistic: it did not delve into the mystery of creation, it accepted the idea of a Creator, and it enhanced the belief in design though the manner in which it was executed was not Paleyean. Still others, seemingly unconcerned with religion and its relation to science, edged their way towards a public defense of evolution (but not necessarily Darwinism) or towards the accumulation of evidence that would speak for itself. By 1871 Edward Drinker Cope had championed "neo-Lamarckism" before the American Philosophical Society. By 1872 the New York Academy had made its first direct contribution to the subject in a paper entitled "Carpus and Tarsus of Birds"; and Othniel Charles Marsh of Yale, who studied under Dana, had announced his discovery in the West of fossil birds with teeth, stunning proof of a genetic relationship between birds and reptiles. The trend was unmistakable. Dana's limited acquiescence in the 1874 edition of his *Manual* was significant, if almost anticlimatic.

Concurrent with the slow and little dramatized conversion of the scientists were the winning over of intellectuals and the rising appeal of popular science. Thinkers in pre-Civil War America had been exposed to natural theology, deism, transcendentalism, and vestigarianism as had English thinkers, and many had accepted the idea of evolution in one field of thought or another. As the 1870s approached, they came increasingly to believe in evolutionism, whether persuaded by the work of Darwin, as was Charles Loring Brace, or of Spencer, as was William Graham Sumner. Conservatives like Edwin P. Whipple might hold Darwinism repulsive, but time was with Oliver Wendell Holmes, no radical, who could write sympathetically in *The Poet at the Breakfast-Table* (1872):

What is the secret of the profound interest which "Darwinism" has excited in the minds and hearts of more persons than dare to confess their doubts and hopes? It is because it restores "Nature" to its place as a true divine manifestation. It is that it removes the traditional curse from the helpless infant lying in its mother's arms. It is that it lifts from the shoulders of man the responsibility for the fact of death. . . . If development upward is the general law of the race, if we have grown by natural evolution out of the cave-man and even less human forms of life, we have everything to hope from the future.[2]

His statement revealed the avenues of approach traveled by innumerable thinkers including Walt Whitman and Ralph Waldo Emerson.

In 1869 Emerson wrote to Anna Botta, "Natural Science is the point of interest now."[3] And so it was. Science seemed to be carrying all before it, to the point of extinguishing poetry. In 1867 Edward Livingston Youmans had persuaded D. Appleton and Company to launch a popular periodical stressing scientific news. *Appleton's Journal* fed readers with lengthy articles on Darwin, Spencer, and associated subjects, but appetites were better whetted when Youmans started the *Popular Science Monthly* in 1872. He supplemented his editorial work by planning and supervising, again for Appleton, the International Scientific Series, which printed books by the leading English and American scientists. In an age becoming Verne conscious, Youman's Series contributed its share to swelling the sales of volumes on science that soared impressively year by year.

The daily newspapers, to which apparently most people confined their reading for about a decade after the Civil War, gave science greater and greater coverage. As lecturers on evolution took to the platforms, their words reached a wider audience. John Fiske's Harvard lectures in the fall of 1869 and spring of 1871 (later published as *Outlines of Cosmic Philosophy*) stirred up immense excitement when printed in the New York *World*. Tyndall's tour in the winter of 1872–73, a prelude to a procession of devotees, was reported in detail by the New York *Tribune*. The regular issues in which it reprinted his addresses enjoyed enormous sales that were supplemented by eager readers snapping up more than fifty thousand copies of a special sheet containing the entire Tyndall series. Among the quality magazines of the day, the *Nation* and *Atlantic Monthly* made bold to stand with Darwin, though taking pains to avoid bold front-page leaders. Not without reason did George E. Pond comment in the *Galaxy* of May, 1873: "The Taine of the twentieth century . . . will discover . . . the ultimate dominant tinge in our era . . . to be Darwinism. . . . Journalism is dyed so deep with it that the favorite logic of the leading article is 'survival of the fittest,' and the favorite jest is 'sexual selection.' "

As scientists were quietly accepting evolution and facilitating its entry into the halls of higher learning, as intellectuals and the general public were being more exposed to evolution and the advancement of science, the tocsin was sounding in the camp of religion, additionally alerted by sundry developments. The *Origin* fell upon an agrarian America which, within ten years, was on the road to vast transformations. The rise of modern industrialism, together with the growth of monopoly capitalism, mechanization, and the labor movement, was to be coupled with an extraordinary rise of cities. While the frontier regions lured some and opportunities in the reconstructed South beckoned others, it was to the urban centers that people flowed in staggering num-

bers from the countryside and abroad.   The unanticipated rush
of population brought the city governments face to face with
problems ranging from slums to sanitation.   Social welfare, too,
commanded consideration, for the mobility and ferment everywhere affected individual relationships not only in business, industry, and government, but in the home.   As it became difficult
to adjust to so many changes in so many directions, there were
persons who drifted dangerously close to losing their footing, or
who lost all sense of ethics, or who condoned lapses from moral
standards.   Washington, New York, and Philadelphia offered
some deplorable examples.

The economic and social changes were matched by cultural
and intellectual changes.   And the defenders of religion were
caught up in them all.   At the very time when moral uncertain-
ties and material certitudes were spreading themselves, things
spiritual seemed headed for a decline.   Religionists, many faced
with denominational schisms due to the prewar slavery controversy, watched with uneasiness an apparent decreasing importance
of religion, and the spread of higher criticism and comparative
religion, which robbed Christianity of its unique features.   They
sensed a gradual loss of the status they had enjoyed as intellectual and moral leaders before 1861 and saw, in the brightening
flame of the educational renaissance, more institutions established
on nonsectarian bases, more liberal thinkers installed as presidents, and more bankers, lawyers, and businessmen—rather than
ministers—appointed to boards of trustees.   The tide of seculari-
zation was bad enough, but the popularization of science was
worse.   Darwinism, the great offender, had been initially politely
squelched.   But as the 1870s dawned and change manifested itself in all of American life, as the churches, facing resultant problems knew not exactly where to turn or what to do while the lower
classes slipped away from their hold, as campaigns opened against
established religious institutions and dogmatism, and groups like
the Free Religious Association grew and opened its membership
to agnostics, atheists, and positivists, as rationalists began to deify
science at the expense of everything, as the writings of Huxley,
Tyndall, and Spencer were more and more purveyed, as scien-

tists, long quoted against evolution, began to bow before it, and as a few liberals tried to reconcile evolution with religion, orthodoxy roused itself.   Movements that threatened full observance of the Lord's Day were vigorously combatted; publications of the Anti-Infidel Library found ready readers; attempts were made to "put God into the Constitution" by the amendment process; and articles unfavorable to Darwinism appeared in popular religious journals, the *Baptist Quarterly* leading off as early as 1869.

If any deluded souls had been unaware of the workings of a plot to subvert religion, spearheaded by evolution, their eyes were opened when, in 1871, Darwin gave the world his *Descent of Man*. (The fact that James Freeman Clarke's *Ten Great Religions* was issued in the same year reinforced the belief.)   It is true that the general thought of the *Descent* was already familiar to the public and that Darwin added little weight to his former arguments.   It is true that Owen's *On the Anatomy of the Vertebrates* (1866–68), Wallace's *Contributions to the Theory of Natural Selection* (1870), and Mivart's *On the Genesis of Species* (1871)—all critical of Darwinism—had preceded its publication and contained battering rams.   Still, the fact that Darwin's two massive volumes on man now stood on the shelves, that his theory rested on no demonstrable proof of a link between man and the animals, and that his ingenious explanation of matters such as conscience were deemed repugnant in many quarters and fraught with terrible meaning, all was sufficient cause for alarm.

There were peals of thunder from press and pulpit.   Even the New York *Times,* receptive to the *Origin,* drew back a bit on this one.   Conservatives wished to think the thing through.   Not so the extremists.   More sure of themselves on man than on plants and animals, they let fly with regrettable phrases that eventually boomeranged by opening the door to ridicule.   Reckless allegations of the Reverend Justin Dewey Fulton (a Baptist) of Tremont Temple in Boston were matched by the remarks of "a not unintelligent speaker" at a New York meeting who pounced on Darwin for saying "that a sheep could be transformed into a cow." [4] Others denounced evolution as "the tendency of favourable varieties of turnips to become men," and as the theory that "man, having first been a tadpole, became a monkey, and then wore off his tail by sedentary habits." [5] Such unbridled effusions had a two-fold effect. They brought a counterattack from those sympathetic to science and secularism, to intellectual fair play and tolerance, to reasonable religion or no religion whatsoever—a body growing since the *Origin* and coalescing rapidly. Orthodoxy, on the defensive, could only think of offensive and in the lull following the explosion over the *Descent* girded for the battle. In 1874, as two different publishers brought out large reprintings of the *Descent*, orthodoxy rushed into the arena led by at least one general of formidable reputation, who supplied the banners with inscriptions.

Charles Hodge, member of the Board of Trustees and leading professor in the Theological Seminary at Princeton, and editor of the *Princeton Review*, was a powerful writer, a victorious controversalist, and a stalwart of Presbyterianism and evangelical Christianity. He was proud to repeat often, of Princeton, "A new idea never originated in this seminary." [6] His stout three-volumed *Systematic Theology* (1872–73)—judged "the greatest system of dogmatics in our language"—had not diminished his influence throughout Protestantism, though it was criticized as not representative of Westminster theology. In 1874, at the age of seventy-seven, Hodge set out to annihilate the enemy, publishing *What Is Darwinism?*, in which, having demolished arguments to his satisfaction and caused heads to roll, he gave the answer "It is Atheism." His asseveration reached thousands who, not having read Darwin, took these words as gospel and passed the pronouncement along with telling effect. Although reviewers, Catholic and Protestant alike, feared materialism and atheism—and were divided among themselves as to evolution—they were not as carried away by Hodge's book as was the *Princeton Review*.

The evolution controversy was now upon the country, and the presses were kept busy supplying both sides with books and articles. The centennial year brought, among others, James T. Bixby's *Similarities of Physical and Religious Knowledge,* Asa Gray's *Darwiniana,* James McCosh's *The Development Hypothesis,* and Minot J. Savage's *The Religion of Evolution.* It also brought Huxley's visit to America. The doughty advocate of Darwinism had gone through the fight in England, and had arrived at more daring conclusions that the author of the *Origin*. In 1868 he had written *On the Physical Basis of Life* to show that he was not a materialist, and its readers had come away convinced that he was. He had never made a secret of his agnosticism, and to undiscriminating minds he was therefore an atheist. When Daniel Coit Gilman invited him to speak at the Johns Hopkins University exercises, a New York divine upbraided the president with, "It was bad enough to invite Huxley. It were better to have asked God to be present. It would have been absurd to ask them both." [7] Not only did the New York *Tribune* reprint Huxley's address in Baltimore, it regularly reported all of his addresses and then published them in their entirety as an extra number that easily reached a potential of 100,000 readers. These lectures were exceedingly important, for Huxley's forceful statements could not be lightly brushed aside, and, almost as he spoke, fossil evidence came to light that supported some of his conjectures. His addresses compelled a deep reconsideration of evolution.

The Tennessee Conference of the Southern Methodist Church made a solemn resolve in 1878:

This is an age in which scientific atheism, having divested itself of the habiliments that most adorn and dignify humanity, walks abroad in shameless denudation. The arrogant and impertinent claims of this "science, falsely so-called," have been so boisterous and persistent, that the unthinking mass have been sadly deluded; but our university alone has had the courage to lay its young but vigorous hand upon the mane of untamed Speculation and say: "We will have no more of this." [8]

But before this J. D. Ball had started a journal of liberal opinion in Boston called *Evolution* (1877) and enlisted Thomas Wentworth Higginson among his writers; and Alexander Winchell, noted geology professor, had followed his *Doctrine of Evolution . . . and Its Theistic Bearings* (1874) with the significantly titled *Reconciliation of Science and Religion* (1877).

By 1879 famed scientists like Winchell in Minnesota, Joseph

Le Conte in California, and Dana in Connecticut had openly accepted evolution. Ministers like Henry Ward Beecher of New
York and Francis Howe Johnson of Andover, educators like
James McCosh of Princeton, and philosophers like John Fiske of
Cambridge were effectively arguing for theistic evolution or, as
Fiske called it, "God's way of doing things." It was even difficult
to raise the monkey issue without losing face, save in the South
and rural backwaters. As a lady reprimanded a senator orating
against evolution in Henry Adams's novel *Democracy* (1880):
"You are very hard on the monkeys. . . . The monkeys never
did you any harm; they are not in public life; they are not even
voters; if they were, you would be enthusiastic about their intelligence and virtue. After all, we ought to be grateful to them, for
what would men do in this melancholy world if they had not inherited gaiety from the monkeys—as well as oratory."

Orthodoxy could maintain no united front. It lost the support of science and had to face growing contingents of liberal
thinkers in all walks of life who either completely divorced science
from religion and let them go their separate ways, or by various
paths—among them immanence of God and pantheism—brought a
reconciliation that enhanced evolution. The margin of acceptance of Christian evolution was widest among the liberal Congre-
gationalists. Though it varied among other denominations, it increased with the passage of time. Some like the Catholics, whose
four-way interpretation of Scripture preserved them from the
shock felt by literal interpreters of the Word, drew the line firmly
at human evolution. The Hodgians, who wished to draw the line
at all evolution, fought a rear-guard action. In 1880 Archibald
Hodge, who had succeeded his late father at the Princeton Theological Seminary, refused to countenance those who identified
evolution with atheism and avowed his acceptance of theistic evolution but not Darwinism. His stand was heartening, for he was
one of the editors of the influential *Presbyterian Review,* which
represented the conservative viewpoint. Soon, at Princeton, theologians would join in the approach of Professor Patrick Macloskie
who "went on to show . . . that the whale's exploit in swallowing

Jonah and giving him shelter for three days and nights was feasible biologically, and hence scientifically credible." [9]

In the 1880s, a heyday of Spencerian optimism, scientific Darwinism almost went into eclipse as conservative (social) Darwinism bid for public approval. Spencer's extension of evolution to society with its "struggle for existence," and "survival of the fittest," provided a rationale for the rampant individualism and the rampant laissez-faire of the time. It also opened the door to reform Darwinism and the controversy that still continues between cosmic determinism and human choice. In sum, by the 1880s evolution had come to stay, owing to Darwin's expositions; and its influence as evolutionism would soon be felt in shattering old and constructing new approaches to knowledge in philosophy, sociology, political science and economy, psychology, literature, art, and religion. It had come to stay, no matter how hard, for example, the scientists might debate theories, whether of Lamarckism, orthogenesis, or heterogenesis; and the philosophers might argue as catastrophists, Hegelians, Spencerians, Lamarckians, or Darwinians.

By 1890 orthodoxy had faced the alternatives and realized the need for compromise; it had adopted the "social gospel" and placed itself once more in touch with the people of the cities; it had passed the midpoint of an inquisitional period of trials and excommunications that did it little credit; and it had recovered from its panic to find its worst fears unrealized despite Francis E. Abbot and Robert Ingersoll. In 1891 and 1892, respectively, Washington Gladden published his popularization of higher criticism, *Who Wrote the Bible?*, and Lyman Abbott his *Evolution of Christianity.* Both men, almost entirely self-trained in theology, were able writers and enthusiastic adherents to evolution. In issuing works comprehensible to the general reader they encountered no outcry. Times had indeed changed when Abbott, Beecher's successor at Plymouth Church, in referring to the New England Primer verse, "In Adam's fall we sinned all," could say, "Adam did not represent me—I never voted for him." [10] By 1893, the year of the Spencer-Weismann debate that attracted little public interest, not only had leaders in the liberal theology movement accepted evolution, but, at the World's Parliament of Religion, the leaders of general orthodoxy followed suit. All the while Henry Drummond, whose visit to America in 1887 had been a triumph for the reconciliation of evolution and evangelism, was lecturing on the subject by express invitation of the New York Chautauqua to responsive audiences composed largely of non-urban churchgoers.

Dwight Moody and Ira Sankey might have been preaching old-time religion to millions throughout the land since 1870, and the Sears Roebuck catalog—a useful index to the mind of rural and small-town America—might not, as late as 1905, have listed any book that would offend them. But it was undeniable that evolution in some form or the other had, after bitter controversy, been accepted by the overwhelming majority of educated people. Only at the portals of the fundamentalist temples, in which Hodgism found refuge, was it refused entrance. There, ill-educated pastors, products of educational short cuts which the Disciples, Baptists, and other groups permitted, earned the eventual gibes of Sinclair Lewis and H. L. Mencken and the praise of William Jennings Bryan by continually turning it away. Their mission has not ended.[11]

The mass of material and the confusion of terms that characterize the whole subject alone give validity to an attempt at separating the literature *on,* from the literature *of,* the evolution controversy induced by Darwinism. Little purpose is served in listing the writings of the second category, since they are inevitably drawn upon by the authors in the first category who, in cumulative fashion, cite them as part of the baggage in their bibliographical wagons. The first category then deserves major emphasis.

The tone of the literature was set in two works which long dominated the field: John W. Draper's *History of the Conflict between Religion and Science* (New York, 1874) and Andrew D. White's *A History of the Warfare of Science with Theology in Christendom* (New York, 1896; 2d ed., 1900). White's book, in a way a tract for the times, was the outgrowth of a lecture tellingly titled "The Battlefields of Science," which he delivered at the Cooper Union in 1869 and subsequently expanded into a periodical article and then a booklet. The popularity of Draper's volume is indicated by the fact that it went through eight separate editions in the two-year period 1875–77. Within the Draper-White frame of reference came numerous contributions, including Charles Hodge, *What Is Darwinism?* (New York, 1874) and George F. Wright, "Recent Works Bearing on the Relation of Science to Religion" (*Bibliotheca Sacra*, XXXV [1878], 46–75). In 1909 John Dewey came out for a wider interpretation with "The Influence of Darwinism on Philosophy," *Popular Science Monthly*, LXXV (1909), 90–98. The controversy was not between science and religion; the clamor in theological circles had hidden its real nature. Where ideas arose to combat Darwinism, they arose not in religion but in science and in philosophy. While Dewey tended to emphasize the argument for philosophy, he made it impossible for all but fundamentalists to continue writing in the old vein. The rise of organized fundamentalism, especially after 1916, when the World's Christian Fundamentals Association was founded, and the dramatic Scopes trial of 1825, led to an outpouring of writing that put the monkey and modernism again in the news; among them Henry Fairfield Osborn's *Evolution and Religion in Education; Polemics of the Fundamentalist Controversy of 1922–1926* (New York, 1926) and Maynard Shipley's *The War on Modern Science; a Short History of the Fundamentalist Attacks on Evolution and Modernism* (New York, 1927). The early 1920s not only saw the depression that sent many seeking solace to religion and the appearance in America of "new orthodoxy," espoused by Reinhold Niebuhr and Paul Tillich. It also saw the pioneer work of Bert James Loewenberg, who sought to strike a balance in dealing with aspects of the great controversy. He published two articles, "The Reaction of American Scientists to Darwinism" (*American Historical Review*, XXXVIII [1933], 687–701) and "The Controversy over Evolution in New England, 1859–1873" (*New England Quarterly*, VIII [1935], 232–57), based on research embodied in his doctoral dissertation of 1934 at Harvard,

The Impact of the Doctrine of Evolution on American Thought, 1859–1900. There soon followed an article by Sidney Ratner, "Evolution and the Rise of the Scientific Spirit in America" (*Philosophy of Science,* III [1936], 104–22); Windsor Hall Roberts's *The Reaction of American Protestant Churches to the Darwinian Philosophy, 1860–1900,* abstract of a dissertation submitted to the University of Chicago in 1936 (Chicago, 1938); Kenneth Franklin Gantz's *The Beginnings of Darwinian Ethics: 1859–1871,* a University of Chicago dissertation of 1938 reprinted in the University of Texas *Studies in English* (1939, pp. 180–209); and William Ebenstein's paper, "The Early Reception of the Doctrine of Evolution in the United States" (*Annals of Science,* IV [1939], 306–18). In his *The Modern Movement in American Theology* (New York, 1939) Frank Hugh Foster saliently discussed the controversy with some new insights. Hardly had the next decade opened than Loewenberg led off with his "Darwinism Comes to America, 1859–1900" (*Mississippi Valley Historical Review,* XXVIII [1941], 339–68). There came too, Conrad Wright's "The Religion of Geology" (*New England Quarterly,* XIV [1941], 335–58). Extended treatment of the subject appeared in such general works as Merle Curti's *The Growth of American Thought* (New York, 1943, rev. ed., 1951). Richard Hofstadter's survey of the controversy in the first chapter of his *Social Darwinism in America* (Philadelphia, 1944; rev. ed., Boston, 1955; New York, 1959) was followed by such useful publications as Herbert W. Schneider's "The Influence of Darwin and Spencer on American Philosophical Theology" (*Journal of the History of Ideas,* VI [1945], 3–18) and his *A History of American Philosophy* (New York, 1946), which coupled an analysis of the effect of evolution on philosophy and theology in Chapter VI, "Evolution and Human Progress," with a lengthy annotated bibliography. Philip P. Wiener added to the subject in his *Evolution and the Founders of Pragmatism* (Cambridge, 1949) and in his reply to points raised by Herbert Schneider in a review of his book (*Journal of the History of Ideas,* XI [1950], 244–47). Stow Persons's work, *Free Religion: An American Faith* (New Haven, 1947), incidentally contained a criticism of some of Loewenberg's analyses.

As the 1950s moved towards the memorable centennial date there appeared a volume edited by Stow Persons called *Evolutionary Thought in America* (New Haven, 1950), a valuable collection of essays by eminent authorities; John L. Morrison's *A History of American Catholic Opinion on the Theory of Evolution, 1859–1950,* a 1951 doctoral dissertation at Missouri University published by University Microfilms (Ann Arbor, 1952); Edward A. White's *Science and Religion in American Thought; the Impact of Naturalism* (Palo Alto, 1952), containing a particularly provocative explanation of the "resurgence of the war between science and religion" in the twenties; Kenneth K. Bailey's *The Antievolution Crusade of the Nineteen-twenties,* a doctoral dissertation of 1953 at Vanderbilt University published by University Microfilms (Ann Arbor, 1953); Philip Gilbert Fothergill's *Historical Aspects of Organic Evolution* (New York, 1953); LeRoy Johnson's *The Evolution Controversy in the 1920s,* a New York University doctoral dissertation of 1954 published by University Microfilms (Ann Arbor, 1955); a paper by Alvar Ellegard, "The Darwinian Theory and Nineteenth-Century Philosophies of Science" (*Journal of the History of Ideas,* XVIII [1957], 362–93); and Edward Justin Pfeifer's *The Reception of Darwinism in the United States, 1859–1880,* a doctoral dissertation accepted by Brown University in 1957 and published by University Microfilms (Ann Arbor, 1958), which does not portray Agassiz in his usual role of champion of orthodoxy. General works touching on the evolution controversy included Henry Steele Commager's *The American Mind: an Interpretation of American Thought and Character since the 1880s* (New Haven, 1950); Harvey Wish's *Society and Thought in America* (2 vols., New York, 1950–52); and Eric F. Goldman's *Rendezvous with Destiny* (New York, 1952), which argued convincingly for the term "conservative" rather than "social" Darwinism. Although the book by Richard Hofstadter and Walter P. Metzger entitled *The Development of Academic Freedom in the United States* (New York, 1955) gives extended attention to the controversy and rather maintains the views of those who held the colleges and universities as important battle grounds, hardly any such impression is conveyed by John S. Bru-

bacher and Willis Rudy in their *Higher Education in Transition*
(New York, 1958) who, indeed, make little mention of the mat-
ter.   In his article entitled "An Indian Perspective of Darwin"
(*Centennial Review of Arts and Science,* III [1959], 357–63) J. B. S.
Haldane concludes that "Darwin was too great a man to assess just
yet.   In each succeeding generation, new aspects of his work
appear important."   Certainly the assessment goes on.   The tor-
rent of literature for the Darwin Centennial is reviewed by Bert
J. Loewenberg in his "Darwin Scholarship of the Darwin Year"
(*American Quarterly,* XI [1959], 526–33).   A rich mine of agreement and conflict will be the three-volume publication, in 1960,
of the speeches and papers delivered at the November, 1959, Darwin Centennial Celebration at the University of Chicago.   They
will be edited by Sol Tax with the general title *Evolution after
Darwin.*   Not only will they highlight the fact of continuous assessment, they will highlight the fact that, a century after Darwin, the
two great mysteries of evolution remain: the advent of life itself
and the origin of man.

The field is by no means exhausted.   Studies are going on.
Already Michael McGiffert has completed a doctoral dissertation
at Yale on Christian Darwinism; the Partnership of Asa Gray and
George Frederick Wright, and Shirley Phillips at Wyoming University is at work on The Doctrine of Evolution in American
Fiction, 1860–1865.   New light will doubtless be shed in corners
still fairly dark.   For example, most people in mid-nineteenth-
century America belonged to evangelical churches.   Where can
one find a comprehensive and scholarly history and analysis of
those churches during the period of the controversy?   Orthodoxy
has not always been viewed from the best of angles.   Scholarly
and sympathetic biographies of leaders like Charles Hodge—or
better yet, one of father and son—would be invaluable.   Some
authors state that Hodge's voice in the early 1870s carried great

weight; others that he had already lost a good deal of his influence. It is possible that the full consequences of the evolutionary hypothesis have not yet been experienced and that some religionists were more right than wrong in estimating the consequences. What Hodge foresaw ought not, perhaps, to be lightly brushed aside. We need, too, a thorough examination of the reconciliation by evolutionary sects of science and religion. What do we know quantitatively of popular reading tastes in America with respect to religion between 1859 and 1879? There is much comment to the effect that Darwin was not read first hand, the implication usually being that Spencer was. More certainty would be welcome. Considering, also, the Atlantic Community approach, it would be interesting to know how many of the men who championed Darwin and evolution were thoroughly familiar with the arguments of Darwin's proponents in England, and how many who were opponents in America took their inspiration and ideas from the British. Profitable, too, might be a comparison of the rate of acceptance of Darwinism and evolution in England with that in the United States—where it was certainly more rapid—as influenced by the existence of a national church which long controlled education, especially on the higher level.

NOTES

1. L. E. Elliott-Binns, *Religion in the Victorian Era* (London, 1936), p. 164.
2. O. W. Holmes, *Works,* III (Boston, 1892), 304–5. It reflects his anti-Calvinism.
3. R. Rusk, ed., *The Letters of Ralph Waldo Emerson,* VI (New York, 1939), 63.
4. New York *Times,* March 13, 1871.
5. *The Index,* III, Supplement, April 13, 1872.
6. R. H. Nichols, "Charles Hodge," *Dictionary of American Biography,* IX (New York, 1932), 98–99.
7. D. C. Gilman, *The Launching of a University* (New York, 1906), pp. 22–23.
8. Quoted in Virginius Dabney, *Liberalism in the South* (Chapel Hill, N.C., 1932), p. 193.
9. E. S. Corwin, "The Impact of the Idea of Evolution on the

American Political and Constitutional Tradition," in Stow Persons, ed., *Evolutionary Thought in America* (New Haven, Conn., 1950), p. 188.

10. Quoted in A. L. Drummond, *Story of American Protestantism* (Boston, 1951), p. 341.

11. There is still sensitivity on both sides. When *Life* magazine in the recent past undertook a series of articles on evolution (organic and inorganic), fundamentalist readers sent in letters that left no room for inference. As late as January 26, 1958, the Bishop of Coventry, England, felt compelled to write a letter to the London *Times,* which had reported one of his sermons under the headline "Bishop Attacks Scientists" in abbreviated form. Although he had commented on the attitude of certain scientists, letter writers, believing he had attacked scientists in general, had begun to pepper the Bishop, who wished his stand to be clearly known. Interestingly enough, the identical issue of the *Times* carried an article by the Reverend C. W. Butterworth entitled "The Limits of Science."

PRAGMATISM IN AMERICA

by Sidney Ratner
RUTGERS UNIVERSITY

PRAGMATISM is more than "a new name for old ways of thinking." It is a profoundly American union of philosophy with life; an application of the methods of science to the problems of philosophers and men in all walks of life. Pragmatism is an expression of modern America's faith in man's ability to remold nature and society through intelligence, will power, and social cooperation. This philosophy arose in post-Civil War America as a revolt against "the genteel tradition" and all other philosophies that exalt the unity of the universe, predestination, eternity, the certainty of knowledge, and entities or powers outside space and time. Pragmatism, however, is far more important for its constructive contributions to an understanding of science, art, philosophy, religion, politics, economics, and education as human activities in an ever-changing universe.

The Pragmaticism of C. S. Peirce. To William James must go the credit for first publicly using the word "pragmatism" in a lecture he gave at the University of California in 1898 on "Philosophical Conceptions and Practical Results." There he spoke of Charles Sanders Peirce's principle, "the principle of practicalism —or pragmatism as he [Peirce] called it, when I first heard him enunciate it at Cambridge in the early 70's." [1] Peirce later wrote of an informal Metaphysical Club that used to meet in his or James's study in Cambridge. These philosophical discussants formed a brilliant group, most of whom were or became famous. There were three scientists: Peirce, William James, and Chauncey Wright; three lawyers: Oliver Wendell Holmes, Jr. (later

Justice of the Supreme Court), Nicholas St. John Green, and
Joseph Warner; a historian-philosopher, John Fiske, and a gifted
logician and theologian, Francis Ellingwood Abbot. It was for
this group, Peirce tells us, that "I drew up a little paper expressing some of the opinions that I had been urging all along under
the name of pragmatism." This essay was expanded and appeared as two essays, "The Fixation of Belief," and "How to Make
our Ideas Clear" in the widely-read *Popular Scientific Monthly*
for November, 1877, and January, 1878, respectively.

In the first of these justly celebrated essays, Peirce points out
how human thinking arises from the irritation of doubt and the
struggle to attain a stable state of belief. He affirms that the sole
object of inquiry is the settlement of opinion or belief. Then he
describes four methods of settling belief. The first is the "method
of tenacity"—the clinging by an individual to a set of opinions
which satisfy him emotionally until social differences, the expression of different opinions by other men he respects, cause him to
question his original belief and to seek another method of fixing
belief. The second is the "method of authority," historically associated with states and churches. But doubts will arise in the
minds of reflective men, especially as they study or come into
contact with other cultures and authorities in other countries and
ages. This unsettlement leads thinkers to the third method:
adopting opinions that seem "agreeable to reason," an expression,
as Peirce says, which "does not mean that which agrees with experience, but that which we find ourselves inclined to believe."
This a priori method is best exemplified in the history of metaphysical philosophy from Plato to the present day. The shock of
conflicting opinions based upon differing tastes and intuitions,
however, causes some men to seek the fourth method: "the method
of science." The use of this method—hypothesis, inference, observation, and experiment—leads to beliefs that are based upon
publicly testable evidence and logical analysis and that acquire a
remarkable success in settling conflicts of opinion.

Then Peirce proceeded in the essay on "How to Make Our
Ideas Clear" to formulate this most important principle: "Consider what effects, that might conceivably have practical bearings,

we conceive the object of our conception to have. Then, our conception of these effects is the whole of our conception of the object." [2] This view of Peirce's was inspired in part by his reflections on Kant's *Critique of Pure Reason,* with its definition of pragmatic belief as that judgment of a situation upon the basis of which one acts in the hope of attaining certain ends, as a physician does in diagnosing a disease. Kant recognized that the touchstone or test of belief is the *bet,* the wager, on which the happiness of our whole life may be staked.

Peirce was also influenced by his discussions with Chauncey Wright, the most penetrating philosophical exponent of Darwinism and scientific method in the 1860s and 1870s, and with Nicholas St. John Green, whom Peirce called "the grandfather of pragmatism." Green often urged the importance of applying Bain's definition of belief as "that upon which a man is prepared to act," from which definition, Peirce asserted, "pragmatism is scarce more than a corollary." [3]

Peirce's 1878 pragmatic maxim was received with a deafening silence, despite the brilliant illustrations he gave of how it clarified the meaning of difficult scientific and philosophical terms like "force" and "reality." Twenty years later James revived Peirce's formula and made pragmatism into an important twentieth-century philosophical movement. His reformation of pragmatism, however, was radically different from Peirce's in many ways, as were some of the doctrines of the two other leading pragmatists: John Dewey at the University of Chicago and F. C. S. Schiller at Oxford. Peirce felt impelled to distinguish his ideas on pragmatism from those of his more influential and popular associates in America and Europe. In 1905 he coined the term "pragmaticism" because it was "ugly enough to be safe from kidnappers." [4]

In contradistinction to James and Schiller, Peirce asserted that pragmaticism was "no doctrine of metaphysics, no attempt to determine any truth of things," but "merely a method of ascertaining the meanings of hard words and of abstract concepts . . . upon the structure of which, arguments concerning objective fact may hinge." [5] The purpose of pragmatism, as he saw it, is to bring to an end prolonged disputes between philosophers which no observations of fact could settle. This he hoped to achieve by persuading philosophers to emulate experimental scientists. He proposed that philosophers undertake to put to the test of observation and experiment the theses they debated by acting upon this improved version of his earlier pragmatic maxim; namely,

In order to ascertain the meaning of an intellectual conception one should consider what practical consequences might conceivably result by necessity from the truth of that conception; and the sum of these consequences will constitute the entire meaning of the conception.[6]

This proposal is important for its emphasis upon the temporal and experimental aspects of philosophical propositions. The rational meaning of a word, proposition, or sign consists of the various words, propositions, or signs into which it can be logically translated or restated. Consider the various definitions that have or can be given of terms like space, time, force, man, democracy, nationalism. The Peircian pragmatist advises choosing that translation, definition, or interpretation of a word, proposition, or sign that is applicable to human conduct and subject to the analyst's "control under every situation, and to every purpose."[7] As a rigorous logician and experimentalist with long years of laboratory training and experience, Peirce argued: "If one can define accurately all the conceivable experimental phenomena which the affirmation or denial of a concept could imply, one will have therein a complete definition of the concept, and *there is absolutely nothing more in it.*"[8]

This stress upon experimentally verifiable statements had been interpreted by some as meaning that the chief end or value of man's life lies in action. Against this Peirce protested that for him the *summum bonum* did not consist in brute action but in that process of evolution whereby the existent universe comes to be governed increasingly by laws or regularities and to embody more and more general ideas made part of social life through action by individuals guided by scientific, ethical, and esthetic ideals.[9] Human reason, as Peirce saw it, becomes a part of the universe through ideas expressed in signs that modify human behavior and help to establish regularity, continuity, and generality in human affairs and in physical nature. The role of action through experiment—in the laboratory or the calculating room—is intermediary to the appreciation of verifiable generalizations and the rational reorganization of life. This position is a far cry from the glorification of action for its own sake or the subordination of thought and scientific activity to commercial profit and individual aggrandizement.

Peirce in addition to being the first theorist of pragmatism, developed a cosmology and metaphysics of great speculative brilliance and power in a remarkable series of articles, some written for the *Monist* (January, 1891—January, 1893) and others published only after his death. He attacked mechanism and determinism as universal principles of explanation, defended the reality of absolute chance, and advanced intriguing theories concerning the origin of the laws of nature and the nature of an evolutionary universe. James, Dewey, and Royce appreciated their importance and acknowledged his influence. But Peirce's grand philosophical structure did not command wholehearted acceptance by any established philosopher during his lifetime. Only since the publication in 1931–35 of six volumes of his *Collected Papers* by the Harvard University Press has Peirce come to be widely appreciated as a philosophical mind of the first magnitude. The wave of adulation that first greeted everything in his *Collected Papers* has now ebbed, and many of his admirers are critical of his cosmology and metaphysics. But his contributions to logic, pragmatism, and scientific methodology, despite the great advances made since his death in 1914, stand as enduring monuments to his genius.

The Pragmatism of William James. In sharp contrast to Peirce, William James had an amazing gift for very vivid statement of philosophical ideas. Like T. H. Huxley in England and Henri Bergson in France he had the ability to simplify complex ideas, to give graphic, easily understood examples, and to make the subjects he dealt with seem a matter of vital concern to all who heard or read him. Peirce has been called "the philosopher's philosopher." James might have been called, in the best sense, "the American people's philosopher."

James came from a family that regarded moral and theological problems of supreme importance. He was a many-sided genius, had a research career in biology, medicine, and psychology, and was predisposed to view philosophical problems in the light of their human origins and consequences. The philosophy of life and logic that he created reflected these influences and his own success in having fought when a young man against prolonged moods of suicidal depression.

When James formally inaugurated the new pragmatic movement in his 1898 lecture on "Philosophical Conceptions and Practical Results," he not only quoted Peirce on beliefs as really rules for action, but went on to reinterpret Peirce's formula. As James put it, "the effective meaning of any philosophic proposition can always be brought down to some particular consequence, in our future practical experience, whether active or passive; the point lying rather in the fact that the experience must be particular, than in the fact that it must be active." [10] But this reformulation of pragmatism did not achieve the éclat of a world-wide movement until James published his *Pragmatism; a New Name for Some Old Ways of Thinking* in 1907. Few works in the history of ideas aroused such a storm of interest in America, England, France, Germany, and Italy. James presented with tremendous effectiveness his view of the pragmatic method as a method of settling metaphysical debates that otherwise might go on forever: e.g., Is the world one or many?—fated or free?—material or spiritual? The way out is to trace the practical consequences if one theory rather than another were true. "If no practical difference whatever can be traced, then the alternatives mean practically the same thing, and all dispute is idle." [11]

In an essay written in 1908 James explained that whenever he employed the phrase "the practical," he meant by it "the distinctively concrete, the individual, particular and effective, as opposed to the abstract, general, and inert." [12] He repudiated the charge that pragmatism was a revolt against reason or theory. The aim of pragmatism, he asserted, was to understand ideas by inferring and testing their particular theoretic as well as practical consequences. Pragmatism to James was a proposal to philosophers to adopt the *"attitude of looking away from first things, principles, 'categories,' supposed necessities; and of looking towards last things, fruits, consequences, facts."* [13]

Although James and Peirce shared some basic beliefs, they differed profoundly on many points and developed sharply divergent philosophical systems. James's restatement of Peirce's pragmatic principle involved crucially important differences that every person interested in philosophy should keep constantly in mind. While both agreed that pragmatism was a theory of meaning, James stressed the sensory perceptions obtained through observation and experiment to which the implications or consequences of that idea or statement lead. Here is the way open to each individual to verify or disprove for himself the assertion under question. As James wrote in 1884, scientific theories "always terminate in definite percepts. You can deduce a possible sensation from your theory and, taking me into your laboratory, prove that your theory is true of my world by giving me the sensation then and there." [14]

This emphasis of James upon the individual's perception and personal experience is as legitimate as Peirce's exaltation of logical generalization and rational habits of action. Each complements the other, and those who champion one at the expense of the other have failed to profit from Kant's dictum: Concepts without percepts are empty, percepts without concepts are blind.

James, in accordance with popular usage, also regards as part of the meaning of an idea or statement the personal reactions evoked by that word or statement, whether in the form of feeling or action-effects. Here he parts company with Peirce, who explicitly excludes these "emotional" and "energetic" interpretations or, as he preferred to say, "interpretants" from the "pragmatistic purport." James was inspired in this direction by his own passionate interest in moral, religious, and theological questions. As an educator and humanist, he wished to awaken the general public to the realization that even abstract philosophical debates are of great importance to mankind because the problems discussed lead to very different beliefs and modes of conduct. As a result he was tempted into formulating some of his views in a forcible, dramatic way that brought out the vital implications of these doctrines but also led him into certain ambiguities and errors that his critics made the most of.

James's most vulnerable application of his pragmatic principle occurs in his discussions of the metaphysical problem of theism versus materialism.   Assume, James writes, that the world with all its contents is once for all irrevocably given, ends at this very moment, and has no future.   Then a theist shows how a God made the world, and a materialist, with equal success, explains how it resulted from blind physical forces.   To a pragmatist, the sensible consequences of the two theories being the same, the two theories mean exactly the same thing despite verbal differences. Consequently, the name we give to the primary cause of the world is entirely arbitrary.   But the situation changes once we take the future into account.   God then means a power that guarantees an eternal moral order while matter becomes the power that brings humanity and human values into existence, but also will eventually bring the extinction of life and all its achievements. To James the real, the vital meaning of materialism and theism resides *"in these different emotional and practical appeals, in these adjustments of our concrete attitudes of hope and expectation, and all the delicate consequences which their differences entail."* [15]

This stress upon a doctrine's feeling- and action-effects was in harmony with the theory advanced by James in his volume, *The Will to Believe* (1897), or as he preferred to call it, "The Right to Believe."   James argued that men in certain situations are forced, or feel forced, in the absence of adequate proof, to make decisions between two or more hypotheses.   These decisions are genuine when the choice has to be made because it involves issues that are momentous to the individual.   These decisions may affect narrowly personal affairs or philosophical and religious questions about the character of man, society, and the world, e.g., the belief in freedom, or in God.

James himself and his best disciples did not use the doctrine of the right to believe as a justification for believing in theories that, though counter to the weight of conclusive scientific evidence, might make certain individuals or groups happy, rich, or powerful; for example, the theory of Aryan racial superiority. A willful or ignorant misuse of the "right-to-believe" doctrine might indeed open the floodgates to superstition and fantasy. But James never intended his views to be used to block the advance of science. He repudiated charges by rationalists like Josiah Royce at Harvard and F. H. Bradley at Oxford that the mere pragmatist does not feel any duty to think truly or that "he must hold any idea, however mad, to be the truth, if any one will have it so." Today we can see that James's theory of the right to believe anticipated one element in the revolutionary work of the great mathematician, John von Neumann, and other scientists on the theory of rational choice and behavior in the decision-making process.[16] James has been branded an irrationalist, but he saw more deeply into the presuppositions of logic than many of his rationalist opponents.[17]

In *Pragmatism* James extends the use of the pragmatic method to the much debated problem of the nature of truth. The most popular theory of truth defines it in terms of the correspondence of an idea with a thing: "a true idea must copy its reality." Another influential theory defines truth as the coherence of any term or statement with all the terms or statements in a philosophical or scientific system. According to followers of Hegel, truth in all its fullness is realized only in the one systematic, coherent whole they call the Absolute.

The pragmatist's theory of truth seeks to bring out what is valid in each theory and to offer important corrections. James asks the seemingly impertinent, yet relevant, question:

Grant an idea or belief to be true . . . what concrete difference will its being true make in any one's actual life? How will the truth be realized? What experiences will be different from those which would obtain if the belief were false? What, in short, is the truth's cash-value in experiential terms?[18]

James's answer is that of a naturalist and laboratory scientist who in his daily work is accustomed to calling true ideas *"those that we assimilate, validate, corroborate and verify. False ideas are those that we cannot."* Truth then "means" what is verified or verifiable, and verification, either actual or possible, becomes both the criterion and definition of truth. Often, especially in everyday life, our verification of a theory involves direct face-to-face confirmation through our perceiving the object, for example, a previously unknown house at the end of a certain path. But often the object discussed may be beyond immediate verification: a distant country like Japan, historical characters long dead like Julius Caesar, objects in interstellar space or in the submicro-scopic world that cannot be seen directly (e.g., atoms, protons) but the effects of which are perceptible. In these cases the copy or correspondence theory of truth is not adequate to describe the situation.

Hence James realizes that in many cases our ideas can only be symbols and not copies of objects that we believe to be realities— things whose existence is made indubitable or highly probable by our sense—experiences and logical analysis. As James puts it, true ideas agree with realities. But "to 'agree' in the widest sense with a reality *can only mean to be guided straight up to it or into its surroundings, or to be put into such working touch with it as to handle either it or something connected with it better than if we disagreed.*" [19]

To this statement few scientists could or would object. But various formal logicians like Bertrand Russell objected as strenu-ously to James's asserting: " *'The true'* . . . *is only the expedient in the way of our thinking,*" as they did to F. C. S. Schiller's saying the true is that which "works" or John Dewey's saying truth is what gives "satisfaction." We cannot go into an extended discussion of James's debates with opponents like Josiah Royce and Arthur Lovejoy in America or F. H. Bradley, G. E. Moore, and Bertrand Russell in England. But the analysis we have made demonstrates that the Jamesian theory of truth accords more with the contem-porary scientists' practices and procedures in the construction and use of theories than do the correspondence- and coherence-theo-ries of truth that James attacked a half-century ago.

James is aware that a temporary confirmation of a theory is not a guarantee that further investigation may not lead to another theory being preferred. He appreciates the point that sometimes alternative theoretic formulas are equally compatible with all the truths we know, and then we choose between them for such reasons as "elegance" or "economy." He also acknowledges that theories which give emotional satisfaction and are useful in non-scientific ways may prove to be falsehoods. The final test is the evidence that acting upon one theory or another establishes in the long run. Any theory claiming truth must be compatible with the whole body of the scientifically established truths. James on the one hand asserts the right to test speculative hypotheses such as his theory about a finite God; on the other, he is willing to reject any of his own hypotheses when the weight of the evidence is against it.

Striking as James's pragmatic method and theory of truth are, the insights and theories he offers on the nature of the universe and man's place in it have proved equally fruitful to his admirers. His pragmatic interpretation of meaning so stresses the value of consequences as to lead to a drastic reevaluation of the importance of time, especially of the future. For him the universe or reality is "still in the making," "in the process of becoming." He rejects the conception of a block-universe, fatalistic determinism, and the polar life-philosophies of pessimism and optimism. In his eyes the evidence of science does not preclude belief in the existence of chance, novelty, and exercise of free human choice. Human beings can add to the variety and novelty in the world by the ideas they formulate and put into action. Physical nature and society consist of pluralities of individual things and beings, each with its own center and distinctive qualities; each independent to a certain degree of the whole physical universe and society. James urges that we shape our lives on the possibility of the world being made better or spiritually saved through human belief and action.

Most contemporary philosophers disagree with both the substance and form of James's theological arguments, partly on temperamental, partly on philosophical grounds. Many take exception to the inadequately precise formulation he gave to his views on pragmatism and truth, but there is much that they find still perceptive and suggestive in his writings. For a time in the 1930s and 1940s all metaphysics, including that contained in James's *Pluralistic Universe, Radical Empiricism,* and *Some Problems of Philosophy,* was out of fashion. Logical empiricists like Rudolf Carnap taught that all statements about metaphysics were "nonsense," that is, unverified or unverifiable. In the last few years this position has been abandoned by many. In any case, recent philosophy has an empirical, pluralistic character that reflects the influence of James's thinking. James's writings have insights that still offer much toward an understanding of our complex world.

The Experimentalism of John Dewey. James had given a new turn to the empiricism of Locke, Berkeley, Hume, and Mill by calling attention to the need for organizing future observations and experiences as well as for reporting and reflecting upon past experiences. In his great treatise, the *Principles of Psychology* (1890), James had suggested that human intelligence had evolved as an instrument of adaptive response to stimuli. This approach aided him in developing his pragmatic positions on meaning, truth, moral idealism, and pluralism. But James never developed a complete pragmatic theory of how human thinkers function in the experimental determination of future consequences.

This task was taken up by John Dewey and his associates, first at the University of Chicago, and after 1904 at Columbia University. Their special set of doctrines became known as instrumentalism or experimentalism. They have dominated pragmatism from 1910, the year in which James died, until the present.

John Dewey (1859–1952) had gifts and a temperament that made him an ally of James and Peirce but very different from both. Unlike James, Dewey had no magic phrases and few vivid images or dazzling intuitions. But this profoundly simple yet complex, ruggedly honest yet worldly-wise Vermont Yankee achieved an influence on both professional philosophers and the general public in America and the rest of the world that exceeded the impact of any other philosopher in American history since Emerson. Dewey's influence became marked as early as the 1890s. In 1903 James hailed him as a philosophic equal and ally; after James's death in 1910 he became the preeminent exponent of democracy, naturalism, and scientific method in America.

Many of his philosophical writings are involved and difficult to follow, in part because of the originality of his ideas, in part because of the technical vocabulary which he acquired in the late nineteenth century and used to convey his own radically new ideas. Nevertheless, his numerous closely knit, systematically developed volumes convinced an impressive number of philosophers that he had a great vision and method of approach to man in nature and to nature-in-man's-experience. At the same time Dewey became a vital force in the remolding of education from the kindergarten to the university in the United States, Mexico, Turkey, China, and even Soviet Russia in the 1920s. He also participated in progressive political and economic movements from the Square Deal of Theodore Roosevelt to the New Deal of Franklin D. Roosevelt and the democratic socialism of Norman Thomas. He was one of the first liberals in America to stress the danger to democracy from both communism and fascism, yet to insist on maintaining civil liberties.

Dewey's pragmatism, like that of Peirce and James, involves a theory of meaning and truth or "warranted assertibility." In Dewey's path-breaking *Studies in Logical Theory* (1903) and *Essays in Experimental Logic* (1916), he starts with the doctrine that human thinking arises out of specific needs and frustrations. When it is successful, it leads to a control of the environment through acts based upon an analysis of the original complex situation into its elements and upon the projection of a plan of action or experiment. This plan of action or experiment embodies ideas as working hypotheses for attaining particular empirical results. The "meaning" of an idea, in its simplest terms, Dewey calls the plan of action it proposes as a solution to a given problem. This "operational" or "experimental" definition of meaning is an extension of Peirce's pragmatic maxim that the meaning of a statement is the sum of its verifiable consequences.

Dewey's approach spells out the fact that ideas arise from concrete problem-situations and serve as guides to observations and experiments. He rightly asserts:

There is no way to know what are the traits of known objects, as distinct from imaginary objects, or objects of unanalytic common-sense, save by referring to operations of getting, using, and testing evidence—

the processes of knowledge-getting . . . for the working scientist, "objects of knowledge" mean precisely the objects which have been obtained by approved processes of inquiry.   To exclude considerations
of these processes is thus to throw away the key to understanding
knowledge and its objects.[20]

This experimental approach to meaning leads to the experimental theory of truth.   This theory starts from the recognition
that truth, in some sense, is the correspondence or agreement of
beliefs or statements with "reality."   But Dewey, like James, refused to take "correspondence" by itself as an adequate explana-
tory principle.   It does not cover the many cases in life, history,
and science where we cannot make a point-to-point correspondence between the various parts or elements of a statement and
the elements in the situations to which they refer.

The true idea or hypothesis is the idea that "agrees" with
reality because it is a successful solution to a problem.   The
agreement or correspondence is established by evidence obtained
through action involving projection of a plan, deducing its consequences, and testing them by observation and experiment.   The
"true" hypothesis, in Dewey's writings, is called good or satisfactory, and is said to "work" or be "useful," only in the sense that the
idea is a tool or clue to the scientific solution of a problem.   Here
Dewey avoids the confusions of James and F. C. S. Schiller between the religious, emotional, or narrowly practical satisfactions
of an idea and the satisfaction it yields in terms of evidence for a
hypothesis.

Truth for Dewey does not exist in a Platonic realm of essences
or as an abstract entity isolated from events in space-time.   Truth
is simply the collection of truths or hypotheses that have been or
will be confirmed or verified by "the best available methods of inquiry and testing as to matters-of-fact; methods, which are, when
collected under a single name, science." [21]   Truth or warranted
assertibility emerges as the end-product of the complex processes
of scientific inquiry.

Truth and knowledge are interdependent because one does
not make sense without the other.   Dewey stresses verification
or verifiability as the test of each warranted assertion, but urges

attention to the importance of new theories, not yet confirmed, that may lead to new discoveries and new evidence. Individuals originate fruitful hypotheses within a given social and cultural situation, but the testing and establishment of hypotheses as a warranted assertion of fact has to be a public and social process if individual caprice, error, and prejudice are to be avoided.

Science is a self-corrective process, without any self-evident truths or unquestionable logical principles or facts. Within the potentially endless self-corrective system of science, however, there are well-determined specific inquiries, each with a definite beginning and conclusion, represented by a solution to a problem. Although no eternal guarantee can be given for the correctness of any single solution, that solution or opinion which is agreed to by all who have persistently investigated the problem in question is what Dewey and scientists call the "truth" or "warranted assertion," and the object represented by the warranted assertion is regarded as "real." [22]

Dewey's experimental theory of meaning and truth has been criticized by champions of the "spectator" theory of knowledge, notably Morris R. Cohen, Arthur Lovejoy, and Bertrand Russell. They have argued that much thought, especially in pure science, art, and philosophy, arises out of idle curiosity; is purely contemplative; and involves no action, experiment, or change in the object studied, e.g., a star. Truth, they contend, cannot be identified with the verification of a hypothesis, since several alternative theories to explain the same event are possible, but must involve a direct correspondence or confrontation between a statement and the objects to which it refers.

Dewey's most careful writing on what he means as practical and useful, e.g., in *Logic: The Theory of Inquiry* (1938) and *Art as Experience* (1939), refutes the charge that he does not do justice to art, science, and philosophy as ends-in-themselves. In many of his writings, however, his stress on the utilitarian, survival, or social-welfare function of thought lays him open to criticism. But even then his utilitarian account of thinking is correct if taken as a general, but not a universal, statement: it holds for the thinking of most people most of the time and of pure scien-

tists, artists, and philosophers a larger part of the time than they
are aware of.   Even a pure theory develops in one *direction*
rather than another because of the special interest or purpose of
the theorist.

The role of action or experiment in thinking seems not applicable to those who write literary or mathematical symbols on
paper; who gaze at tables, neighbors, or scenery; or who observe
through telescopes or microscopes objects they cannot touch or
change.   But I suggest that Dewey's position can be vindicated
when one realizes two things: (1) All philosophic and mathematical thinking involves "ideal experimentation": the creation and
manipulation of diagrams, signs, and symbols that represent either
actual or ideal entities or situations; (2) Observation of stars,
mountains, or microscopic life involves in all cases the movement
of our eyes and bodies, in some cases the creation or use of spe-
cially contrived instruments.   We may not change physically the
star, mountain, or microscopic form of life that we study, but we
change the situation—our position or instruments—by means of
which we carry on our observations.   In short, the "object" we
know is never known immediately or by intuition but is known
always as the outcome and objective of a specific inquiry.

Significant as Dewey's theory of scientific inquiry is, it is
rivaled, in my judgment, by his work in a dozen other fields.   His
naturalistic ethics, as presented in *Human Nature and Conduct*
(1922) and other works, makes a sharp break with traditional religion and moral philosophy.   Moral systems, acts, and choices
are shown growing out of and changing with biological and social
conditions.   Dewey agrees with George Santayana that everything
ideal has a natural basis, and everything natural a possible ideal
development.   But Dewey disagrees with two important rival
ethical theories: the view of G. E. Moore, the English analytical
philosopher, that goodness, while an objective and real quality, is
indefinable, incapable of being validly described by other psychological terms; and the view of Ralph Barton Perry, the American
philosopher, that any thing has value if it is the object of an interest by some person or persons.   Dewey's own theory asserts
that an object desired by a human being ought to be considered

desirable or valuable when analysis shows that the consequences of satisfying the desire yield more benefit than harm.   In other words, the experimental method has to be applied to the judgment of moral values, e.g., the sanctity of private property or the rights of labor unions, just as it has been to conceptions of physical objects.

This experimental theory of ethics has been applied by Dewey with amazingly fruitful results to the practice and theory of education.   His *Democracy and Education* (1916) persuaded educators in America, Europe, and Asia that students (1) should make doing a part of learning; (2) should achieve self-discipline by having their interest in various subjects elicited; (3) should practice cooperation in their day-to-day school activities; and (4) should be given an opportunity to explore a wide range of subjects from the natural and social sciences to arts and crafts.   One may disagree with specific proposals of Dewey's and criticize the distortions of his teachings by some of his followers.   But few scholars devoted to the extension of democracy and scientific method on the broadest possible basis should object to the basic principles of Dewey's educational philosophy.   Severe attacks have come from sincere champions of the old classical tradition in education.   But the most vitriolic opposition to Dewey has been voiced by spokesmen for (1) certain business groups; (2) supernaturalism; (3) Communist or Fascist totalitarianism.

In politics, economics, and law, Dewey has stood for the maximum use of free, experimental intelligence in establishing and preserving political, economic, and social democracy.   That is why he stands for the most thoroughgoing reforms within our own society and at the same time opposes dictatorship in all its forms, left or right, unlike such myopic liberals and radicals as George Bernard Shaw and the Webbs who see all the evils of capitalism and democracy but few of the far worse evils of Soviet Russia, Communist China, and their satellites.   The best of Dewey's many proposals for social change are embodied in his *Public and Its Problems* (1927), *Liberalism and Social Action* (1935), and *Freedom and Culture* (1939).

The impact of Dewey upon political science is best seen in

the work of Arthur F. Bentley, Charles E. Merriam, and T. V.
Smith on the group-pressures in government and in the programs
for reform that they have sponsored.   In economics Rexford Tugwell, A. A. Berle, Jr., and other members of F. D. R.'s Brain Trust
applied their interpretation of Dewey's experimental method to
the problems of New Deal recovery and reform.   Other followers
of Dewey have inclined towards or favored democratic socialism.
Prominent exponents of this position have been Sidney Hook and
Clarence Ayres in philosophy and economics.   David Dubinsky
and Walter Reuther in the trade-union movement have worked
within and outside the Democratic party for more drastic reforms
than the New Deal carried out, yet have stopped short of socialism.
Wesley C. Mitchell, John R. Commons, and Walton H. Hamilton
—each in his own special way—have done much to bring realism
into the study of economic institutions and experimentalism into
governmental policy-making.

The profound affinity between Dewey and the greatest figures
in American jurisprudence of the last half-century can be traced
in the decisions, essays, and letters of Justices Holmes, Brandeis,
and Cardoza.   Similarly, the key formulators of sociological jurisprudence and legal realism in America—from Roscoe Pound to
Jerome Frank and Felix S. Cohen—share with Dewey a concern
for solving the conflicts arising from the diverse interests of men
and for judging the value of decisions in terms of the ascertainable
or predictable consequences to specific human beings.   Since the
mid-1930s the Supreme Court has become an increasingly active
factor in social change, notably in the field of race relations, civil
liberties, and antitrust action.   These decisions, whatever one's
evaluation of the proper role of the Court may be, are in accord
with Dewey's life-long fight against social and religious discrimination; the suppression of free speech, press, and assembly; and the
excessive concentration of economic power in any one group's
hands.

There is much in Dewey's philosophy that we cannot explore,
for example, his philosophy of art as an integral phase of human
experience, or his presentation of the generic or generally pervasive traits of existence-as-experienced by human beings, or his hu-

manistic religion of shared experiences and ideal goals.   Not all
of Dewey's admirers agree with the specific positions he takes on
the aesthetic experience, metaphysics, or religion.   Ernest Nagel
and Sidney Hook, for example, scorn metaphysics as a futile quest
for an unintelligible "Being," while John Herman Randall, Jr.,
and Justus Buchler defend the legitimacy of a naturalistic metaphysics.   Horace Kallen and Irwin Edman have developed chal-
lengingly independent but equally pragmatic theories of art and
the aesthetic experience.   J. H. Randall holds that the ritual and
other institutional aspects of religion need to be given greater
weight as organized communal activities than Dewey does, but
here Hook and Nagel tend to disagree.

   The Future of Pragmatism.   New and old winds of doctrine
have been sweeping America in the last two decades: Marxism,
neo-Catholicism, existentialism, logical positivism, and the lin-
guistic-analysis philosophies of G. E. Moore and Ludwig Wittgenstein.   Dewey, Kallen, and Hook have written effective replies to
the supernaturalists, Marxists, and existentialists.   C. I. Lewis,
Ernest Nagel, Willard Quine, and Morton White have written
powerful critiques of various weaknesses in logical positivism and
the philosophies of G. E. Moore and Wittgenstein.   There is a
ferment and fluidity in the current philosophical scene that for-
bids a final judgment on the new philosophical systems that are
now in the process of formation.   But pragmatism, I am convinced, will survive as an indispensable method of clarifying ideas
and processes of decision-making in all phases of life.

BIBLIOGRAPHICAL NOTE

Interesting studies of the development of American philosophical
thought can be found in Morris R. Cohen, *American Thought; a
Critical Sketch* (New York, 1954); Merle Curti, *The Growth of American Thought* (New York, 1943); and Herbert W. Schneider, *A History of American Philosophy* (New York, 1946).   Additional background and critical perspective on the post-Civil War American
intellectual scene are furnished by Charles A. and Mary R. Beard,
The American Spirit (New York, 1942); Henry Steele Commager, *The
American Mind* (New Haven, 1950); Ralph Henry Gabriel, *The*

Course of American Democratic Thought (New York, 1940); Sidney Ratner, "Evolution and the Rise of the Scientific Spirit in America," *Philosophy of Science,* III (1936), 104–22; Morton G. White, *Social Thought in America* (Rev. ed., Boston, 1957); and Philip P. Wiener, *Evolution and the Founders of Pragmatism* (Cambridge, Mass., 1949).

The philosophical writings of Peirce are best approached by the general reader through two selections of his essays: *Chance, Love, and Logic,* ed. by Morris R. Cohen (New York, 1923), and *The Philosophy of Peirce,* ed. by Justus Buchler (London, 1950). Those interested in exploring Peirce's profoundly original but difficult system should consult *The Collected Papers of Charles Sanders Peirce,* ed. by Charles Hartshorne and Paul Weiss (6 vols., Cambridge, Mass., 1931–35); Volumes VII and VIII, ed. by Arthur W. Burks, appeared in 1958. The best biographical sketch is Paul Weiss's article in the *Dictionary of American Biography.* Among the helpful critical expositions of Peirce's thought are Justus Buchler, *Charles Peirce's Empiricism* (London, 1939); W. B. Gallie, *Peirce and Pragmatism* (Penguin ed., Harmondsworth, Eng., 1952); T. A. Goudge, *The Thought of C. S. Peirce* (Toronto, 1950); Manley Thompson, *The Pragmatic Philosophy of C. S. Peirce* (Chicago, 1953); Philip P. Wiener and Frederic H. Young, eds., *Studies in the Philosophy of Charles Sanders Peirce* (Cambridge, Mass., 1952).

Horace M. Kallen provides an introduction to James's thought through his admirable anthology, *The Philosophy of William James* (New York, 1925). The standard biography is Ralph Barton Perry, *The Thought and Character of William James* (2 vols., Boston, 1935). It contains valuable chapters on Peirce, Schiller, and Dewey; it should be supplemented by H. M. Kallen, *William James and Henri Bergson* (Chicago, 1914). The student should consult for himself James's main philosophical writings, especially *The Will to Believe* (New York, 1897); *Pragmatism* (New York, 1907); *The Meaning of Truth* (New York, 1909); and *Some Problems of Philosophy* (New York, 1911). Horace Kallen has done important, original work in aesthetics, education, the economics of the consumer movement, and international relations, bringing to fruition more ideas in James's philosophy than the work done by any other contemporary philosopher. For an introduction to these developments see Sidney Ratner, ed., *Vision and Action: Essays in Honor of Horace M. Kallen* (New Brunswick, N. J., 1953).

The main points of Dewey's thought are presented extremely well in two volumes of selections: Irwin Edman, ed., *John Dewey: His Contribution to the American Tradition* (Indianapolis, 1955) and Joseph Ratner, ed., *John Dewey's Philosophy* (New York, 1939). Valuable historical accounts of the origins of pragmatism by Dewey are to be found in his essay "The Development of American Pragmatism," *Philosophy and Civilization* (New York, 1931), in Jane M. Dewey, "Biography of John Dewey," in *The Philosophy of John Dewey,* ed. by Paul A. Schilpp (Evanston, 1939); and in Dewey's essays on William James in *Problems of Men* (New York, 1946). For an exposition of the leading themes in Dewey's thought, see Sidney Hook, *John Dewey: an Intellectual Portrait* (New York, 1939); and Sidney Ratner, "The Evolutionary Naturalism of John Dewey," *Social Research,* XVIII (1951), 435–48, his "The Development of Dewey's Evolutionary Naturalism," *Social Research,* XX (1953), 127–54, and his "Dewey's Contribution to Historical Theory," in *John Dewey: Philosopher of Science and Freedom,* ed. by Sidney Hook (New York, 1950). Cf. George R. Geiger, *John Dewey in Perspective* (New York, 1958), and Jerome Nathanson, *John Dewey* (New York, 1951).

The most important volumes setting forth Dewey's experimentalism are his *Essays in Experimental Logic* (Chicago, 1916); *Logic: the Theory of Inquiry* (New York, 1938); *Problems of Men;* and (with Arthur F. Bentley) *Knowing and the Known* (Boston, 1949). But every reader interested in Dewey's impact upon American civilization should read some of his other major works: *Human Nature and Conduct* (New York, 1922); *Experience and Nature* (Chicago, 1925); *The Public and Its Problems* (New York, 1927); *The Quest for Certainty* (New York, 1929); *Art As Experience* (New York, 1934); *Liberalism and Social Action* (New York, 1935); *Freedom and Culture* (New York, 1939).

The special variety of pragmatism represented by F. C. S. Schiller's Humanism has not been explored because most of his long life he lived at Oxford and is properly part of English philosophic history. But the relations between him and James were intimate, and students should read his *Studies in Humanism* (London, 1907) to get his special voluntaristic point of view. Reuben Abel has written an incisive critique, *The Pragmatic Humanism of F. C. S. Schiller* (New York, 1955), that does justice to his place in England and America. Equally, if not more, important in the history of pragmatism is the work of George Herbert Mead, a seminal mind of the first order in the opinion of both Dewey and Whitehead. His influence through his teaching at the University of Chicago was as profound as that of Dewey at Columbia. Mead's major writings include: *The Philosophy of the Present* (Chicago, 1932); *Mind, Self, and Society* (Chicago, 1934); *Movements of Thought in the Nineteenth Century* (Chicago, 1936); and *The Philosophy of the Act* (Chicago, 1938). Valuable support to Dewey and Mead was given by Addison W. Moore, *Pragmatism and Its Critics* (Chicago, 1910), and by the numerous writings on ethics by James H. Tuft, especially his co-authorship with Dewey of *Ethics*

(New York, 1908; rev. ed., 1932), and his *America's Social Morality* (New York, 1933).

Significant additions to the clarification of pragmatism were made by the contributors to *Studies in Logical Theory,* ed. by John Dewey (Chicago, 1903); *Creative Intelligence,* ed. by John Dewey (New York, 1917); *Essays in Honor of John Dewey* (New York, 1929); *The Philosopher of the Common Man,* ed. by Sidney Ratner (New York, 1940); and *John Dewey: Philosopher of Science and Freedom,* ed. by Sidney Hook. *The Philosophy of John Dewey,* ed. by Paul A. Schilpp (Evanston, 1939), has an illuminating reply by Dewey to his critics, pp. 515–608. The support given Dewey by writers on operational logic can be studied in P. W. Bridgman, *The Logic of Modern Physics* (New York, 1927), and his later writings. The confluence of Arthur F. Bentley (1870–1957) and Dewey can be seen in their joint *Knowing and the Known,* in Bentley's last work, *Inquiry Into Inquiries,* ed. by Sidney Ratner (Boston, 1954), and in the essay on Bentley by Sidney Ratner in *Life, Language, Law,* ed. by Richard W. Taylor (Yellow Springs, Ohio, 1957). Some recent notable works by pragmatists or their allies are C. I. Lewis, *An Analysis of Knowledge and Valuation* (Chicago, 1946); Ernest Nagel, *Sovereign Reason* (Glencoe, Ill., 1954), and *Logic without Metaphysics* (Glencoe, Ill., 1956); Willard V. O. Quine, *From a Logical Point of View* (Cambridge, Mass., 1953), and Morton White, *Toward Reunion in Philosophy* (Cambridge, 1956).

Out of the vast literature of criticism of pragmatism, the following philosophical works may be regarded as representative: Morris R. Cohen, *Studies in Philosophy and Science* (New York, 1949); Arthur O. Lovejoy, "The Thirteen Pragmatisms," *Journal of Philosophy,* V (1908), 1–12, 29–39; Jacques Maritain, *True Humanism* (New York, 1938); William Pepperell Montague, *The Ways of Knowing* (London, 1925); Bertrand Russell, *A History of Western Philosophy* (New York, 1945); George Santayana, *Character and Opinion in the United States* (New York, 1920); W. T. Stace, *The Destiny of Western Man* (New York, 1942); and Harry K. Wells, *Pragmatism: Philosophy of Imperialism* (New York, 1954). Attacks by literary critics, political and social philosophers, and theologians will be found in Randolph Bourne, *Untimely Papers* (New York, 1919); Waldo Frank, *The Rediscovery of America* (New York, 1929); Lewis Mumford, *The Golden Day* (New York, 1926); Van Wyck Brooks, *Three Essays on America* (New York, 1934); in William Yandell Elliott, *The Pragmatic Revolt in Politics* (New York, 1928), Frank H. Knight, *Freedom and Reform* (New York, 1947); Walter Lippmann, *Essays in the Public Philosophy* (Boston, 1955); Reinhold Niebuhr, *The Children of Light and the Children of Darkness* (New York, 1950); and John U. Nef, *The United States and Civilization* (Chicago, 1942). The chief opposition to Dewey or progressive education or both has been expressed in Robert M. Hutchins, *The Higher Learning in America* (New Haven, 1936), Mortimer J. Adler, "This Pre-War Generation," *Harper's Magazine,* CLXXXI (1940), 524–34; Alexander Meiklejohn, *Education between Two Worlds* (New York, 1942); Mark Van Doren, *Liberal Education* (New York 1943). Arthur Bestor, *The Restoration of Learning* (New York, 1955), tries to strike a balance but falls far short of this goal.

Powerful counterattacks to these diverse critics have been made by John Dewey in *Characters and Events* (2 vols., New York, 1929) and *Problems of Men;* by Sidney Hook in *Education for Modern Man* (New York, 1946) and *Reason, Social Myths and Democracy* (New York, 1940); by Horace M. Kallen in *Art and Freedom* (2 vols., New York, 1942), *The Education of Free Men* (New York, 1949), and *Secularism Is the Will of God* (New York, 1954); by Ernest Nagel in *Sovereign Reason* and *Logic without Metaphysics;* by Morton White in the epilogue to *Social Thought in America* and *The Age of Analysis* (New York, 1955); and by the contributors to *Naturalism and the Human Spirit,* ed. by Y. H. Krikorian (New York, 1944).

NOTES

1. William James, *Collected Essays and Reviews* (New York, 1920), p. 410.

2. Charles Hartshorne and Paul Weiss, eds., *Collected Papers of Charles Sanders Peirce* (6 vols., Cambridge, Mass., 1931–35), V, par. 402.

3. *Ibid.,* V, par. 12.   4. *Ibid.,* V, par. 414.
5. *Ibid.,* V, pars. 464, 467.   6. *Ibid.,* V, par. 9.
7. *Ibid.,* V, par. 427.   8. *Ibid.,* V, par. 412.
9. *Ibid.,* V, par. 433.

10. James, *Collected Essays and Reviews,* p. 412.

11. William James, *Pragmatism; a New Name for Some Old Ways of Thinking* (New York, 1907), p. 45.

12. William James, *The Meaning of Truth* (New York, 1909), p. 209.

13. James, *Pragmatism,* pp. 54–55.

14. James, *The Meaning of Truth,* p. 40; see also his *Some Problems of Philosophy* (New York, 1948; 1st ed., 1911), p. 62.

15. James, *Pragmatism,* p. 107 (italics added).

16. John von Neumann and Oskar Morgenstern, *Theory of Games and Economic Behavior* (Princeton, 1944; 3rd ed., 1953); and R. B. Braithwaite, *Theory of Games as a Tool for the Moral Philosopher* (Cambridge, Eng., 1955).

17. See James, "Faith and the Right to Believe," in *Some Problems of Philosophy* (New York, 1911), pp. 221–31.

18. James, *Pragmatism,* p. 200.   19. *Ibid.,* pp. 212–13.

20. John Dewey, *Essays in Experimental Logic* (Chicago, 1916), p. 65.

21. John Dewey, *Experience and Nature* (New York, 1929), p. 410.

22. John Dewey, *Logic: The Theory of Inquiry* (New York, 1938), p. 345 *n.*

POPULISM: ITS SIGNIFICANCE IN
AMERICAN HISTORY

by Everett Walters

OHIO STATE UNIVERSITY

ALONG with reinterpretations of earlier democratic movements, such as that of the Jacksonian period, the political movement in the United States termed Populism has been the subject of reappraisal by historians, economists, and others. What was the significance of this turbulent and dramatic phenomenon of American politics that flared up in the latter part of the nineteenth century, carrying repercussions into the twentieth century?

Past and recent interpretations fall into two main categories. Historians, economists, and others have viewed the Populist movement on the one hand as socialistic and on the other extreme as old-fashioned pioneer doctrine. Other judgments usually range within these extremes. The present essay seeks to summarize these varied interpretations, to indicate their major trend, and also to venture a brief personal conclusion.

That a similarity existed between Populism and Socialism was emphasized in a study in the early nineties made by Frank L. McVey.[1] McVey's slender volume, published in 1896 before the political campaign of that year, reflected the conservative economic views then prevailing. McVey had little sympathy with the Populists. He examined their platform tenets and concluded that the Populist party was not a party of constructive principles but was a movement merely of protest against the existing economic system. The party failed to state any basic views on the large national problems. McVey attacked all the main beliefs of the Populists: ownership of railroads, free silver, the abolition of na-

tional banks, the subtreasury scheme, and curtailment of the existing mortgage and loan procedures.   He censured the leaders for
their failure in the Omaha Platform to say anything about the
tariff.   Many of their demands, he claimed, were merely efforts
to secure political allies.   The call for a shorter working day and
the restriction of immigration—sops offered to please the labor
unions—were not popular with the farmer of Kansas, since he
worked many more than eight hours and an increased population
would mean additional consumers for his products.

McVey implied that, if the silver advocates were not so powerful in the party, the similarity between Populism and Socialism
would be even closer.   "Its whole tone is socialistic," he declared
of the Omaha platform.   To support this contention he prepared
a chart to show the similarity in the demands of the Socialist and
Populist parties.   Although he admitted that there was the great
difference of common ownership and equality of income, he
believed that "national ownership of the railroad and telegraph,
coupled with a demand for increased state action, can only characterize the platform as socialistic in its tendency." [2]   He held
that the party's hope lay in casting aside halfway measures and
following the logic of its underlying tendencies, boldly announc-
ing itself as the Socialist party in America, confessing paternalism
as its principle of constitutional interpretation, advocating the
socialization of industry as its economic doctrine, and ignoring
politics as its political program.   "Thus it may become a party of
principle, and possess all the elements of a great one; but it must
rest with the future to say whether such a party, however great,
can be right." [3]

Apparently believing that the future would prove the party to
be wrong, McVey concluded that its existence was transient; a
party must be based on more lasting qualities than mere discontent.   It had added nothing "but variety to our political life." [4]

The view that Populism was an old-fashioned pioneer phenomenon found impressive presentation by the renowned historian and creator of the frontier theory, Frederick Jackson
Turner.[5]   So great was his prestige that his interpretation had

general acceptance for many years.   The Populist was "a survival
of the pioneer, striving to adjust present conditions to his old
ideas.   The ideals of equality, freedom of opportunity, faith in
common man."   The task of the Middle West, the home of the
Populist, was "that of adapting democracy to the vast economic
organization of the present [1901]." [6]   Always conscious of the
role of the West in what has been "distinctive and valuable in
America's contributions to the history of the human spirit," Turner contended that "Populism is a manifestation of the old pioneer ideals of the native American, with the added element of increasing readiness to utilize the national government to effect its
ends." [7]   Many of the Populists, he went to considerable lengths
to show, were native Americans "of the New England and New
York current."   They were of the breed who had fought at Con-
cord Bridge.   As they went West they had taken their ideals with
them.   Mary Ellen Lease might sound raucous to the New Englander, but she was an echo of the Revolutions of '76—and, indeed, of "the leaders and sectaries of Cromwell's army." [8]   Later,
Turner stressed that the Grangers and the Populists were prophets
of the reform movement of the early twentieth century.   Their
emphasis on the need for "governmental regulation of industrial
tendencies in the interest of the common man" was reflected in
"Mr. Bryan's Democracy, Mr. Debs' Socialism, and Mr. Roosevelt's Republicanism." [9]

"The disappearance of the frontier, the closing of an era,"
Turner wrote, convinced the Western radical that he "must sacrifice his ideals of individualism and free competition in order to
maintain his ideal of democracy."   "The former safety valve of
abundant resources" had brought on a "new national development."   The Populist came to believe that government was the
people and that the powers of the various governments must be
extended to preserve "his historic ideal of democratic society."
Capital, labor, and the Western pioneer had abandoned competitive individualism in order to organize their interests in more
effective combinations.[10]   Of course, it was the Westerner who
began the movement.

Turner's interpretation was largely accepted by John D. Hicks in his scholarly volume *The Populist Revolt*,[11] which, published in 1931, frequently has been termed the definitive history of the movement. Sparing in interpretation, Hicks presented the history of the agrarian movement of the last decades of the nineteenth century from its frontier background and initial grievances to the national election of 1908. As he summarized their doctrines, the Populists insisted that American laborers, farmers, and factory workers were entitled to a decent living in return for their labors. When farm prices fell and their economic situation became critical, farmers began to find fault with the existing order, the prevailing economic and political conditions, especially such factors as the power of the railroads, the grasping practices of loan companies, and the widespread corruption in government. Like Turner, Hicks declared that, since there was no frontier with available lands where they might begin life anew, the farmers turned to the government for assistance. "Now with the lands all taken and the frontier gone, this safety valve was closed. The frontier was turned back on itself. The restless and the discontented voiced their sentiments more and fled from them less." [12] When they found the government in the hands of the plutocrats, they felt compelled to obtain control. The two fundamental propositions of Populist philosophy, Hicks indicated, are, "one, that the government must restrain the selfish tendencies of those who profited at the expense of the poor and needy; the other, that the people, not the plutocrats, must control the government." [13] He observed that many of the Populist demands, "while despised and rejected for a season, won triumphantly in the end." Thanks to this triumph, "one may almost say that, in so far as political devices can insure it, the people now rule." Granted the existence of some corruption, "on the whole the acts of the government have come to reflect fairly clearly the will of the people." Hicks admitted that to the radicals of 1931 the Populists' reforms seem totally inadequate. Indeed, he concluded, in view of the proposed drastic changes of the dark days of the great depression, the demands of the Populists seem quite conservative; they have been accepted, in the main, by both political parties.[14]

But Turner's frontier theory was not to remain undisturbed; it was increasingly attacked as a whole and in many of its applications. Among the critics was Chester McArthur Destler, who found fault with Turner's interpretation of the rise of Populism. In his book on American radicalism, 1865–1901, Destler developed a new appraisal of the Populist movement.[15] He attacked frontally the idea that Populism was "exclusively the product of repetitive sociological and economic processes at work on the frontier which found expression in a somewhat emotional discontent or in a patchwork of remedial proposals that lacked any philosophical basis other than a desire to restore the working prosperity of a small entrepreneur, rural economy."[16] To secure a better understanding of Western radical thought, he used a concept taken from social anthropology, cultural diffusion. This, he believed, would test "the possibility of ideological transmission between rural and urban areas in both directions, not only of single concepts as culture traits, but of an entire complex of ideas."[17] Destler examined the intercourse between urban and agrarian radicals from the Locofocoism of the Jackson era to the free silver victory of 1896. His conclusion was that Populism was a "re-elaboration of the Jeffersonian tradition in an attempt to meet the problems produced by corporate monopoly and the urban-industrial age," and that its basic concepts (antimonopolism, insistence on equal rights, labor-cost theory of wealth, hostility to finance capitalism and the money power, and the assertion of a community of interest between rural and urban producers) were foreshadowed in the writings of John Taylor of Caroline and of William Leggett. "Grafted into this radical ideology," he asserted, "were other concepts and proposals that re-orient it from political negation to positive but limited state intervention in the economic field."[18]

Destler also stressed at some length the importance of the farmer-labor alliance, a "neglected aspect of the Populist movement." His contention was that the "greatest problem of ideological conflict and adaptation produced by the attempted coalition did not develop out of a conflict between Populism and the half-formulated philosophy of a shattered trades unionism . . .

[but] from the clash of indigenous Populism, produced by decades of cross-fertilization between urban and agrarian radical
movements with an imported, proletarian Socialism which made
its first great appeal to English-speaking wage earners in America
in the depression-ridden nineties." The clash, he pointed out,
was partly responsible for the People's party declaration for free
silver at the St. Louis convention in 1896.[19] Destler's examination of the agrarian labor alliance deserves the careful attention of
the student of Populism. His detailed articles on the Labor-
Populist alliance in Illinois during the election of 1894 do indeed
point out a "neglected aspect of the Populist movement." Earlier writers, such as Turner, Buck, and Hicks, barely mention the
significance of the labor groups.

Destler's emphasis on the influence of "imported, proletarian
Socialism" on the rise of Populism drew replies from other students of the period. Hicks, writing eighteen years after the publication of his magnum opus on the Populist revolt, conceded the
effectiveness of liberal humanitarianism and "imported socialism."
He hastened, however, to reaffirm his belief that "American radicalism would simply never have been what it was but for its long
and sturdy line of Granger-Greenback-Populist progenitors." In
support of this view he traced at length the influence of Populism
on such early twentieth-century leaders as Robert La Follette, Albert B. Cummins, John A. Johnson, Joseph W. Folk, and even
Theodore Roosevelt.[20] Several years later Hicks insisted that
the "middle western agrarians were not socialists; on the contrary, they were, or at least aspired to be, small capitalists." Their
antimonopoly views, he added, were developed naturally from
their long-existent hatred of monopolies, especially the railroads,
and their interest in government regulation and control was a
logical consequence.[21]
Other historians have examined the relation of Populism and
Socialism during recent years and in general conclude that the
influence of Socialism was slight. George Harmon Knoles pointed
out, in his analysis of the political campaign of 1892, that Socialism and Populism were basically antithetical although they had a

common opposition to industrial capitalism; the former expressed radical views concerning individualism, whereas the latter represented radical agrarianism. "Populists, as a rule," he declared, "did not recognize the fundamental cleavage dividing the two; the radical socialists did." As Knoles saw it, the differences between the two proved irreconcilable. Populism had its roots deep in that distinct social entity, the American farmer, who could not become a proletarian, and who, when his way of life was seriously invaded, turned to familiar remedies—managed currency, control of monopolies, and land legislation. Socialism, a new development in America, "drew upon Marx for its theory and upon European and American labor strife for its experience." "Populism was the natural expression of farmer protest; Socialism was the natural expression of the dissent of industrial labor." [22]

In his recent examination of the roots of American Communism, Theodore Draper reiterates the thesis that Populism and Socialism were poles apart. Populism, he claimed, was an expression of "a dream of recapturing an imaginary idyllic past of independent freeholders," but one which never threatened the foundations of private property. "The demand for government ownership and control that came out of the Populist tradition was not a step toward collectivism, Socialism, or Communism," he stated, but "a peculiar American device to defend the capitalism of the many against the capitalism of the few." Although Populism and Socialism "spurned each other," Draper concluded, the latter could take over from the former. Some Populist leaders, such as Eugene Debs, became Socialist leaders; indeed, in 1909 former Populists accounted for fifteen percent of the Socialist party members, and many popular Socialist songs of the West were Populist in origin.[23]

Another recent trend of interpretation has been the stress placed on the democratic nature of Populism or, conversely, on its antidemocratic nature. A. Whitney Griswold, in his *Farming and Democracy*, published in 1948, pointed out that the Populists sought "to enforce through direct legislation the classic democratic principles of individual liberty, equal opportunity, and popular sovereignty." In this, Griswold held, they were indeed conservative. Their radicalism, he added, "consisted largely in their militancy and in their rejection of laissez-faire tactics for a deliberate use of government and public policy as means to their ends." [24]

Grant McConnell, writing in 1953, extends this view, contending that the subsequent decline of agrarianism brought on a decline in democracy.[25] The farm movements of the late nineteenth century, including Populism, were a protest "against the system of power growing out of the raw and turbulent capitalism of the era. The protest was made not merely against injustices to farmers but against injustice to all men. Agrarianism spoke in the name of all." This voice of democracy, McConnell charged, has lately been lost because a power structure (the American Farm Bureau Federation and other farm organizations) has developed and sharpened class lines so that there now exists an elite in agriculture.

In commenting on the books by Griswold and McConnell, as well as books by other writers who stressed the theme of democracy in Populism, Charles M. Hardin expresses doubt that Populism was a real democratic mass movement for all men. First, he points out that, because of its political and economic demands, the movement would have required a formidable organization of power, which was certainly not democratic. Second, he contends that its prejudices against aliens, townspeople, and, in many areas, Negroes were inimical to democracy. Finally, Hardin claims, the Populist demand for a scapegoat (Wall Street, bankers, and the railroads) "must be considered inhospitable to democracy." [26]

Although not a historian of the period, the literary critic Irving Howe has offered a picture of Populism that reflects a popular antidemocratic theme. He asserts that in Populism there was an "insistently programmatic mindlessness, a mindlessness that was sometimes its only program; a xenophobic scorn of city slickers and intellectual 'long hairs' . . . an occasional stereotyped identification of the Jew with the odious Wall Street banker; a sentimental glorification of mere solidarity at the expense of thought . . . it comprises an authoritarian tendency buried deep within a certain kind of plebeian revolt." [27]   It would appear that, in striving so earnestly for rhetorical effect, Howe has failed to understand the real issues of Populism.

Most Southern historians have stressed the unusual sectional aspects of Populism.   They have examined in considerable detail the economic appeal of the movement in the South, but they always emphasize the influence the Populists had on the established parties, especially the Democratic party.[28]   Thus Populism in many areas of the South represented a certain wing of Democrats that broke away in an effort to split the tight machine or "ring" control of the Democratic leaders who had gained political dominance in the last decades of the nineteenth century.   Although the pattern varied from state to state, the Populists usually used the Negro problem to their own advantage.   John B. Clark, writing in 1927, maintained that the Negro was a "tool, a pawn for which white parties contested, and that the negro, more than other factors, was responsible for the Populist party in Alabama.   Economic questions fell into the background."   C. Vann Woodward, in summarizing the role of the Populists, points out that the leaders openly spoke of the conflict of class and section and "ridiculed the clichés of Reconciliation and White Solidarity."   Some of the leaders, he added, attacked the cult of racism and stressed the hope of common action by farmers and workers from both classes.[29]   Thus in many parts of the South the movement challenged the one-party system as well as white solidarity. All writers agree, however, that with few exceptions, the Populist leaders assumed that the South would continue to be controlled by the white class even if the new party attained political power.

Since the era of Roosevelt and the New Deal, historians generally have come to interpret Populism as one of the first steps in the modern American reform movement, a movement culminating in the New Deal.   Only the reaction of the twenties interrupted the movement from Populism to Progressivism to New Dealism.   One of the most colorful historians of this movement is Eric Goldman, whose *Rendezvous with Destiny* pictures the stream of reformers, contrasting Populism with the liberalism of the eighties and nineties.[30]   While Populists and liberals had a common desire for reforms in existing governmental procedures, the former were much too extreme for the latter.   The "obvious socialism" of the Populist demands, he points out, brought the most anguished of all cries from liberals."   The liberals of the period emphasized "liberty, the freedom of the individual in political, economic, and social relations, either with another individual or with the government."   The Populists, on the other hand, considered liberty to be "the freedom to escape poverty and to rise in economic and social status."   They stressed economic opportunity rather than political liberty.[31]

Goldman brings out the interesting fact that both Populists and liberals found their hero in Thomas Jefferson.   The Populists looked to him as the man who despised capitalist groups as the greatest enemy of the people, and the liberals saw him as the great political thinker who feared centralized power.[32]

A recent illuminating analysis of Populism has been offered by Richard Hofstadter in his excellent volume *The Age of Reform*.   Despite his urban, somewhat cynical, attitude toward the agrarian group as a whole, Hofstadter presents effectively an interpretation of Populism from the perspective of today.   In his examination of the three great reform movements of the past sixty-five years, he characterizes Populism as an intense expression of the first movement, the agrarian uprising of the latter part of the nineteenth century.   Hofstadter discusses two other movements for reform, the Progressive movement from 1900 to 1914 and the New Deal, "whose dynamic phase was concentrated in a few years of the 1930's." [33]

Hofstadter views Populism as a heightened expression of the discontent of the farmers and others with the economic changes that were taking place.   He believes that this dissatisfaction has persisted, and is now expressed "partly as an undercurrent of provincial resentments, popular and 'democratic' rebelliousness and suspiciousness, and nativism."   He admits that, in reexamining the chief tenets of the Populists and Progressives, he found much that was "retrograde and delusive, a little that was vicious, and a good deal that was comic."   By his critical examination he hopes to stimulate "safeguards against the political misuse" of some of the alleged values of these ideas and to salvage the real values that are still meaningful.[34]   Hofstadter constructs what he calls the "agrarian myth"—the dominance of the Jeffersonian concept of the self-reliant, independent yeoman who could satisfy virtually all his needs on his own farm, and the belief that only an agricultural society was perfect.   Then he shows how illusory was this myth, since the independent yeoman had virtually disappeared by 1860 and had been supplanted by the commercial farmer.   Thus, because of its peculiar development, American rural society neither preserved the Jeffersonian farmer nor gave rise to the European type of farm village community.   Rather, it developed a "harassed little country businessman who worked very hard, moved all too often, gambled with his land, and made his way alone." [35]

The Turnerian explanation of Populism is rejected by Hofstadter.   The notion that Populism was the logical product of the frontier spirit, he contends, is "a deceptive inheritance from the Turnerian school."   To justify his refutation, Hofstadter describes the decisive role of the South, the limited support Populism received from the West as a whole, the influence of the world agrarian movement, and the weakness of the so-called valve theory of the Turner school.

In his essay on "The Folklore of Populism," Hofstadter describes the dominant themes in Populist ideology that were nurtured by the tradition of the agrarian myth.   As he sees it, these themes were the dream of a golden agricultural community, the concept of the natural harmony of interests among the productive classes, the dualistic version of social struggles, the idea that history was a conspiracy working against the farmer, and the doctrine of the primacy of money.[36]   Inevitably, these motifs reflect what he calls the delusive aspect of Populism, the general view of society in which the Populists were held to be "most credulous and vulnerable."   He dwells upon what he believes to be neglected aspects of the movement—its provincialism as revealed in the stress on nativism and nationalism and "its tincture of anti-Semitism."   Another neglected aspect is the jingoism of the 1890s that arose concurrently with Populism.[37] In his essay "From Pathos to Parity," Hofstadter examines the People's Party as a political movement and explains why it failed.[38] Its failure derived from its basic limitations: its inability to capture the vote of the laboring classes, its meager following among farmers east of Indiana, its inability to obtain sufficient financial backing, and, finally, its championing of free silver. But although it failed politically, the successes of Populism are impressive; plank after plank of its platforms has been adopted, not through its own efforts but through the efforts of the major parties.

Perhaps Hofstadter's most important contribution to our understanding of Populism is his account of the "soft" side of agrarianism, which gave way to the "hard" side. In other words, the farmer of the agrarian myth was replaced by the farmer of commercial actuality. Fortunately for the farmer, this change, which had been developing slowly and came to a climax sharply in 1896, was accompanied by the great prosperity of the era that preceded World War I.

For the student of American history, Populism remains an ever fascinating movement, open for fresh speculation and for reinterpretation. It had, and it retains, political and historical significance. Whether it is viewed as a farmers' protest against a changing society, as a native socialist expression, as a reactionary, even totalitarian, demonstration, or simply as a senseless revolt of a benighted farming group, the blunt truth remains that many of the demands made by the Populists have become accepted in our tradition and have become law. Theirs was not an intellectual movement; it was emotional, pragmatic—and effective! Populists were leaders in the fight for reforms needed in American democracy; although their movement failed to acquire political acceptance, yet what they sought for themselves and others has been widely accepted in the years that followed. More than fifty years later Populism may be viewed as a movement of protest against injustice and inequality, a protest typical of Americans since pre-Revolutionary War days.

NOTES

1. Frank L. McVey, *The Populist Movement* (American Economic Association, Economic Studies, Vol. I, No. 3; New York, 1896).

2. *Ibid.*, p. 184.   3. *Ibid.*, p. 190.   4. *Ibid.*, p. 195.

5. Frederick Jackson Turner, *The Frontier in American History* (New York, 1920).

6. *Ibid.*, p. 155.   7. *Ibid.*   8. *Ibid.*, pp. 239–40.

9. *Ibid.*, p. 281.   10. *Ibid.*, pp. 280, 305–6.

11. John D. Hicks, *The Populist Revolt* (Minneapolis, 1931). James C. Malin, a careful student of agrarianism, sharply criticizes this volume, especially the author's failure to deal with the international economic situation of the nineties, to give a comprehensive survey of United States agriculture of the period, and to investigate Populism in Kansas and several other states. Malin also comments briefly on other early writers on Populism. "Notes on the Literature of Populism," *Kansas Historical Quarterly*, I, No. 2 (1932), 160–64. Solon J. Buck's *The Agrarian Crusade* (New Haven, Conn., 1920), a slender history of the agrarian movement with virtually no interpretation, remains a brief and useful account.

12. *Ibid.*, p. 95   13. *Ibid.*   14. *Ibid.*

15. Chester McArthur Destler, *American Radicalism, 1865–1901: Essays and Documents* (New London, Conn., 1946).

16. *Ibid.*, p. 2.   17. *Ibid.*

18. *Ibid.*, p. 222.   19. *Ibid.*, p. 30.

20. John D. Hicks, "The Legacy of Populism in Middle West," *Agricultural History*, XXIII (1949), 235–36.

21. Theodore Saloutos and John D. Hicks, *Agrarian Discontent in the Middle West, 1900–1930* (Madison, Wis., 1951), p. 30.

22. George Harmon Knoles, "Populism and Socialism, with Special Reference to the Election of 1892," *Pacific Historical Review*, XII (1943), 295–304.

23. Theodore Draper, *The Roots of American Communism* (New York, 1957), pp. 36–39. Another Midwesterner who gave up Populism for Socialism after 1896 was Julius A. Wayland. See Howard H. Quint, "Julius A. Wayland, Pioneer Socialist Propagandist," *Mississippi Valley Historical Review*, XXXVI (March, 1949), 585–606.

24. A. Whitney Griswold, *Farming and Democracy* (New York, 1948), pp. 145–46.

25. Grant McConnell, *The Decline of American Democracy* (Berkeley, Calif., 1953), p. 1.

26. Charles M. Hardin, "Farm Politics and American Democracy," *Journal of Politics*, XVII (1955), 655.

27. Irving Howe, *Sherwood Anderson* (New York, 1951), pp. 87–

88. The quotation appears in Howe's comment on Anderson's *Marching Men,* an account of the restlessness of the nineties and the attempts made to organize labor.

28. Alex M. Arnett, *The Populist Movement in Georgia* (Columbia University Studies in History, Economics, and Public Law, No. 235; New York, 1922); John B. Clark, *Populism in Alabama* (Auburn, Ala., 1927); Roscoe C. Martin, *The People's Party in Texas: a Study in Third Party Politics* (University of Texas Bureau of Research in the Social Sciences Study, No. 4; Austin, Texas, 1933); William DuBose Sheldon, *Populism in the Old Dominion: Virginia Farm Politics, 1885–1900* (Princeton, N.J., 1935).

29. C. Vann Woodward, *Origins of the New South, 1877–1913* (Baton Rouge, La., 1951), Chap. IX.

30. Eric F. Goldman, *Rendezvous with Destiny* (New York, 1953).

31. *Ibid.,* p. 51.　　　　　　32. *Ibid.,* pp. 51–52.

33. Richard Hofstadter, *The Age of Reform; from Bryan to F. D. R.* (New York, 1955), p. 3.

34. *Ibid.,* pp. 5–11.　　　　　　35. *Ibid.,* p. 46.

36. *Ibid.,* p. 62.　　　37. *Ibid.,* pp. 85–93.　　　38. *Ibid.,* pp. 94–109.

IMPERIALISM AND RACISM

by James P. Shenton
COLUMBIA UNIVERSITY

AT THE BEGINNING of the twentieth century establishing empires seemed the duty of the white man. Even as outspoken an anti-imperialist as William Graham Sumner believed that the creation of empires was the inevitable "penalty of greatness" that obliged the ascendant nation to extend "law and order for the benefit of everybody." [1] In the middle of the twentieth century the white man surrenders his empires—sometimes in dignity and at other times in violence. He does so knowing that if he persists in holding fast to his colonial possessions no opprobrium will be sufficient to describe his behavior. He knows also that he stands indicted among the former and the remaining colonials by the very ideals which he ostensibly went forth to bring to the "earth's dark places." [2] And if this were not enough, as George Orwell reminds us, the imperialist in his declining days seeks also to escape "looking a fool" to his subjects. This result was indeed forseen by Andrew Carnegie who predicted that "in teaching our history, we supply [the colonials] with the most deadly explosives, sure some day to burst and rend the teacher." [3]

It is now evident that the "ascendant nation's" rule of law is established only to be supplanted by "the heterogeneous compound of inefficient [colonial] humanity" bent upon becoming its own law enforcement agency.[4] The colonial justifies his aspiration by invoking the ideals which gave to the original imperial ventures their high moral purpose. No matter how inadequately understood, how corruptly practiced, how imperfectly articulated, the rationale used and the goals to be reached once freedom is achieved are those set forth in western liberal and democratic doctrines.   The aftermath of imperialism for the former colonial powers may be uncomfortable, but it is a discomfort that has its origins in the now ignored side of imperialism; namely, in the presumption, whatever its basis, of the inferiority of the colonial peoples.   An examination of the United States' entrance into empire building makes this point strikingly evident.

American historians have generally agreed that the United States became an imperial power with the annexation of the Philippine Islands.   It was, they agree, the unexpected result of the Spanish-American War—at least for everyone but "the young imperialists who had espoused the 'large policy' of Lodge and Roosevelt." [5]   If correct, this position insinuates that American imperialism came without the active assistance of the American people.   The explanation has overtones of a "conspiracy thesis." It also assigns to the democracy a role of flaccid passivity.   Furthermore, the historian has subscribed, although with variations, to A. K. Weinberg's conclusion that annexation marked the moment when "the fulfillment of expansionist desires could no longer be left to fate but required force—conceived by John Morley as an inevitability of imperialism." [6]   Implicit in this statement is the idea that expansionism before 1898 differed fundamentally from that which occurred afterwards.   The former was a "natural overflow of nationality" while the latter was "a great national aberration."   In effect, one is being invited to accept the assertion that American imperialism is a historical phenomenon without a past.   The event was perhaps "a breach" in American "traditions," but it is my intention to show that it was no "shock to their established values." [7]

No American at the time seriously considered the possibility that the newly annexed territories would become full-fledged states.   The fact that the native populations were colored precluded this possibility.   Consequently, it is doubtful whether "established values" were at stake.   Although the historian of the antiimperialist movement has emphasized that its membership opposed expansion "because they thought that an imperialist policy ran counter to the political doctrines of the Declaration of

Independence, Washington's Farewell Address, and Lincoln's Gettysburg Address—the doctrines which asserted that a government could not rule peoples without their consent," the evidence indicates that both imperialist and antiimperialist invoked traditional American biases against colored peoples.[8] Both the Indian and the Negro had been excluded throughout most of our history from full participation in American life. Only the brief experiment of Reconstruction stands out here and there as an exception. Contemporaneously with our excursion into imperialism came the systematic segregation of the Negro through Jim Crow laws. The two events were not unrelated; exclusion was the binding theme.[9]

I do not mean to reject the idea that economic grievances play a major role in exacerbating relations between white and nonwhite. It is however true that the expropriation of colonial property had as its ultimate justification not economic necessity but the belief in the colored man's inferiority and incompetence. Furthermore, it appears increasingly that the belief in the colored man's inferiority provokes the deepest outrage towards Americans among former colonials and wounds their violated egos most profoundly.

That color was the factor which conditioned the thinking of nearly all Americans was strikingly evident in the debate over the annexation of the Philippines. On one point there was near unanimity: that the colored man was a burden. Whatever debate occurred was over whether it was the white man's responsibility to assume that burden. Henry Cabot Lodge put it succinctly when he observed: "Bryan and his party think we should abandon the Philippines because they are not fit for self-government. I believe that for that very reason we should retain them." [10] Indeed, the pervasiveness of this sentiment leads one to conclude that the imperialism which followed the Spanish-American War marked the moment at which the racial experiments of Reconstruction were confirmed a failure.

This development was not immediately evident when agitation for war was reaching its climax. If anything, it was the appeal to the humanitarian ideals embodied in Reconstruction that determined the event.   This fact is most evident in the reaction of the business community to the speech of Vermont's Senator Redfield Proctor.   As Julius W. Pratt notes, that speech carried "great weight" in breaking down business opposition to the war.[11] Without using "a lurid adjective," Proctor "aroused the nation" and made "intervention the plain duty of the United States on the simple ground of humanity." [12]

Proctor concerned himself with two distinct problems.   He reported what he had seen and heard of conditions in Cuba, and he described the ethnic and racial derivations of the Cuban population.   Although he did not specifically advocate intervention against the Spaniards, he assumed that America would have to intervene somehow if Cuba were to be free.   Since he preferred self-government for Cuba, his concern with race was designed to convince the listener that the Cuban was racially fit for self-government.   His description of the "desolation and distress, misery, and starvation" that had brought death to "two hundred thousand . . . within Spanish forts," the infamous *reconcentrados*, shocked the humanitarian sentiments of the nation.   But he had to reassure Americans that Cuban freedom would not inaugurate another "prostrate state."

He noted that the Cuban whites were "like the Spaniards, dark in complexion, but oftener light or blond."   An ambivalence is evident in his description of the Cuban Negroes, whom he described as declining in numbers though "by nature quite the equal mentally and physically of the race in this country [and] physically . . . by far the larger and stronger race on the island." Although he stated he did not fear the consequences of annexation, Proctor opposed it as it was "not wise policy to take in any people of foreign tongue and training, and without any strong guiding American element."   He believed that the Cubans, aided by their own virtue and the "large influx of American and English immigration and money," contrary to the "impression . . . prevailing in this country, even among those who sympathize with them," would prove capable of self-government.[13]

As yet muted, the attitude of Anglo-Saxon superiority was present—a sentiment that would move one of the earliest historians of the Spanish-American War to describe it as a logical culmination of the "racial" incompatibility between the Spaniard and the "North-American Anglo-Saxon." [14] It was a sentiment that would increasingly express itself in more strident tones.

For the reluctant businessman who had viewed war with skepticism, the newly conquered empire now brought visions of ample profits. It did not matter that there was little evidence to justify his expectations—the wish fathered the belief. Subsequently there would be second thoughts, but the decline of business opposition to war and then the active espousal of imperialism by a considerable number of businessmen were vital factors in deciding both events.[15] Significantly, however, the debate over imperialism did not stress, in the main, the economic consequences of empire but rather the moral obligations and racist consequences.

The tone of the debate was established by Utah's Senator Rawlins who reminded his colleagues that they had "enacted laws which stand like cherubim with flaming sword at the gateways of the Republic to drive back the hordes of the dark and degenerate races of the East, lest they may enter in to infect and degrade us." [16] Pitchfork Ben Tillman, who represented himself "as a Senator from Africa, if you please, South Carolina, with 750,000 colored population and only 500,000 whites," warned against "the injection into . . . [the United States] of another race question which can only breed bloodshed and a costly war." The general Southern opposition to annexation developed because "we of the South have borne this white man's burden of a colored race since their emancipation and before." [17] Senator Money of Mississippi saw no chance that "the Asiatic mind . . . will conceive the idea of self-government, as we understand and as we practice it." Without this understanding the white man would never be able to lay down his burden. The school house, which was the symbol used to designate the intention of the white man to educate the colored man, would never succeed in its purpose.[18] The Old Dominion's Senator Daniel conjured up "a witch's cauldron" made up of "black spirits and white, red spirits and gray . . . not only of all hues and colors, but . . . spotted peoples, and . . . striped peoples . . . with zebra signs upon them." To plunge into such a cauldron could only signal the fall "of our great, broad, Christian, Anglo-Saxon, American land." [19]

Northern Senators were no less forthright in cautioning their colleagues about the racial consequences of annexation. George Frisbie Hoar of Massachusetts foresaw "terrible results" should the United States absorb "a distant people, dwelling in the tropics, aliens in blood, most of them Moslem in faith, incapable to speak or comprehend our language, or to read or write any language, to whom the traditions and the doctrines of civil liberty are unknown." Senator Turner of Washington foretold a "mongrelizing [of] our citizenship . . . (a) debauching [of] our institutions . . . by an assimilating miscegenation." [20] The expectation among antiimperialist Senators was that "our country" was about "to be overrun by . . . a horde of people unassimilable by reason of turbid and passionate natures." [21]

The imperialist Senators countered with the assurance that the relationship between the United States and the Philippines was to be unlike that with previous territories. Henry Cabot Lodge bluntly defined the new relationship when he observed: "We have full power and are absolutely free to do with those islands as we please." [22] No alien hordes would come unless we invited them.

Since the alteration in territorial policy was justified as necessary to bring to the Philippines "the principles of law, order, and good government," Tillman questioned whether the unwillingness of the proponents of annexation to give the Filipinos the same self-government that had been given the former Southern slaves was not an acknowledgement by the North "that you were wrong in 1868." Minnesota's Knute Nelson, to whom the question was directed, promptly renounced the "dead past" which he would not revive to make the Southern "burden" of Negroes "heavier." Having conceded Tillman's point by default, Nelson turned upon the one-time abolitionist, Hoar of Massachusetts, who opposed annexation, to demand why Hoar had voted to annex the Hawaiian Islands when he knew that "95 per cent of [its] people were of inferior races." The xenophobic qualities of New

England life were amply evident when Hoar replied: "I expect that Hawaii will be filled within fifty years with Americans, and, I will add, a Northern and largely a New England population." [23]

Beyond the Senate a larger debate continued as the nation's press and public figures hastened to make their feelings about imperialism known. William Jennings Bryan, whose conception of a political campaign was always monistic, abandoned silver and began preaching the case against imperialism. Somewhere in the morass of argument that Bryan martialed in his antiimperialist crusade there was probably a strand of sincere belief. Whatever the case, the man who would editorialize "that liberty was designed for the brown man as well as for the white man and the black man," warned also of "the yellow peril"—a warning which was heartily endorsed by Samuel Gompers—that endangered the American workingman as a result of annexation. The same Bryan would insist approvingly, when challenged to explain the difference between the Southern treatment of the Negro and the evils of imperialism, that "when conditions force . . . two races to live under the same government in the same country the more advanced race never has consented, and probably never will consent, to be dominated by the less advanced." He would argue disingenuously that Jim Crow was temporary while imperialism would be permanent. As to the idea that an American president should entertain a Negro at lunch, even so illustrious a one as Booker T. Washington, Bryan warned that the president should not become an advocate "of social equality." One of the rare souls who denounced imperialism because it went contrary to the innate equality of mankind, Thomas Wentworth Higginson, who had also headed Bryan's electoral ticket in Massachusetts during the 1900 election, was impelled to characterize Bryan's racial attitudes as "utterly retrograde and medieval." [24]

Through all arguments both imperialist and antiimperialist there moved an almost unquestioning acceptance of the innate superiority either of the Anglo-Saxon or the American experience. The absorption of another race it was assumed by the antiimperialist would corrupt that experience. Carl Schurz questioned whether the fate of the Filipino was to be "more hopeless than the colored man now living among us." He asked publicly whether the very "troublesome race problem in the United States," whose solution seemed distant, would become vexed beyond hope should we take in "Spanish-Americans, with all the mixtures of Indian and Negro blood, and Malays and other unspeakable Asiatics . . . and all of them animated with the instincts, impulses and passions bred by the tropical sun." [25] Along with William Graham Sumner, Schurz foresaw "the conquest of the United States by Spain." [26] Moorfield Storey, although bitterly hostile to the revocation of American Negro rights, feared that imperial expansion would result in "the annexation of new regions which, unfit to govern themselves, would govern us." [27] Grover Cleveland concluded sardonically that "Cuba ought to be submerged for a while before it will make an American State or Territory of which we will be particularly proud." [28]

The staunch antiimperialist Andrew Carnegie expressed himself as "quite resigned to our own and the negro races occupying the South together." His expectation was that the Negro under the leadership of Booker T. Washington would "continue to ascend morally, educationally, and financially." As for the use of lynch law against the Negro, Carnegie cautioned a Scotch audience:

It is easy for those thousands of miles away, surrounded by the machinery ready to punish crime, to preach patience with and obedience to all forms of the law's delay, but were we present, and the victim in the hands of the incensed neighbors, it may be doubted whether we could preserve the judicial spirit needed to preach patience. "Judge" Lynch is rarely, if ever, accused of punishing the innocent—undue haste or excessive "efficiency" is his fault. The number who suffer, not from injustice but undue haste, is not great.[29]

Although reconciled to the existence of the American Negro, Carnegie actively opposed the annexation of the Philippines which he feared would endanger the amalgamation of the Anglo-Saxon peoples "under the American flag and the American Constitution." With a fine sense for the appropriate description, Carnegie termed his expectation that the Anglo-Saxons would reunite, undoing the rupture of 1776, as "race imperialism." [30]

But Carnegie was not alone in his expectations of Anglo-Saxon reunion. Endless numbers of words pronounced the inauguration of "the Anglo-Saxon century." Both imperialist and antiimperialist heartily concurred with the idea that "to that race [the Anglo-Saxon] primarily belongs in a preponderating degree the future of mankind, because it has proved its title to its guardianship." [31] Disagreement developed over whether the United States was to do its duty through "the cruelty and bondage of the empire or the friendship and freedom of the republic." [32] Those that supported the latter course argued that the American was the culmination of the Anglo-Saxon experience and, as such, would conquer.[33] More often, it was proposed that the Anglo-Saxon mission would be fulfilled through an exercise in English and American "interdependence." Richard Olney accepted the proposition that "there is a patriotism of race as well as of country —and the Anglo-American is as little likely to be indifferent to the one as to the other." [34] The old Populist James B. Weaver noted the "similarity of thought" between Joseph Chamberlain, secretary of state for the British colonies, and William McKinley on the decision of "Providence" to make the United States "a great governing power, conquering in order to civilize, administer and develop vast areas of the world's surface, primarily to our advantage, but to their own advantage as well." He drew the pointed conclusion that "there is an entente cordiale existing between the two governments." [35]

The need for unity among the Anglo-Saxons was accepted as urgent because it was assumed that the decline of Great Britain had become evident. America had now to grasp the sceptre of Anglo-Saxon world dominance or share in the British collapse. Brooks Adams believed that there was no alternative but "to compete for the seat of international exchange, or, in other words, for the seat of empire." [36] Ties of blood and kinship were similarly invoked to justify expanded American and British cooperation. An antiimperialist, Senator Augustus O. Bacon of Georgia, assured his listeners that despite his opposition to the creation by the United States of a British-like empire, he was proud that "all

the blood that I have in me comes from English ancestry." En-
thusiastically he continued:

I am proud of the English race; I am proud of the grand civilization
given to the world by England; I am proud of her history; I am proud
of her achievements; and if the time came that the great powers
leagued themselves together to destroy her, I would be willing to go
to her side and bare our breasts in her defense. Whenever her life
was at stake I think we would owe that much to the mother country.[37]

The annexation of the Philippines was the test which Henry
Cabot Lodge believed would establish whether the United States
was prepared to meet its new "responsibilities." He was in agreement with his friend Theodore Roosevelt that the white man was
obliged to bring "liberty with order" to the earth's "dark places." [38]
Yet, fulfillment of that mission did not mean the various races
would ultimately come together, for Lodge was convinced that
racial intermarriage would result only in mutual corruption.[39]
Roosevelt anticipated that the American "imperialist" would educate and guide the Filipinos so "that beautiful archipelago shall
become a center of civilization for all eastern Asia." [40]   Ulrich B.
Phillips's conclusion that slavery was a school house in which the
American Negro had been prepared for civilization had been preceded by the imperialist's argument that they came to teach the
retrograde natives the benefit of Anglo-Saxon institutions.

The originally antiimperialist Woodrow Wilson reconsidered
and decided it was the duty of the United States to "moralize" the
Philippines. He warned that the Filipinos "can have liberty no
cheaper than we got it. They must first take the discipline of
law, must first love order and instinctively yield to it. . . . We
are old in this learning and must be their tutors." [41] The Episcopal Bishop of New York, Henry Codman Potter, had declared
before an antiimperialist audience of 3,000 that imperialism
"threatens equally the moral integrity of the nation and the conditions on which its prosperity has hitherto rested." After a visit
to the Philippines, he no longer believed that the Filipinos were
"competent to govern themselves." He challenged those who believed otherwise:

I believe them [the Filipinos] to be exposed to the unscrupulous, ignorant and ambitious men, among themselves—many of whose representatives I have seen and conferred with. I think it was ill-advised and unfortunate that originally we held the Philippines; but I think also that, to abandon them *now,* would be to abandon them to internal warfares of rival leaders and rival tribes. At present they are no more fit to lead themselves, or organize a government, than a parcel of children. It does not follow that because you think otherwise persons who differ from you are frauds and time-servers. They have seen the Philippines.[42]

Charles W. Eliot, president of Harvard, had identified himself with misgivings as an antiimperialist. His name frequently appeared on petitions advocating the granting of independence to the Philippines. To one such petition submitted to both the 1904 Republican and Democratic national conventions, Theodore Roosevelt warned Eliot that it might receive favorable attention only from the Democrats. Its reception by them would depend upon Southern Democrats who Roosevelt observed "were willing to prate about the doctrines contained in the Declaration of Independence, as applied to the brown men in the Philippines," while "they embody a living negation of those doctrines so far as they concern the black men at home." Eliot may have known some uneasy stirrings as he read Roosevelt's comments, for he favored the segregation of Negro from white students in Boston should the number of Negroes in the city increase enough to warrant it. As for Harvard College, Eliot would subsequently declare publicly: "If more than half the students . . . were negroes perhaps we should think of separating the majority from the minority. At present there are so few negroes they are absolutely lost in the mass of the 5,000 whites, and they have no influence of any sort for evil on the mass of whites." [43] The fate of the Southern Negro was being determined as Roosevelt noted "by the present day representatives of the old copperhead and dough-face vote in the North." [44]

Other academicians expressed unease over the implications of imperialism for the United States. Stanford's David Starr Jordan described the Philippines as lying "in the heart of that region which Ambrose Bierce calls 'the horrid zone, nature's asylum for degenerates.'" He was certain that "the Anglo-Saxon or any other civilized race degenerates in the tropics mentally, morally, physically." To annex such territory was to complicate the growing domestic racial problems. "Wherever degenerate, dependent or alien races are within our borders today," Jordan announced, "they are not part of the United States." Their presence constituted "a menace to peace and welfare." Gloomily, he predicted: "There is no solution of race problem or class problem, until race or class can solve it for itself." A solution was predicated upon the ready access to the traditional rights and privileges given to American citizens.

Unfortunately, as a Cornell professor emeritus was noting, "in the United States the white man has a burden, such perhaps as no other nation has been called upon to bear . . . that of the two races in the South." Nor did the retired professor believe a solution was possible, for "where intermarriage is out of the question, social equality cannot exist; without social equality political equality is impossible, and a Republic in the true sense can hardly be." [45] Like the water that erodes but does not nourish the soil, the American racial question revealed the bleak truths that underlay the facade of American democratic rhetoric.

At home even the true humanitarian did not cry out against racism; he could only wonder in apprehension at what the future held "when hatred of race has mounted to such a pitch that the people of one race go out by thousands to see a man of the race burnt alive, and carry away his charred bones or pieces of his singed garments as souvenirs." [46] It is therefore not surprising that the nation managed to conceal from itself the full horrors of an event like the Philippine Insurrection. It took the Commanding General of the United States Army, Lt. General Nelson A. Miles, to jolt the national complacency. On February 19, 1903, he issued a report that he had seen great devastation in large areas of Luzon, that Filipinos had complained to him of the American "reconcentrado policy" and of various indignities, one of which Roosevelt described as the "old Filipino method of mild torture, the water cure." Americans read about Filipinos being suffocated after 600 of them had been crowded into a 70 by 20 ft. building, of torture and cremation, and of unjustified executions with gun and bayonet.   The publication of an order by an American field commander in the Philippines directing his troops "to kill and burn and make a howling wilderness of Samar" led to a Congressional investigation which established that the troops had fully complied.   *The Nation* concluded that "this remarkable document, full as it is of tales of horror, rivalled only by the cruelties in Cuba about which we went to war in 1898," had brought the crusade of 1898 full circle.[47]

The public response to these revelations followed "well-defined and firm convictions" on Philippine policy.   The antiimperialist chortled over this latest twist in "benevolent assimilation," while the imperialist doubted whether it would be possible "to convince the American people that our soldiers are not as humane and honest as any on earth."   Henry Cabot Lodge questioned whether the barbaric behavior of the Filipino guerrillas did not explain the "nasty" actions of American troops.   The President of the United States concluded "that we had been far more merciful to the Filipinos than . . . toward the Indians of the plains."   He "did not intend to repeat the folly of which our people were sometimes guilty . . . when they petted the hostile Indians." [48]

And so the white American carried his dark burden.   The black and brown ciphers sometimes protested the rationalizations of the white man's injustice towards them; othertimes, they waited patiently for the inevitable day when the American would abandon his burden.   North Carolina's last Negro congressman wondered how the white man could accuse the Negro "of shiftlessness and idleness when the accuser of his own motion closes the avenues for labor and industrial pursuits to us . . . of ignorance when it was made a crime under the former order of things to learn enough about letters even to read the Word of God."   Thousands of miles to the golden west, General Emilio Aguinaldo, although conquered, declined to learn English.   His reason was simple: "I thought the Americans would leave us alone . . . after the Spanish-American War and, since then, for over half a

century, I expected them momentarily to pull up stakes and depart." In London there appeared a bitter parody of Rudyard
Kipling's "The White Man's Burden" which linked the past and
present plight of the colored man. It enjoined:

> Pile on the brown man's burden,
> And if his cry be sore,
> That surely need not irk you—
> Ye've driven slaves before.[49]

NOTES

1. William Graham Sumner, *War, and Other Essays* (New Haven,
Conn., 1911), pp. 292–93. He did not believe that American institutions were equipped to sustain such an effort. He believed it would
be better to allow Great Britain to continue her police function
throughout the world.

2. Howard K. Beale, *Theodore Roosevelt and the Rise of America
to World Power* (Baltimore, 1956), p. 72. The words are those of
Theodore Roosevelt.

3. George Orwell, *A Collection of Essays* (New York, 1954), p. 162;
Andrew Carnegie, *The Negro in America* (Inverness, Scotland, 1907),
p. 7.

4. William Jennings Bryan, *Republic or Empire?* (Chicago, 1899),
p. 184; the description of the colonial was that of the vehemently antiimperialist Senator from California, Stephen M. White.

5. Julius W. Pratt, *Expansionists of 1898* (New York, 1951), p. 232.
Beale, *Theodore Roosevelt*, p. 55, asserts: "A few men in powerful positions were able to plunge the nation into an imperialist career that
it never explicitly decided to follow." Joseph E. Wisan, *The Cuban
Crisis as Reflected in the New York Press* (New York, 1934), concluded
that "the Spanish-American War would not have occurred had not
the appearance of Hearst in New York journalism precipitated a bitter battle for newspaper circulation." George W. Auxier, "Middle
Western Newspapers and the Spanish-American War, 1895–1898,"
The Mississippi Valley Historical Review, XXVI (March, 1940), 523–
34, rejected sensationalism, but developed the Mid-Western editor's
emphasis "on the basic interests of the United States in the Caribbean,
their repeated laments that Spain violated these interests . . . and the
evident partisanship reflected in their discussion of the Cuban question." Richard Hofstadter, "Manifest Destiny and the Philippines,"
in Daniel Aaron, ed., *America in Crisis* (New York, 1952), p. 189,

notes: "The real decisions were made in the office of Theodore Roosevelt, in the Senate cloakroom, in the sanctums of those naval officers from whom the McKinley administration got its primary information about the Philippines. . . . The public was, by and large, faced with a fait accompli that, although theoretically reversible, had the initial impetus of its very existence to carry it along."

6. Albert K. Weinberg, *Manifest Destiny* (Baltimore, 1935), p. 283.

7. *Ibid.*, p. 8, which states: "The expansion of the United States was of a character which can be viewed with minimal moralistic prepossession. In the pages of its history there is relatively little of tragedy which, though it induces reformist emotion, interferes with correct interpretation of human motives. Although Filipinos and Haitians can well deny that 'the shadow of a sigh' never 'trembles' through the story, it is perhaps the most cheerful record of such ambitions that one can find." J. A. Hobson, *Imperialism: a Study* (London, 1905), pp. 6–8, stresses the differentiation between colonialism and imperialism. The former, according to Hobson's presentation, characterized American development until we chose to leap the ocean; Samuel Flagg Bemis, *A Diplomatic History of the United States* (New York, 1950), p. 475; Hofstadter, "Manifest Destiny and the Philippines," in Aaron, ed., *America in Crisis,* p. 173. A striking departure from traditional accounts and one which relates "imperialism" to the developing progressive mood of the country is that of William E. Leuchtenburg, "Progressivism and Imperialism; the Progressive Movement and American Foreign Policy, 1898–1916," *Mississippi Valley Historical Review,* XXXIX (December, 1952), 483.

8. Fred Harvey Harrington, "The Anti-Imperialist Movement in the United States, 1898–1900," *Mississippi Valley Historical Review,* XXII (September, 1935), 211.

9. *Congressional Record,* December 12, 1898, pp. 94–96, contains Missouri's Senator George Vest's argument which best states the territorial issue. He insisted: "I do deny that territory can be acquired to be held as colonies, peopled by millions of subjects not citizens, with no hope or prospect of its ever becoming a state of the Union." Senator John W. Daniel of Virginia, although opposed to the annexation of the Philippines, justified the Indian's fate with the argument: "The Indian of one hundred and twenty-five years ago is the Indian of to-day—ameliorated, to a certain extent civilized, and yet . . . separate and distinct from the great dominant race which had come to take this land and to inhabit it, this is indicated in what we are still doing and must forever do with them so long as they maintain their tribal relations and so long as they are Indians. Racial differences, differences of psychology, the subtle analyses of man have put them asunder." Bryan, *Republic or Empire?*, p. 377.

10. John A. Garraty, *Henry Cabot Lodge* (New York, 1953), p. 206.

11. Pratt, *Expansionists of 1898*, p. 246. The intriguing aspect of Pratt's analysis of business's attitude toward the coming of war is not only that business had mixed emotions about a war with Spain, but also that its support among others was necessary before a war could come.

12. *Dictionary of American Biography*, XV (New York, 1943), 246; *The Literary Digest*, XVI (March 26, 1898), 361–63. A cursory examination of the press and magazine reaction to Proctor's speech confirms that it was profound. See the New York *Times*, March 19, 1898; Emporia *Daily Gazette*, March 18, 1898; the Chicago *Daily Tribune*, March 18, 1898. *Public Opinion*, XXIV (March 24, 1898), 358–60, has extensive coverage of press reaction that indicates nationwide shock at Proctor's revelations; *The Independent*, April 14, 1898, p. 14, commenting on Proctor's indictment of Spanish colonial policy concluded that "it is no wonder that even the poor degraded natives of the Philippine Islands should rise in rebellion." See also *Wall Street Journal*, March 19, 1898.

13. *Congressional Record*, March 17, 1898, pp. 2916–19. A question which interested many newspapers was why Proctor had made his investigation. Several emphasized that he was "a close friend of the President" and "one of . . . McKinley's most trusted advisers and friends." From this they drew the conclusion that he was acting either as the official or unofficial agent of "the administration." See the summary of news comment in *Public Opinion*, XXIV (March 24, 1898), 358–60.

14. French Ensor Chadwick, *The Relations of the United States and Spain* (New York, 1909), p. 4.

15. Bernard Baruch, *My Own Story* (New York, 1957), pp. 107–8, who recalls: "Thinking of how American arms had been victorious on land and sea from Cuba to the Philippines, halfway around the world, I felt the surge of empire within me. No thought entered my head of the problems and responsibilities that an 'American Empire' might bring in years to come." His enthusiasm was further stimulated by the prospect of "sizable profits." Pratt, *Expansionists of 1898*, pp. 230–78; Hobson, *Imperialism*, pp. 73–79. The division of sentiment among businessmen at the beginning of the war raises questions about the sufficiency of a term like "business" when used to explain why an event occurred. To find businessmen like Mark Hanna, Andrew Carnegie, Jacob Schiff, and James J. Hill "strongly anti-war and anti-imperialist" does little to support Hobson's conclusion that "American Imperialism was the natural product of the economic pressure of a sudden advance of capitalism which could not find occupation at home and needed foreign markets for goods and

investments." Carnegie anticipated that American industry would dominate world markets without colonization. See James M. Swank MSS, Pennsylvania Historical Society, Carnegie to Swank, March 11, 1898.

16. *Congressional Record,* February 1, 1899, p. 1348.

17. *Ibid.,* February 2, 1899, p. 1389; Bryan, *Republic or Empire?* p. 123. Tillman's conservative colleague, John Lowndes McLaurin, agreed with Tillman's views and proposed: "The experience of the South for the past thirty years with the negro race is pregnant with lessons of wisdom for our guidance in the Philippines. It is passing strange that Senators who favored universal suffrage and the full enfranchisement of the negro should now advocate imperialism . . . . If they are sincere in their views as to the Philippines, they should propose an amendment to the Constitution which will put the inferior races in this country and the inhabitants of the Philippines upon an equality as to their civil and political rights, and thus forever settle the vexed race and suffrage questions." *Congressional Record,* January 13, 1899, pp. 638–42. Similar sentiments were expressed by Senator Gorman of Maryland who foresaw an even greater "misfortune" than that "which came to us by the injection into our body politic of the slave." *Ibid.,* February 6, 1899, pp. 1486–87.

18. *Congressional Record,* February 3, 1899. Doubts were often expressed about the length of time it would take to educate the colored man to appreciate the values of the Anglo-Saxon. Henry Cabot Lodge, although an avowed imperialist, agreed that "Not even education . . . could change a man quickly." Quoted in George E. Mowry, *The Era of Theodore Roosevelt* (New York, 1958), p. 40. The symbol of the school house was used frequently in magazine and newspaper cartoons. The natives were most often depicted as being dragged or driven to school by American soldiers. A subtle insight into racial thinking was the frequency with which Filipinos were depicted as Negroes speaking in a minstrel man's drawl. Aguinaldo whose photos showed a sensitive, fine-featured young man was portrayed as a cannibal. See the selection of cartoons taken from various journals and magazines that appears in *The Literary Digest,* XVIII (1899) 141, 180, 216, 240, 260, 331.

19. *Congressional Record,* February 3, 1899, pp. 1422–32.

20. *Ibid.,* January 9, 1899, pp. 493–503; January 19, 1899, pp.783–89.

21. Bryan, *Republic or Empire?,* pp. 292–94. These were the sentiments of Nebraska's Senator William V. Allen.

22. *Congressional Record,* January 24, 1899, pp. 958–60.

23. *Ibid.,* January 20, 1899, pp. 836–38.

24. *The Commoner,* I (January 30, 1901), 1–2; I (December 6,

1901), 1; II, (February 21, 1902), 3, in which Bryan notes that "the race question which we have in the South will sink into insignificance in comparison with the race question that we have to meet in the Philippines if we give them a territorial government and attempt to insure white supremacy." *Ibid.,* I (November 1, 1901), pp. 1–3, deals with the Washington affair. The New York *Times,* October 20, 1901, p. 6, editorialized on the incident that "the notion that . . . [Roosevelt] was indorsing the idea of social equality between all white and all colored men, is absurd." Southern sentiment was summed up in the flat assertion: "Race supremacy precludes social equality." *The Literary Digest,* XXIII (October 26, 1901), 486–87. See Bryan, *Republic or Empire?,* pp. 209–10, on Gompers, who wondered: "If the Philippines are annexed . . . how can we prevent Chinese coolies from going to the Philippines and from there swarm into the United States and engulf our people and our civilization?" Higginson MSS, Houghton Library, T. W. Higginson to W. J. Bryan, Nov. 27, 1901; *Speeches of William Jennings Bryan* (New York, 1909), II, 11, which rejects imperialism because it would change the United States from "a homogeneous republic" into "a heterogeneous empire." For a view that treats Bryan as a hypocrite in the debate, see that of a major actor of the Filipino Insurrection in Emilio Aguinaldo and Vincente Albano Pacis, *A Second Look at America* (New York, 1957), pp. 87–89.

25. Carl Schurz, *Speeches, Correspondence and Political Papers* (New York, 1913), V, 503–4, and VI, 6–13.

26. Sumner, *War and other Essays,* pp. 297–334.

27. Mark DeWolfe Howe, *Portrait of an Independent, Moorfield Storey, 1845–1929* (Boston, 1932), pp. 194–95.

28. Allan Nevins, ed., *Letters of Grover Cleveland* (Boston, 1933), pp. 526–27.

29. Carnegie, *The Negro in America,* pp. 28–29, 43.

30. Burton Hendricks, *The Life of Andrew Carnegie* (New York, 1932), I, 422.

31. John Dos Passos, *The Anglo-Saxon Century* (New York, 1903), p. 47. The contemporary literature on this subject is extensive. See especially A. V. Dicey, "A Common Citizenship for the English Race," *Contemporary Review,* LXXI (April, 1897), 457–76, which advocates what its title suggests; James Bryce, "The Essential Unity of Britain and America," *Atlantic Monthly,* LXXXII (July 1898), 22–29, agreed with Dicey's proposal and emphasized that this right not be accorded to "other foreigners." A. W. Tourgee, "The Twentieth Century Peacemakers," *Contemporary Review,* LXXV (June 1899), 886–908, provides an interesting comment on the racial views of a Reconstruction carpetbagger when he notes: "The Anglo-Saxon alone offers to the semi-civilised people that come under his control the advantages of

intellectual and material development. . . . Political and material betterment are the prizes it offers to the laggards in civilization who come beneath its rule. . . . That is what . . . the United States offers in the West Indies and the Philippines." Carl Schurz, *Speeches, Correspondence and Political Papers,* V, 514.

32. Bryan, *Republic or Empire?* p. 328; Charles A. Towne, former Minnesota Congressman, who had abandoned the GOP over the silver issue in 1896, posed the question. He viewed the American as the end of the march of "our Aryan forefathers" in their "story of human progress."

33. *Ibid.,* pp. 37–39. So thought Bryan.

34. James K. Hosmer, "The American Evolution: Dependence, Independence, Interdependence," *Atlantic Monthly,* LXXXII (July 1898), 29–36; Richard Olney, "International Isolation of the United States," *Atlantic Monthly,* LXXXI (May 1898), 577–88; also cited in Edward Weeks and Emily Flint, *Jubilee: One Hundred Years of the Atlantic* (Boston, 1957), p. 413.

35. Bryan, *Republic or Empire?,* pp. 108–9. Weaver expressed particular indignation that "the Right Hon. Englishman spoke first and blazed the way in these recent discoveries concerning the ways of Providence with imperialism."

36. Brooks Adams and Marquis Childs, *America's Economic Supremacy* (New York, 1947), p. 104.

37. Bryan, *Republic or Empire?,* p. 539.

38. Garraty, *Henry Cabot Lodge,* p. 206; Beale, *Theodore Roosevelt,* pp. 72–73.

39. Higginson MSS, Henry Cabot Lodge to Mrs. Thomas Wentworth Higginson, February 8, 1915.

40. Elting E. Morison, ed., *The Letters of Theodore Roosevelt,* Vol. II (Cambridge, Mass., 1951), T. R. to Lala, June 27, 1900, p. 1343.

41. Woodrow Wilson, "The Ideals of America," *Atlantic Monthly,* XC (December 1902), p. 730; Arthur Link, *Wilson: the Road to the White House* (Princeton, 1947), pp. 27–28. Significantly Wilson shared the "southern view of race relations." His promise to do the Negro "justice" was kept with the establishment of "Jim Crow" in federal employment. Arthur Link, *Wilson: the New Freedom* (Princeton, 1956), pp. 245–54.

42. *City and State* (Philadelphia), IV (January 26, 1899); Henry Codman Potter MSS, Synod House, New York, Potter to Franklin Pierce, April 4, 1900.

43. Garraty, *Henry Cabot Lodge,* p. 200, n 3; Morison, ed., *Letters of Theodore Roosevelt,* Vol. II, Roosevelt to Eliot, November 14, 1900, pp. 1415–16; Vol. IV (Cambridge Mass., 1951), Roosevelt to

Eliot, April 4, 1904, p. 768; *Boston Herald,* February 15, 1907. Eliot's sentiments were expressed at a meeting called to aid Berea College of eastern Kentucky.   That Eliot's attitude toward the Negro was not unique at Harvard is indicated in the experience of W. E. B. Du Bois during that time.   See Eric Goldman, *Rendezvous with Destiny* (New York, 1953), pp. 182–83.

44. Morison, ed., *Letters of Theodore Roosevelt,* Vol. IV, Roosevelt to James Ford Rhodes, November 29, 1904, p. 1050.

45. Bryan, *Republic or Empire?,* pp. 276–77; David Starr Jordan, *Imperial Democracy* (New York, 1901), p. 44.   Responsibility for improvement in their lot was also assigned to the Negro by Charles Francis Adams, *"The Solid South" and the Afro-American Race Problem* (Boston, 1908); Goldwin Smith, *Commonwealth or Empire* (New York, 1902), pp. 42–43.

46. Smith, *Commonwealth or Empire,* p. 43.   *Congressional Record,* January 10, 1899, pp. 528–34, contains the speech of Senator William Mason of Illinois which questioned what the United States had to offer as an example to the Philippines: "Shall we send special instructors to teach them how to kill postmasters, their wives and children, if their complexion does not suit the populace? Shall we have illustrated pictures showing the works of the mob in Illinois, North Carolina, and South Carolina?" Despite his questions, Mason voted to annex the Philippines.

47. *Army and Navy Journal,* XL (May 2, 1903); Morison, ed., *Letters of Theodore Roosevelt,* Vol. III (Cambridge, Mass., 1951), Roosevelt to Herman Speck von Sternberg, July 19, 1902; Mowry, *The Era of Theodore Roosevelt,* p. 168; *The Nation,* LXXVI (April 30, 1903), 343.

48. *The Literary Digest,* XXVI (May 9, 1903), 675–76.   *The Outlook,* LXXIV (May 9, 1903), 100, also charged that General Miles was motivated by his aspirations "for the Presidency." *Public Opinion,* XXXIV (May 7, 1903), indicated the report as hearsay evidence—a charge which could have been applied to the well-received Proctor report.   The New York *Times,* April 28, 1903, wondered why Miles advertised for complaints which could only cast reflection upon the institution he represented.   It recalled the "proverb about the manner of bird which fouls its own nest." Garraty, *Henry Cabot Lodge,* p. 210; Morison, ed., *Letters of Theodore Roosevelt,* Vol. III, Roosevelt to Elihu Root, February 18, 1902, pp. 232–33.

49. Guion Griffis Johnson, "The Ideology of White Supremacy, 1876–1910," *Essays in Southern History* (Chapel Hill, N.C., 1949), p. 155; Aguinaldo and Pacis, *A Second Look at America,* p. 16; *The Literary Digest,* XVIII (February 25, 1899), p. 219.

THE MUCKRAKERS:
IN FLOWER AND IN FAILURE

by Louis Filler

ANTIOCH COLLEGE

YELLOW SPRINGS, OHIO

ONLY intellectual monopolists will rejoice in the circumstances which have attended muckraking since the First World War and see it as a "field" for solitary tilling and exploitation. If history is a responsibility as well as a trade and is relevant to our society and its operations, then the citizen who happens to be an historian will wish to consider what muckraking has contributed or failed to contribute to our affairs.

It is difficult to say where he might best look. *Contemporary American History, 1877–1913,* by Charles A. Beard (1914), was an interesting survey and was written for the "large numbers of students" whom its author was constantly meeting, who had "no knowledge of the most elementary facts of American history since the Civil War" (page v). But it found no occasion to mention muckraking, even in connection with the passage of the Pure Food Law. Paul Leland Haworth's *America in Ferment* (1915) was more vibrant with a sense of society in motion and of several of its less orthodox leaders; however, it, too, showed no awareness of muckraking, or its dramatic disappearance.

Harold L. Stearns spoke for the new youth, in his *Liberalism in America: Its Origin, Its Temporary Collapse, Its Future* (1919), and eloquently of the descent of liberalism into pragmatic opportunism. But Stearns and his set had cut loose from the grass roots and lacked the simplest knowledge of the actual workings of reform. Their attitude was more than a matter of knowledge;

it was a matter of will. They were uninterested in reform.[1]
Mark Sullivan, himself one of the old-style liberals, wrote depre-
catingly of muckraking in Volumes II and III of his *Our Times*
(1927, 1930), attempting, confusedly, to distinguish "sensationalism" from the reporting of "facts," in terms which only a partisan
segment of his old co-workers would have accepted.

   The Era of the Muckrakers, by C. C. Regier (1932), a doctoral
thesis, was braver in title than in treatment. With small grasp
and uncertain information, it held muckraking to have been no
more than a "fad"—a thing of a season, rather than of an era.
John Chamberlain's *Farewell to Reform* (1932) walked progressively away from muckraking; by its last page, it had fully established the "failure of reform," at no more expense than of logic,
understanding, facts, and consistency.[2]   Silence became the rule
thereafter.   There were sound and relevant pages in Harold U.
Faulkner's *The Quest for Social Justice, 1898–1914* (1931).   But
even such pages and paragraphs failed to take into account the
fact that the subject was heavy with controversy and that no
reference to muckraking could be truly sound which did not
come to grips with the pertinent pros and cons.[3]

   George Seldes not only kept the muckrakers in mind, but
more or less attempted to build upon them, in his books and
other writings. But Seldes was a publicist, not an historian. It is
more puzzling to determine what the editors of the *Monthly Review* might best be called. They helped distribute David Graham Phillips's *The Treason of the Senate* (the high point of
muckraking), originally published in *Cosmopolitan* during 1906
and reproduced between covers in unappetizing offset in 1953.
Harvey O'Connor's appreciation of Phillips's articles, in the
Monthly Review for October of that year, vaguely but vigorously
equated the Senate of Phillips's time with that of the since late
Joseph R. McCarthy, in terms which served neither history, biography, civil liberties, nor, it may be, enough wide-awake readers
to make any difference.

   No, the muckrakers are not well remembered. Clichés of
accomplishment are, to be sure, still identified with several of
their names.   Tarbell, Steffens, and Baker, of *McClure's* and the

American, and a few others in desultory formation, are still cited as notable in an age of exposé, still credited with generous and desirable civic traits. But others are as regularly condemned for intemperateness or shallowness or sensationalism. This would be true of Thomas W. Lawson and David Graham Phillips and Upton Sinclair. A typical and widely used work distinguishes the muckrakers from the progressive movement which it is said to have helped publicize, and even from the "literature of revolt," "a fictional literature dedicated to advancing the cause of democracy." It credits *McClure's* writers with accuracy and readability, but concludes:

It was inevitable, however, that the muckraking technique should be adopted by publishers and writers of dubious integrity and exploited merely for financial gain. As muckraking turned [*sic*] into yellow journalism around 1906, public interest was at first tremendously stimulated. But soon readers tired of the excitement; and by 1908 the entire muckraking movement was discredited.[4]

This study finds a line of distinction between muckrakers and progressives such as the naked eye cannot perceive, though there were muckrakers who preferred Wilson or Debs to Theodore Roosevelt, in 1912. It distinguishes between muckrakers and the "social justice movement," though there were muckrakers active in every one of its folds. Brand Whitlock, for example, was crusader, mayor, and, not incidentally, novelist, and anything but alone in his many-sidedness. The juxtaposition of muckraking and yellow journalism is patently inadequate, and the date of 1908 patently inaccurate. In 1908, the Ballinger affair had not yet taken place. *Hampton's, Everybody's, Collier's, Success,* the *American,* and a dozen other muckraking magazines were still being distributed to mass audiences. But the purpose of these observations is not to argue a point; it is merely to indicate that the muckrakers have not been well remembered.

The greater number of them have been thoroughly forgotten, the few others who are generally cited serving no particular end. They are mere names—Charles Edward Russell, Norman Hapgood, Samuel Hopkins Adams—or mere titles—*The Story of Life Insurance, The Women Who Toil, People of the Abyss, The*

Color Line. They fill out the paragraphs in textbooks, or add *décor* to analyses of twentieth-century trends. C. P. Connolly, Josiah Flynt, Herbert N. Casson, Frederic U. Adams, John K. Turner, Benjamin B. Hampton are several of many personages who were significant to, or central in, muckraking operations, and whose names never appear in commentary respecting the era.

But this is not the bottom fact of forgetfulness. The muckrakers' works have not survived their heyday. It is not only that they have not been reprinted; they are unread. This is as true of Lincoln Steffens as of Charles Edward Russell. Many of the muckrakers thought of themselves as literary figures as well as students of society and commentators. They have received regard in neither area. (Ray Stannard Baker is curious in this respect in that his David Grayson books continue to sell to the type of reader who is not influenced by official literary criticism.) Finley Peter Dunne would seem to be an exception to the generalization, in that he is frequently quoted, and in a variety of sources. However, a recent, parochial stir of interest in his work, sponsored by the *New Republic,* only revealed that publication's glaring lack of contact with the reality of Dunne and also the enthusiastic incapacity of its readers.[5]

The loss of contact with the detail of muckraking has affected individual and historical perspective. Thus, Edwin Markham was the poet of reform and also the prophet of the child-labor crusade. The numerous references to his most famous poem have only underscored how completely buried are his achievements as both poet and reformer, to say nothing of his long and significant personal odyssey.[6] How does one assess his work? Is it diminished by comparison with that of the socialists of his time? of the politicos? Does it lose stature when placed beside the writings of the revolutionary youth of the 1910s? Or beside permutations of similar elements in the 1920s or after? The fact is, of course, that these nonmuckraking elements have not themselves escaped the unsympathetic judgment of time. A few reform and radical reputations remain, from the ruins of our past decades: La Follette, Eugene V. Debs, Big Bill Haywood, John Reed, and Randolph Bourne are credited with integrity and ac-

complishment.   But whether any of them are better read than
Markham, or *McClure's,* may be questioned.[7]

The reputations of the muckrakers need to be recaptured and
described; but even more, they need to be explained.   For if it
should appear that they represented something real in the American people—something permanent and unavoidable—and reflected
it in accurate and connotative terms, it might be that they have
been too hastily prejudged and insight into our very own times
lost.

Although muckraking suddenly confronted a startled and receptive public, many of its elements were rooted in American attitudes and experiences, extending back to John Peter Zenger's
time or beyond.   Like earlier reformers, the muckrakers were to
blend utopian and sentimental aspirations with hard and immediate concerns.   They were to carry over into their crusade
remnants of every manner of earlier movement of dissent and so
establish a firm continuity with past experience.   Cooperatives,
Negro rights, socialism, humanitarianism, the nationalization
schemes of the Bellamyites, the single tax—these causes and many
others were to figure in the work of the muckrakers.   Nevertheless, their work contained novelties which stirred their readers
and put them into motion.

The muckrakers were not untried or accidentally assembled.
A significant percentage of them were mature people, who had
accumulated experience on newspapers or with magazines.   An
equally significant number were from the farm and the west: although muckrakers worked in the cities, muckraking did *not* derive primarily from urban conditions.   It was a sophisticated con-
tinuation of the old, nineteenth-century revolt which had culminated in Populism.   With progressivism, its other self, it used
"the same ideas travelling in the same direction, with new leaders,
new vitality, and new weapons, against the old forces of privilege
and corruption." [8]   This statement requires qualification.   True,
the muckrakers came to New York trailing romantic memories of
Republican fathers and families which had been self-reliant, patriotic, and religious.   (Upton Sinclair was the scion of a broken
Southern family; and, indeed, the South's relationship to muck-

raking and progressivism has long wanted individual and inten-
sive treatment.)   They left regions which were not reconciled to
Bryan's defeat.   But their vision was broader than that of their
Populist predecessors.   Writers like Hamlin Garland who could
not progress beyond its horizons would be thrust aside by the
muckrakers.   They had grown up in an untidy and even desperate land: an America of new political entities, of new industry,
immigrations, and cities.   They had little time for nostalgic recollections of an allegedly golden age of peace and plenty.   The
major muckrakers could not afford the naive anti-Semitism of the
Populists; on the contrary, their experience made them enthusiastic partisans of their newer compatriots.   Their America needed
many things, but above all, it needed communication.   The
frontier had been closed with unprecedented rapidity, and the
barest minimum of telegraph wires and roads had not yet been
completed.   The multiplying factories and company towns increasingly employed hands rather than people.   The cities bur-
geoned with neighborhoods which literally could not speak English.

The need for communication—of problems, aims, and simple
circumstances—was central to the needs of post-Civil War America.
It was not satisfied in the established newspapers and magazines.
These, curiously enough, also upheld the values of the Populists,
favoring free enterprise and opportunity; unlike the Populists,
they refused to recognize factors which had narrowed both beyond endurance.   John Hay, once of Indiana and author of *Pike
County Ballads,* was of the New York *Tribune* before he ascended
to glory, and also the bitter antilabor author of *The Bread-Win-
ners.*   Charles A. Dana, late secretary of Brook Farm, was now
the savagely cynical editor of the New York *Sun,* itself once of the
pre-War "penny press" and responsive to its readers' interests.
Thomas Nast, who exposed the Tweed Ring, also pelted Horace
Greeley ruthlessly with editorial mud, in the interests of Grant's
second candidacy.   E. L. Godkin, of the *Nation,* was a lucid and
determined liberal, whose liberalism, however, tolerated neither
radicals nor Grangers.

The future muckrakers, following obscure democratic traces,

fell in with the new popular newspapers and magazines, where they could best observe the disorder of post-Civil War American life, and report it without compunction, as news. The newspapers of the 1890s, and even before, are the best sources for pre-muckraking material, and are yet to be fully and intelligibly examined.

The journalism of the future muckrakers especially helps to explain the novel talents which were to give them so much influence over their readers. Steffens on the New York *Post*, that newspaperman's newspaper, experimented freely with ideas and features. He sought writers, not journalists. He encouraged statements of reality rather than conventional formulations. In effect, he looked outward to his reader rather than attempting to foist a preconceived view of affairs upon him. Charles Edward Russell's staff on the New York *World* avoided neither horror nor confusion, and it treated rich and poor as warranting equal attention. *World* writers learned what subjects, details, and choice of words arrested the general reader; as David Graham Phillips put it, in an ill-used novel:

[Howard] saw that his success had been to a great extent a happy accident; that to repeat it, to improve upon it he must study life, study the art of expression. . . . He must work at style, enlarge his vocabulary, learn the use of words, the effect of varying combinations of words both as to sound and as to meaning. "I must learn to write for the people," he thought, "and that means to write the most difficult of all styles." [9]

But as important as newspaper experience were the points of view which the nascent crusaders—working in a hectic milieu of free enterprise and experiment—developed in the course of their work. Unconsciously, they were profiting from a democratic revolution in journalism. For as the new popular press mushroomed in response to mass demand, so new magazines, for the first time in American history seeking popularity in the broad sense, began to find solid footing and to develop programs for common consumption. It needs to be kept in mind that the purpose of *Munsey's, McClure's, Collier's*—those individualistic concerns—was *not* to produce low-grade reading for the lower classes; it was to produce quality magazines at cheaper prices and for a wider audience than the established magazines recognized. And who could produce articles from which the general reader could derive information and ideas having something to do with him and his actual affairs and thus justifying his serious expenditure of perhaps twenty or more cents? Not the Civil War generals who filled *Century* with their memoirs, not the government bureaucrats, the cultural dilettantes, travelers, clubmen, and dreamers whose stories and articles filled *The Forum, Poet-Lore, Scribner's,* and many another publication. The newspapermen who had tramped the streets, reported catastrophes, interviews, elections skullduggery, stock-market developments, building projects, and other happenings in the workaday world, who had sought human interest stories in obscure corners of the city, were prepared to formulate pieces which were up-to-date, and concerned with living American themes and operations. The new magazines were *not* reform magazines; they were money-making ventures. They were purchased because they gave due regard to the human vocabulary of contemporary affairs. In succeeding, the magazine entrepreneurs forged a weapon of communication, a vehicle for whatever purposes their public might prefer.

From what point of view did the popular reporter write? The Populist would hardly have recognized it. It seemed, essentially, a disenchanted viewpoint. Too much had happened in the Populist's lifetime to leave his successor many illusions. The Darwinian hypothesis compromised much that he had learned at home. His own family troubles—with weather, railroads, monopolistic concerns—infringed upon his optimism. Newspaper work revealed too much that was seamy and uncontrollable. A comparison between Theodore Dreiser and David Graham Phillips is revealing and merits full examination, on its own merits, as well as to neutralize the effects of remarkably misdirected commentary available in the field.[10] That both men came from Indiana is among the minor facts requiring mention. Dreiser was born into a family whose values had been badly frayed by economic and social circumstances and whose relationships had deteriorated. Phillips was the son of a small-town banker, surrounded with loving family and security.   Both Dreiser and Phillips entered journalism.   Dreiser drifted into it, in the sad, dissatisfied way which would be his trademark.   Phillips, out of Princeton, plunged into it, determined to learn the facts of American life.   Both young men were insecure, pessimistic, appalled by the indifference and cruelty which their journalistic experiences repeatedly revealed and which Herbert Spencer's philosophy underscored.   Early in the 1890s, Phillips managed to write a number of articles and sketches for *Harper's Weekly*.   In view of the robust optimism, the indomitable will toward happiness and success which his later fiction and muckraking displayed, his 1890s efforts are strikingly depressed and languid in tone.   Phillips was a Bryan Democrat in 1896, but the fiction to which he subscribed was influenced by Zola and naturalistic determinism.   Dreiser, oddly enough, had not read Zola, when he began to evolve his somber tales.   But he persisted in writing them in the face of the burst of energy and anticipation which muckraking released and for which he had no enthusiasm.[11]

Phillips, on his side, threw over his pessimism and abandoned determinism, to preach with renewed faith the doctrine that the individual counted, that he could make his presence felt, and that society could progress:

The "great battle" was on—the battle he had in his younger days looked forward to and longed for—the battle against Privilege and for a "restoration of government by the people."   The candidates were nominated, the platforms put forward and the issue squarely joined.[12]

One needs to recall—as undiscriminating critics have not—that this is from Phillips's first book, published before muckraking went into effect, written hastily while its author carried his daily burden of newspaper and editorial work, to say nothing of his personal conflicts.   It is a raw production, valuable for many purposes, but at the other extreme from Phillips's finished work. The present passage says something about the frame of mind which the public now assumed, in the satisfaction it took in muckraking.   Was it an unrealistic perspective, conducive to the production of shallow writings?   The present author has elsewhere added up some of the notable works written during the reform period, in social criticism, description of contemporary processes, human and individual documentation, fiction, verse, and other fields.   It seems more important, here, to consider the effectiveness of muckraking which might, or might not, entitle it to attention, and also to ask what qualities defined or limited it, in its own time or after.

The work which the muckrakers did can only be appreciated when seen beside the fact that there were earnest, principled, determined, and powerful forces which freely opposed democracy, in the pre-First World War period.   The articles, books, and other publications frankly and aggressively opposing democratic processes are too numerous, too variegated to indicate.   A major point of concern was the immigrant, who appeared to them slave-minded, unable to understand Anglo-Saxon freedom, prone to radicalism, unionism, and general disorder.   An added impediment to the maintenance of democratic forms and considerations was the atomization of American society.   True, the key elements of monopoly and law operated freely and in harmony in defense of their interest, using, among other ingredients of social control, strikebreakers, the black list, and the antistrike injunction.   But more needful social elements were not united, and were often opposed, on the meaning of civil liberties, the relation of law to economic plight, and the rights of minority groups.   It is an old paradox that "everybody" opposed trusts and that they nevertheless continued to grow; they continued to grow during the reform era.

Was this a failure of reform?   Obviously, the reformers were not agreed on what constituted proper curbs on large business consolidations.   The purpose of their writings, however, was not so much catharsis as it was enlightenment: they were providing their public with information—in all its connotative complexity— necessary to determining its wants.   The public's decisions were often disappointing.   In Upton Sinclair's famous phrase, *The Jungle* had aimed for the public heart and hit it in the stomach. But the public's horrified response to the reality of unclean food is an impressive example of the relationship, in the era of reform, between ideas and action, between writers and the general public.

That public did more than feel a guilty involvement in the ugly and antisocial operations which disfigured city and state political organizations, permitting organized crime, thievery by corporations, fraud by insurance combines, inhumanity by real estate interests, and a long series of exploitative devices by employers large and small.   The public demanded and received action in the ousting of numerous bosses and political machines, in the enactment of a quite endless number of laws and ordinances, from the famous Pure Food Law of 1906 to laws providing for safety measures and devices in public and private places.

All this did not destroy the corporations.   It did not even regulate them.   But it surrounded them with a network of laws which permanently established their responsibility to the public in every field, and were an earnest promise of further intervention whenever occasion might require.   In rousing common citizens to their own interests and duties, the muckraker reaffirmed the reality of democracy, despite giant business and the mazes of modern social organization; and by giving individuals a stake in affairs which did not concern them directly, he gave them a sense of national responsibility which unified and dignified them, at the expense of the blatant "elitists" who presumed to direct their thinking and activities for them.

It has sometimes been observed that the muckraker seemed to put as high a premium upon the process of exposure as upon the subject being exposed; and it has been concluded that he inadequately appreciated the need to deal competently with particular social problems.   Aside from the high competence of muckrakers and reformers in their several fields of inquiry, this criticism misses the mechanism of muckraking, which assumed that nothing could be done of value, permanent or otherwise, which did not start with a regard for freedom of inquiry, freedom of communication, and an impartial control of all elements of society.   It is often assumed that muckraking was easy sport.   Forgotten is the fact that the leading muckrakers were always in danger of violence, vilification, deliberate plots for character assassination; we will shortly note the classic case of successful libel: a deed of darkness perpetrated in open daylight.   This fact assured the highest responsibility of action on the part of the muckrakers. At the very least, they were liable to ruinous law suits; it is a sensational aspect of the era that they were so rarely required to justify themselves in court.[13]

Thus, it was not alone giant thefts, grossly unsanitary methods of manufacture, and corrupt administration of public responsibilities which characterized muckraking, though these were sufficiently noteworthy. It was *the process of social control* which the muckrakers instituted which was a major threat to private interests, a major democratic landmark. This helps explain why later journalistic sensations of the postmuckraking era could seem to be different from those of the tabloid stripe, could look like the original article, and yet lack its original impact and significance. *Collier's* in the 1920s ran numerous series in what seemed to its editors the old tradition, "exposing," for example, the evils of venereal disease. Norman Hapgood, once again an editor in the 1920s, took satisfaction in his exposé of the Ku Klux Klan in *Hearst's International Magazine*. And so many other editors and publications, old and new. But even the still-active editors felt that something had changed since the old days. Their magazines no longer served strategic purposes. They no longer appealed to a cohesive audience, in control of national issues, and jealous of civil liberties. It suffices to recall the extirpation of minority opinion during the First World War, the numerous indignities, and worse, inflicted upon minority groups, and the long, daylight ordeal of Sacco and Vanzetti to realize that muckraking had lost some basic strength and influence.

But in 1910, muckraking still looked down upon a democracy apparently based foursquare on constitutional privileges and heading toward social democracy. With the Ballinger affair behind it—proving that no individual was too insignificant to be protected against political and economic powers—it seemed prepared to institutionalize muckraking and enter upon an era of unexampled promise. As Phillips wrote only a few years before, in words which are surely more tragic than absurd:

Let us read the past aright. Its departed civilizations are not a gloomy warning, but a bright promise. If limited intelligence in a small class produced such gleams of glory in the black sky of history, what a day must now be dawning! [14]

What had the muckrakers not taken into account? We might, at least, attempt not to let their confusions blind us. The domestic achievements of the first Wilson administration are often noticed. It is less often noticed that the period during which Taft was President had also been notable for a long list of legislative accomplishments. The knowing reader understands immediately that many of these achievements had no particular connection with Taft or his official party. It should be evident that legislative triumphs have no necessary connection with attendant administrations. To that extent the muckrakers were correct to concentrate upon men and issues rather than upon theories of bureaucracy. But Herbert Croly was also right, in his famous storehouse of revaluations, when he wrote in scorn of reformers to whom "reform means at bottom no more than moral and political purification." [12] This admirer of Mark Hanna was interested in what he conceived to be a larger program, such as Theodore Roosevelt would, presumably, be able to furnish: a program for the elite, of government intervention wherever required, and, for the less consequential classes, popular unity built around a national ideal.

It is little short of amazing how little thought the muckrakers gave to administrative questions on the national level. They appear to have thought it poor form to examine the personnel with whom the President pleased to surround himself. The People's Lobby which they instituted in 1906 was instrumental in the notable fight against Speaker Cannon of the House of Representatives, but it operated entirely from the outside of government. The muckrakers do not appear to have expected their President to surround himself with Progressives. They accepted Taft as his successor with extraordinary good grace. Their most glaring lack was in the field of foreign affairs. Not that, as a group, they were aggressive nationalists, let alone imperialists. Such muckrakers as Charles Edward Russell were international-minded and antiimperialist in sentiment. But, as a group, they gave too little attention to foreign affairs at all and permitted Roosevelt and

Taft to act as they pleased in these matters, and with associates who were bureaucrats and elitists, and even social butterflies, almost to the last man.

In such of their attitudes, the muckrakers, of course, reflected the indifference of the average man to intricate governmental affairs. That individual had developed a high sensitivity to his own woes and dangers. He had relatively little attention to spare for foreigners or for the mechanisms which at home controlled his existence. By 1910, he was satisfied that the awkward old systems of boss rule had been overthrown, and that the old, heavy-handed operations of trusts were things of the past. Journalists and reformers appeared to be competing for his attention; he needed no more than to choose between them.

No analysis of the precipitous decline of muckraking would be complete which did not take in the psychological aspect of the public's role. But nothing can be shallower than to believe that the public "tired" of muckraking. On the contrary, it assumed that popular magazines, as well as other vehicles of communication, were continuing to deal with essentials in public affairs. It assumed that the victories of free speech and inquiry were established. It failed to become concerned when some of the more aggressive magazines issued warning signals that they were under attack, or to give more than passing attention to the phenomenon of magazines closing down despite subscription lists in the hundreds of thousands. It remained for John Reed, a proud young man with no regard for grass-roots politics or values, and with his coterie's malicious contempt for muckraking, to observe sardonically:

> A silly tale I've heard
> That round the town is flying
> That every monthly organ
> Is owned by J. P. Morgan.
> Now isn't that absurd?
> Somebody must be lying.[16]

Symbolic of this critical period was the overthrowing of La Follette as leader of the Progressive movement, by methods which have not yet been adequately examined. Suffice it here that on the occasion of his well-known speech, significantly to the Periodical Publishers Association, on February 2, 1912, La Follette was maligned from coast to coast.   It was also held that he had suffered a nervous breakdown and thus become unavailable for the Presidential nomination.   It is inconceivable that such an attack could have been maintained successfully two short years before.   The demand for clarification would have been such as to drive La Follette's traducers under cover.   In this instance, no such demand arose.   Theodore Roosevelt, with his supporters led by millionaires Frank A. Munsey and George W. Perkins, took over the Progressive party and put it on what seemed to them a more practical basis.   It was now an organization of the political elite.

As the popular magazines settled down into soft entertainment agencies, uncritical of society's leaders, undemanding of their readers, new organs were founded which did not seek mass circulation and which concentrated upon programs rather than popular sentiment.   *The Masses* did not speak, of course, to the masses, but to a relatively tiny, if select, audience.   Croly's *New Republic* was dependent upon private funds.   Nevertheless, such publications boasted of intellectual status and influence and did not mourn the passing of the muckrakers.

The first Woodrow Wilson administration seemed to justify their choice of exclusiveness, rather than grass-roots content.   It moved smoothly and intelligently.   If anything, Wilson was more aggressive than Roosevelt had been in fulfilling his tariff, currency, agricultural, and other promises.   Even so, the legislative program of what one might call the Democratic and Republican Progressive alliance, from 1913 to 1916, was something less world-shaking, in retrospect, than what was unleashed in Europe during that same period.   A Clayton Anti-Trust Act which did not shackle trusts, a free trade tariff which, thanks to the European war, among other factors, did not initiate free trade, a Federal Reserve System which proved its metal in 1929, and a Federal Trade Commission which firmly protected businesses which could stand on their own feet—these were harbingers of expanded government responsibilities but hardly justified the eloquence of the 1912 campaign.

The truth is that Progressivism had become an efficiency

movement, somewhat comparable, on the side of politics, to the Taylorization movement in industry which was sweeping out old technological and organizational modes from business plants, without necessarily raising concomitant social and economic relations to a more democratic and otherwise valid level.

The harshest thing, then, that one can say of those who succeeded the muckrakers—those who followed Croly's shining lights of the *New Republic*—was not that they were manipulators who planned to dominate affairs from raised platforms. The harshest thing that can be said of them is that they were ineffective: they were insects on the great wheel of events, who persuaded themselves that they were turning it. That Croly and his friends should have scorned the muckrakers and popular reformers as naive and with an inadequate program would be amusing, if it were not so tragic in the light of Croly's own impotence during the First World War and the fight for the League of Nations.

All students of the time are acquainted with Wilson's strange and somber prophecy, when he decided for war, that it would stop thought in this country, promote hysteria, and breed popular evils of antidemocratic action. This was the nation for which both the Creel Committee on Public Information, composed largely of ex-muckrakers, and, on a more seemly intellectual level, the Croly elitists, administered the philosophical side of the war. It is curious that the crusade to save democracy abroad should have had, as a concomitant, so much that was less than democratic back home. The Croly intellectuals were, of course, opposed to lynchings, tar-and-feathering parties, and the gentle game which young girls played of pinning white feathers on young men not wearing uniforms. But Croly and his friends had no means for controlling these popular manifestations of patriotism—a patriotism which they had themselves solicited. And their high-level social thinking had less and less relationship to it. In their worries and dissatisfaction with the great crusade we may find the shadow of what would finally become a characteristic of elements of their following: a plaintive and resentful fear of the numerous people who did not read liberal publications and an untiring search for formulas which would curb their intemperate whims.

In the 1920s, it was possible for Croly liberals to remain visible among the forces of the left and the forces of the right which were building at home and abroad.   Croly liberalism, separating right from wrong, good from bad, efficiency from inefficiency, seemed to express a natural aristocracy of leadership.   It carried the promise of power.   To that extent, it was still possible for it to denigrate the old muckraking technique as naive and irrelevant, since it was alleged to have been bemused by old, outmoded American ideals and experiences, and to be incapable of coping with the pragmatic realities of post-First World War affairs.   In the 1930s, however, it began to appear that liberalism might itself be cashiered as irrelevant and that a new principle of control over public action and opinion might be developed out of the compulsive and immediate needs of the insecure masses.   But these needs turned out to be more complex than the calculations of doctrinaire intellectuals of any persuasion could predict.   The New Deal was a pragmatic patchwork of contradictory programs. It could hardly be anything else, since it was a mere response to apparent needs, rather than to formulated experiences or philosophies, and could be changed and even discarded at will.   There was no public controversy when Dr. Win the War was substituted for Dr. New Deal: no explanation of the points on which they differed.

Public policy, like public need, was not formulated in Washington (to say no more of the liberal publications), but estimated by balancing decisive action by foreign governments against public opinion at home.   This, public opinion polls were cleverly learning to assay.   They could not explain it.   The dream of the elitists of forging policy which the manipulated masses would have to accept had been reduced to a process of trying to read its wants and gain its suffrage by promising to act upon them.

This was obviously no policy at all, and such works as Samuel Lubell's *The Future of American Politics* (1952) were efforts to advance beyond mere guesses and promises: to examine the voter's actual purposes and characteristics and to trace the history of his choices.   Although this was a scientific approach, it did not always produce scientific results.   The "usable past" was not so easy to find or use.   In addition, it did not answer the question of one's convictions.   As Grover Cleveland had asked, "What is the use of being elected or reëlected, unless you stand for something?" [17]   It was a refreshing question, and not indefinitely avoidable.

The intelligence able and willing to meet the question might wish to survey the past decades with a less peremptory attitude toward the experiences they were able to offer.   And, among other experiences, it might wish to come to grips with those of the muckrakers.   The key difficulty with the intellectuals of liberal movements of the twentieth century since the days of the muckrakers had been that they had cut themselves off from grass-roots relationships and avoided truly pragmatic alliances and understandings.   They had dealt in verbalisms.   They had taken on modern problems of industry and social relations, in a context of Marxism, Freudism, and other economic and human disciplines, at the expense of direct contact with the people whom they were presuming to analyze and lead.   The intellectuals of the 1910s did not supplement muckraking methods and projects with their own insights; they treated them with contempt.   The journalists, commentators, analysts of succeeding decades deepened and developed this easy and catastrophic trait.   It was, of course, no mere error of judgment.   It reflected an effort to avoid parochialism, an effort to meet the challenge of mass production and international anarchy with living programs of social study and techniques of social control.   But in taking the larger social setting into its purview, the up-to-date, up-to-the-minute commentator lost control of his domestic circumstances.   His choice was not really between New Deal experimentation on a high governmental level, and Progressive intimacy with traditional American ideals and expectations.   Both were necessary to a program with reasonable possibilities for fulfillment.   If the flowering of muckraking had been an American triumph, its failure had been an American setback.   The problem was not to accept or reject muckraking, but to understand it; and first, to recapture its reality.

NOTES

1. A friend of Randolph Bourne, leader of the "younger generation," read the biography of him by the present writer and was disturbed by a criticism of Bourne based on his disregard of such controversies as that over Secretary of the Interior Richard A. Ballinger: "Why should Randolph have been interested in it?" The present writer explained that Bourne had claimed to be concerned for American democracy and that the Ballinger affair had involved responsible handling of public resources, the rights of little people in government, free speech, the functions of muckraking, and other basic problems in democracy. Bourne's friend interrupted to ask what the muckrakers had accomplished. The writer extemporized some of their achievements: a conservation policy, antitrust legislation, control over insurance companies and "money trusts," the overthrow of outmoded municipal systems, laws governing the preparation of food and patent medicines, housing, working conditions, railroads. "You win," said Bourne's friend; "when I was a young man, I didn't care anything about my country."

2. Louis Filler, "John Chamberlain and American Liberalism," *Colorado Quarterly,* VI (Autumn, 1957), 200–11.

3. This is particularly true of Frank Luther Mott's *A History of American Magazines, 1885–1905* (Boston, 1957), IV, 207–9 and *passim,* which merits a footnote of its own. Although a work of undoubted industry, developing numerous materials of value to the student, it contains no substantial concept of muckraking, lacks understanding of the milieu in which it flourished, and is totally devoid of a sense of controversy.

4. Arthur S. Link, *American Epoch* (New York, 1955), p. 76.

5. William Esty, "The Poised Shillelagh," *New Republic,* CXXXV (October 1, 1956), 17–18; for readers's letters, *ibid.,* CXXXV (October 15, 1956), 31. For an effort to use the "Mr. Dooley" technique in a modern setting, see "Dooley Redivivus," *ibid., CXXXVI* (April 29, 1957), 6.

6. Louis Filler, *The Secret Life of Edwin Markham,* is in preparation for publication by the Antioch Press, Yellow Springs, Ohio.

7. Richard Hofstadter, *The Age of Reform* (New York, 1955), holds the muckraker to have been central to pre-Wilsonian progressivism: "To an extraordinary degree the work of the Progressive movement rested upon its journalism" (p. 185). However, its achievement is also held to have been more cathartic than substantial (p. 212). The inference would appear to be that the muckrakers served a purpose in their own time. This does not contradict the statement that they serve no purpose today. The sobering fact is that there are few

enough examples of past twentieth-century American writings which are treated as serviceable today.

8. Russel B. Nye, *Midwestern Progressive Politics* (East Lansing, Mich., 1951), p. 196. See, also, Filler, "East and Middle West: Concepts of Liberalism during the Late Nineteenth Century," *American Journal of Economics and Sociology,* XI (January, 1952), 180 ff.

9. John Graham [pseud.], *The Great God Success* (New York, 1901), pp. 26–27.

10. The latest and most remarkable, by far, being Kenneth S. Lynn, *The Dream of Success* (Boston, 1955); see Filler, "Dreamers, and the American Dream," *Southwest Review,* XL (Autumn, 1955), 359–63.

11. Foster Rhea Dulles, *Twentieth Century America* (Boston, 1945), p. 67, misreads Dreiser's *The Titan* and *The Financier* as "noveliz[ing] the muckrakers' exposures of financial buccaneering." Dreiser's vision, however, was not that of the reformer but of the pessimist. If anything, Dreiser identified himself with his titan, plagued by compulsions and mocked by life.

12. Graham, *The Great God Success,* 286–87.

13. One case, which went against *McClure's,* is notable simply because of its rarity; see Ray Stannard Baker, *American Chronicle* (New York, 1945), pp. 207, 211–12.

14. David Graham Phillips, *The Reign of Gilt* (New York, 1905), p. 295.

15. Herbert Croly, *The Promise of American Life* (New York, 1909), p. 145.

16. Granville Hicks, *John Reed* (New York, 1936), p. 89.

17. Allan Nevins, *Grover Cleveland: a Study in Courage* (New York, 1933), p. 377.

A CYCLE OF REVISIONISM
BETWEEN TWO WARS

by Harry W. Baehr
NEW YORK HERALD TRIBUNE

THE TELESCOPING of history during the past generation has tele-
scoped the cycles of historiography as well.   After five centuries,
it is quite possible to attack the Tudor version of the reign of
Richard III without anticipating any attempt to restore the jun-
ior branch of the House of York upon the British throne and
thus test the validity of the revised concept.   But those who, in
the 1920s, controverted the orthodox thesis of America's entry
into the First World War found their ideas written into legislation in the 1930s and battered by the guns of the 1940s.   For, to
a considerable extent, the argument over that event passed out of
the hands of the professional historians at an early stage.   It was
taken up by publicists, politicians and the public at large; conclusions were debated with emotion and written into statutes.   And
the interpretation of the existing body of facts on the subject de-
pended far less upon an academic consensus than on the state of
the world.   The Second World War shed a lurid new light on
the First World War; it revised the revisionists.

The official statement of American objectives in the First
World War was given by President Woodrow Wilson, addressing
a joint session of Congress on April 2, 1917, to "advise that the
Congress declare the recent course of the Imperial German Government to be in fact nothing less than war against the Government and people of the United States."

The hard core of President Wilson's war message was the use
of German submarines against merchant shipping; their violation

of the time-tested methods of search and seizure in maritime warfare; the resulting loss of American ships and citizens in spite of Washington's warning that Germany would be held to a "strict accountability" for such acts.

The President also listed other offenses by the German government: espionage, intrigue, and attempts "to stir up enemies against us at our very doors." The last referred, of course, to the Zimmerman Note, the German proposal that in case of war between the United States and Germany, Mexico would be invited to regain its lost provinces north of the Rio Grande, possibly in conjunction with Japan.

Mr. Wilson also went beyond these concrete acts to assert that the object of the United States was "to vindicate the principles of peace and justice in the life of the world as against selfish and autocratic power . . . to fight thus for the ultimate peace of the world. . . . The world must be made safe for democracy." [1]

This mixture of specific and general causes of war was delivered against a background in which Americans—many of them, at least—had come to believe that Germany had launched a war of conquest, had trampled on neutral Belgium, committing many atrocities in the process, and thus represented a moral outrage and a physical threat to the United States. There was much emotionalism behind these beliefs and a tolerance of many charges against Germany that were to seem fantastic at a later time. But Germany had declared war on Russia and France, had invaded Belgium, had destroyed much of Louvain because of alleged civilian resistance, had initiated gas warfare and unrestricted submarine warfare.

Nevertheless, the official and popular arguments for America's declaration of war did not go unchallenged at the time. Most of the arguments that were to be made by later historians were at least adumbrated in the speeches of those Senators and Representatives (six of the former; fifty of the latter) who voted against the war resolution. Senator George W. Norris, of Nebraska, asserted: "We are going into war on the command of gold." He laid the blame for American hostility to Germany at the door of "the great combination of wealth that has a direct financial interest in our participation in the war. We have loaned many hundreds of millions of dollars to the Allies in this controversy."

Senator Robert La Follette, of Wisconsin, based his opposition to war chiefly on the contention that the United States had "assumed and acted on the policy that it could enforce to the very letter of the law the principles of international law against one belligerent and relax them as to the other." In bowing to British infractions of the rules of maritime warfare, including the declaration of the North Sea as a zone of war, the extension of contraband lists to include foodstuffs, interference with mails, and the like, Washington had been, in Mr. La Follette's view, unneutral and had lost "the rights that go with strict and absolute neutrality." He complained that: "It has pleased those who have been conducting this campaign through the press to make a jumble of the issue until the public sees nothing, thinks of nothing but the wrongs committed by the German submarines, and hears nothing, knows nothing of the wrongdoing of England that forced Germany to take the course she has taken or submit to the unlawful starving of her civilian population."

With the origins of the war, the Wisconsin Senator alleged, the United States had no concern. He rejected the assumption of Germany's unique responsibility for the struggle. "For my own part, I believe that this war, like nearly all others, originated in the selfish ambition and cruel greed of a comparatively few men in each government." [2]

In President Wilson's speech and the replies of the dissident Senators lies the crux of subsequent controversy. Either the United States was driven by German disregard of neutral maritime rights into a war between autocracy and democracy from which lasting peace might be secured; or financial involvement with the Entente, unneutral conduct favoring the Allies and an active propaganda which confused the issues led the United States to take part in a quarrel of obscure European origins in which no vital American interest was at stake.

It is a curious fact that all the subsequent studies by historians, Congressional investigators, and publicists, although they adduced an enormous amount of data, have done little to alter the main outlines of this antithesis, as it was presented in the early days of April, 1917. Except on two points—the origins of war in Europe and the peace objectives of the Entente—there have been few revelations of any real importance. It is the subsequent course of events that has caused the major changes in American attitudes toward the First World War.

One may regard the writings on the war of such men as John S. Bassett and John B. McMaster, which appeared between 1918 and 1920, as lacking perspective and accurate detail on the thoughts and acts of the principal figures in the war period.[3] But whether one agrees with their adherence to Wilsonian orthodoxy or prefers the revisionism of Charles C. Tansill's *America Goes to War* (Boston, 1938), will depend less upon the facts presented in each than upon the way those facts are appraised in the light of the Second World War.

The first orthodox tenet of the First World War to come under critical scrutiny was its European origins. This process was fostered by the great outpouring of diplomatic documents as the revolutionary governments of Germany, Austria, and Russia ransacked their archives to prove the errors—or crimes—of their predecessors. It was accelerated by the fact that the Treaty of Versailles had put a price tag on the Allied theory of Germany's sole responsibility—a tag variously estimated at between twenty and two hundred billion dollars.

Article 231 of the treaty read:

The Allied and Associated Governments affirm and Germany accepts the responsibility of Germany and her allies for causing all the loss and damage to which the Allied and Associated Governments and their nationals have been subjected as a consequence of the war imposed upon them by the aggression of Germany and her allies.

It has been disputed whether the *Schmachparagraphen,* as the Germans called them, really were intended as an admission of moral guilt or of specifically economic responsibility for reparations. Either way, the Germans resisted them strenuously, and those among the Allies who either had held aloof from the emotionalism of wartime, or repented it, were prompt to use the emerging documentation of the war's multiple causation as the basis of the revisionist school.

Among the first as well as the soundest of the American revisionists was Sidney B. Fay. He began with some articles in the *American Historical Review* in 1920 and 1921—notably attacking the legend of the "Potsdam Conference" of July 5, 1914, at which the American Ambassador to Turkey, Henry Morgenthau, alleged on the authority of his German opposite number, Baron von Wangenheim, that the war was plotted.[4]

The Fay articles started an avalanche of revisionist studies and claims. Harry Elmer Barnes, perhaps the most passionate and articulate of the school, wrote of himself that "he was actually first awakened from his 'dogmatic slumbers' by Professor Fay's articles in the summer of 1920. Professor Fay's demolition of the myth of the Potsdam Conference was a shock almost equivalent to the loss of Santa Claus in his youth." [5]

Barnes promptly drew on the work of Fay, as well as of such European revisionists as Pierre Renouvin, G. P. Gooch, and Max Montgelas for his *The Genesis of the World War,* which appeared in 1926. It turned the orthodox thesis on its head, ascribing the chief responsibility to Russia, France, Serbia, and Austria, and putting Germany with England at the bottom of the list.

Fay produced a more scholarly and temperate pair of volumes, *The Origins of the World War,* in 1928, which avoided a simple catalogue of offenders against the peace; it by no means exonerated Germany and asserted that "Austria was more responsible for the immediate origins of the war than any other power." But it did bear down hard on Russia's general mobilization as the factor which "precipitated the final catastrophe, causing Germany to mobilize and declare war." In another edition, a year later, Fay took an even more severe view of Russia's responsibility in making a European war inevitable.[6]

The revisionist trend was arrested to some extent by Bernadotte E. Schmitt's *The Coming of the War, 1914* (New York, 1930). It placed the chief guilt on Germany, blamed Austria severely, and regarded the Russian mobilization as inevitable in the light of the Austrian stand.[7]   The revisionists were annoyed, but in one sense their cause had been won.   Regardless of where the chief blame lay, there had been ample demonstration of diffused responsibility for the war's origins.   This made Americans far more critical of their own immersion in the struggle.

The first full-dress attempt to revise the Wilsonian theory of American participation came with C. Hartley Grattan's *Why We Fought* (New York, 1929).   It presented in documented form essentially the arguments that had been made by Senators Norris and La Follette on April 2, 1917.

Grattan was able to use the work of the revisionists on the origins of the war: the knowledge of the secret Entente treaties for dividing the spoils of victory; the published papers and memoirs of such key figures as Woodrow Wilson, J. von Bernstorff, Theobald von Bethmann-Hollweg, Cecil Spring-Rice, Sir Edward Grey, Colonel E. M. House, Franklin K. Lane, D. H. Houston, Walter Hines Page, Theodore Roosevelt, Alfred von Tirpitz, and Brand Whitlock.   He also had the benefit of Harold D. Lasswell's pioneer study in propaganda, *Propaganda Techniques in the World War* (New York, 1927).

The result of the postwar revelations and scrutiny was to heighten the impression of a predisposition among American statesmen to favor the Entente cause, to demonstrate that Allied propaganda had, in fact, been far more effective than the German, and to show that the blacks and whites of wartime had been shot through with a considerable admixture of grey.

But the groundwork for such "blame-mingling"—to use a phrase which the strongly pro-Ally New York *Tribune* employed to characterize this process—had really been laid by disillusionment with results of the war.   Submarine commerce raiding, that "cruel and unmanly business," as Wilson termed it, was accepted as a technique of warfare.   Except for the limitation on capital ships set by the Washington treaty, and on sea and land forces imposed on the defeated nations, the burden of armaments remained heavy.   The world had not been made safe for democracy; there was a Communist dictatorship in Russia and a Fascist counterpart in Italy.   The victorious powers were at odds over war debts, over reparations, over colonies—even when these were termed "mandates." The United States Senate had rejected the Versailles treaty system, including Wilson's League of Nations, and had made separate peace treaties with the late enemy countries. It seemed clear that the war had not produced, for the United States, the positive results at which Wilson aimed. Whether the avoidance of the effect of a German victory on the world balance of power was worth the cost of American intervention was being increasingly questioned.

The questioning was sharpened and accelerated as America slipped from the prosperity of the 1920s to the grim depression of the 1930s. Tumbling stock markets, lengthening lines of unemployed, apple-sellers on the streets and "bonus marchers" in Washington brought home the economic effect of the world catastrophe "in all its *cui bono*" as Hurree Chunder Mookerjee might have said. Economic nationalism and political isolationism marked the initial phase of the New Deal which Franklin D. Roosevelt proclaimed in 1933.

One aspect of the world's preoccupation with economic questions after 1929 was an intensified interest in the influence of the trade in arms upon peace. There was a pronounced Marxist strain in this, as in so many of the other phenomena of the 1930s. In 1929 Americans were mildly shocked when it was charged that the activities of William B. Shearer as a lobbyist for shipbuilding firms had "wrecked" the Geneva naval disarmament talks in 1927. But in the ensuing years there was a spate of books denouncing private trade in arms as an instrument to promote wars. Characteristic were *Merchants of Death*, by H. C. Engelbrecht and F. C. Hanighen (New York, 1934) and George Seldes's *Iron, Blood and Profits* (New York, 1934).

In the same year, a Senate committee headed by Senator Gerald P. Nye began its long investigation into the arms traffic, an investigation which by the beginning of 1936 was to turn to a study of the influence of American financial interests upon our entry into the First World War.

After Germany's "criminal invasion" of Belgium in 1914, said J. P. Morgan before the Nye committee on January 7, 1936, we found it quite impossible to be impartial as between right and wrong. . . . If Germany should win a quick and easy victory the freedom of the rest of the world would be lost. . . . We agreed that we should do all that was lawfully in our power to help the Allies win the war as soon as possible.

"We," in this case, meant Mr. Morgan and his associates who acted to arrange credits, raise loans, and coordinate American purchasing by France and Britain before America's entry into the war.[7]

If their premises—which were essentially the premises on which the United States went to war—were accepted, their conduct had been patriotic. But American public opinion was no longer in a mood to accept those premises. It was reverting rapidly to the prevailing mood of August, 1914, which held that neutrality was good in itself and that anything which contributed to entanglement in the belligerency of Europe was wrong, no matter which side profited by America's abstention.

From this standpoint, it cannot be proved that the American trade in foodstuffs, arms, and raw materials, and the credits and loans by which it was financed, were decisive in producing the declaration of April 6, 1917.   President Wilson himself could hardly have been moved by the Wall Street he had always distrusted.   That the influence of all the economic interests created by trade with one set of belligerents was powerful, in many ways, is almost self-evident.   It certainly was so to the American public of the mid-1930s.

Evidence of this can be found in the popularity of Walter Millis's *Road to War* (Boston, 1935), which presented the revisionist thesis in brilliant narrative and with sustained irony.   An "effort in interpretation rather than research," it laid stress on the intangible atmosphere which many factors—diplomatic, economic, emotional, and propagandist—contributed in favor of American belligerency.   But its implicit thesis assumed that neutrality— "practical, as distinguished from formal, neutrality"—was both desirable and necessary.

Mr. Millis's book was not received uncritically by scholars. There were volumes on the other side at this period, *American Diplomacy during the World War* (Baltimore, 1935), by Charles

Seymour, and *Why We Went to War* (New York, 1936), by New-
ton D. Baker, President Wilson's Secretary of War. These two
writers sought especially to refute the idea that financial interests
affected the decision to enter the conflict; it was the German submarine campaign, they maintained. But *Road to War* was a delight to read, especially in the mood of the hour, and found a
wide audience through serialization in the press.

On April 4, 1937, George Gallup, director of the American Institute of Public Opinion, marked the twentieth anniversary of
America's entry into the war by a national poll on the question:
"Do you think it was a mistake for the United States to enter the
World War?" Seventy percent said yes; 30 percent, no. The
South was least convinced of Wilson's error, registering only 61
percent against the war decision; the Pacific Coast states were
most strongly opposed, with 76 percent. But in no group and no
section, in neither major party, was a majority mustered for the
correctness of the declaration of April 6, 1917.

It was inevitable that this tide of feeling should find vent in
practical action—particularly since the guns were firing in many
parts of the world in the early 1930s and there were omens of another great explosion in Europe.

If neutrality was itself the great good, neutrality must be protected—but not by asserting neutral right by force of arms, since
that might mean the war that neutrality was designed to avert;
not by specific action to prevent aggression, since the stigmatizing
of an aggressor was itself unneutral. The United States would
defend its peace by self-denial, by abstaining from risks, by surrendering rights.

President Franklin D. Roosevelt put the matter strongly—yet
not as strongly as many of his countrymen would have done—in
his message on the state of the union at the beginning of 1936.
He attacked the growth of autocratic regimes abroad: "world
peace and world good will are blocked by only ten or fifteen percent of the world's population." He pointed to the danger of
war, adding:

The United States and the Americas can play but one role: through a
well-ordered neutrality to do naught to encourage the contest, through

adequate defense to save ourselves from embroilment and attack, and through example and all legitimate encouragement and assistance, to persuade the nations to return to ways of peace and good will.[8]

In October, 1937, a Gallup Poll was conducted on the question: "Which plan for keeping out of war do you have more faith in—having Congress pass stricter neutrality laws, or leaving the job up to the President?" Sixty-nine percent favored stricter laws; only 31 percent would have left the President his traditional freedom of action. On this test of opinion, Republicans were more skeptical of presidential discretion than Democrats: 87 percent favored stricter laws, but 60 percent of the Democrats agreed with them.[9] This test followed President Roosevelt's speech at Chicago, on October 5, when he said, "The epidemic of world lawlessness is spreading" and proposed a "quarantine of the patients." [10]

Attempts to codify this sentiment into law had begun with the temporary Neutrality Act of 1935, which was expanded in 1936 and made permanent in a stronger form in 1937. When the President declared a state of war existed, there was to be an automatic embargo on arms and a ban on loans and credit to belligerents. Certain raw materials for belligerents could be barred from American ships. Sales to warring nations were possible on a "cash-and-carry" basis, the American seller surrendering title before the ship sailed. Americans could be barred from belligerent vessels. This seemed to cover most of the points that, in the revised versions of First World War history, had contributed to America's entry.

There was not too much that could be done legally about propaganda. Another volume on this theme appeared in 1935; James Duane Squires's *British Propaganda at Home and in the United States from 1914 to 1917* contended that while British propaganda was not *the* cause for American entrance into the World War, "it was a cause and a powerful one." [11] Four years later, H. C. Peterson in his *Propaganda for War: the Campaign against American Neutrality, 1914–1917* was to charge: "The most important of the reasons for the American action in 1917 . . . was . . . the attitude of mind in this country—the product of British propaganda." [12]

Foreign agents were required to register, but it was perfectly obvious that the subtle flows of argument, the ties of culture, the poisoning of the sources of news, could only be guarded against by a vigilant skepticism.[13]

The climax of the attempt to legislate America into negative neutrality came with the introduction of the proposed Ludlow Amendment to the Constitution. In 1935 Representative Louis Ludlow, Democrat, of Indiana, proposed an amendment requiring a referendum before Congress could declare war, except in case of invasion. He could obtain only seventy-two signatures, in the 74th Congress, of the 218 required to bring the bill before the House. But a Gallup Poll in November, 1935, showed 75 percent answering affirmatively this question: "In order to declare war, should Congress be required to obtain the approval of the people by means of a national vote?" Sentiment remained remarkably constant on this question: 71 percent favored a referendum in November, 1936, and 73 percent in 1937, when Mr. Ludlow was at last able to introduce his joint resolution. It was strongly opposed by President Franklin D. Roosevelt, and the author failed on January 11, 1938, by a vote of 209 to 188, to bring the measure out of committee for debate on the floor.[14]

This was the high tide of the mingled forces of isolationism, pacifism, and neutralism that had so gladly accepted the rewriting of the history of the First World War. But the Second World War was drawing closer. Hitler had already revised the Treaty of Versailles in a manner most revisionists never contemplated; Mussolini had conquered Ethiopia; Japan was on the march in China. Many Americans were already questioning whether neutrality was indeed the key to peace in a world where force made the neutrality of the weak just a "word" and treaties merely a "scrap of paper," as Bethmann-Hollweg had characterized them in the red twilight of the older order. And by analogy, they were wondering whether American opinion had indeed been naive and untutored when it was revolted by Imperial Germany's invasion of Belgium in 1914.

This is indicated by the response to an unpublished survey which the American Institute of Public Opinion made in October, 1939, after Hitler had invaded Poland and drawn on his na-

tion the war declarations of Britain and France.   The question
posed to the public was: "Why do you think we entered the last
war?"

Thirty-four percent responded that "America was the victim
of propaganda and selfish interests."   But 26 percent held that
"America had a just and unselfish cause" and 18 percent that
"America entered the war for its own safety."   Eight percent
plumped for various other reasons, and 14 percent had no opinion.   Although this question was not strictly analogous to that on
the wisdom of America's entry, the replies certainly seem to indicate a marked change in two years.   Nearly half, or 44 percent,
saw valid reasons for American participation, while only a third
held to the basic neutralist concept.[15]

The neutralists continued to draw morals from the First
World War as the "great debate" began over America's role in
the second global war—a debate that was not to be stilled, and
then only temporarily, until the Japanese bombs fell on Pearl
Harbor.

Charles C. Tansill's *America Goes to War,* the most thoroughgoing and scholarly study of the 1914–17 period from the revisionist standpoint, appeared in 1938.   The book did not labor
its conclusions, but clearly implicit in the volume was the thought
that America's entry into the war was a tragedy.   The author believed that many factors contributed to this end; he laid special
stress on the failure of the Wilson administration to distinguish
between armed and unarmed merchantmen in its efforts to curb
submarine warfare.   He also emphasized the pro-Allied preconceptions of so many of the leading men in America—but without
questioning whether that may not have had a valid basis.

Edwin Borchard and William Potter Lage first published their
Neutrality for the United States (New Haven) in 1937; they
brought out a new and extended edition in 1940.   This was a
closely reasoned argument for neutrality as a sound, moral, and
traditional American policy, regarded by many before 1914 as
"the maximum achievement of international law."   The volume
posed frankly the opposing concepts of collective security and
neutrality.   The debate of the later 1930s had crystallized these

concepts, which had barely been recognized as alternative policies prior to 1914, when opposing military blocs represented the closest approach to collective security since the disappearance of the vague Concert of Europe in the mid-nineteenth century.

Meanwhile, Americans saw Japan expanding on the mainland of Asia, Italy in Africa, and Germany on the European continent —all by naked force, all without any check by the United States, which was discovering that neutrality meant paralysis.   The fact that Adolf Hitler comported himself like the worst caricature of a "Hun" out of the Kaiser's war, atrocities and all, heightened the emotions of the hour.   And when the Nazi-Communist invasion of Poland in 1939 set off the second global conflict, the United States promptly junked its brand-new neutrality legislation and set out to give the Western Allies "all aid short of war."   It remained short of war—and that by a strained definition—only until December 7, 1941.

There is a new "revisionism" now, which holds in the main to the old tenet that neutrality would have served the United States and the world better than participation in the war.   But that is certainly not official American policy.   After the Second World War, the United States committed itself to collective security through the United Nations; when the cleavage between East and West rendered the Security Council virtually impotent, regional mutual security pacts were entered into by this country with more than forty other states around the world.   The United States has wavered in its official stand on neutralism in other nations, but it has renounced neutralism for itself.

"I believe," said Secretary of State John Foster Dulles on January 17, 1956, "that there are basic moral values and vital interests for which we stand, and that the surest way to avoid war is to let it be known in advance that we are prepared to defend these principles. . . . This policy . . . is not a personal policy; it is not a partisan policy; it is a national policy." [16]

On that basis, instead of condemning the Wilson administration for declaring that it would hold Germany to "strict accountability" for American lives and property lost in submarine warfare, today's thesis might well be that Wilson erred in not making it crystal clear that this accountability meant war. Carrying the whole idea a step farther, the First World War might have been prevented if Germany had known that the United States was willing and able to assist the Entente in preventing Germany from oversetting the balance of power on the Continent.

It is no longer possible to hold to the "personal devil" theory of the origins of the First World War—although Hitler and Stalin have proved that persons can be devils—or to ignore its many complex causes or the effect of calculated propaganda upon America's entry into the struggle. Dexter Perkins's *America and Two Wars,* published while the second was still raging, stated succinctly the growing appreciation of the failure of neutralism—as it applied to the earlier war. After admitting frankly that American neutrality before 1917 had been "one-sided," he went on to ask (the italics are his):

Would the collapse of Britain have been of no concern to America? Would a shift in the balance of power that gave free scope to German ambition have been a matter of no concern? Would neutrality, if it meant German victory, have been to the interest of the United States? It is doubtful if many Americans would answer that question with a "Yes" today.[17]

Thus Julius W. Pratt, in *A History of American Foreign Policy,* published in 1955, would find a more sympathetic audience than would have been possible in 1935 for his statement: "British propaganda, however, was probably less influential in building anti-German sentiment than authentic words and deeds of German leaders and the German armed forces." [18]

And Oscar Theodore Barck and Nelson Manfred Blake, in *Since 1900,* view 1917 through today's eyes when they write:

Complete German dominance of Europe, followed as it must inevitably have been by mastery of the Atlantic Ocean, would have created such a new situation in world politics as to affect most seriously the security of the United States. Since this was so, "strict and absolute neutrality" was as unrealistic in the years following 1914 as it was in the years following 1939.[19]

This will be contested. Professor Tansill has done so in *Back Door to War,* in which he argues that American intervention in the First World War "completely shattered the old balance of power and sowed the seeds of inevitable future conflict in the dark soil of Versailles." [20]   There are others.   Moreover, the succession of "great debates" that have marked the various stages of America's course through the stormy twentieth century has by no means ended.   They will find their echoes in historiography.   No serious student can now write of the First World War without taking into account the myth-breaking of the 1920s and 1930s. But he will also have to recognize that the myth of neutrality is included among the wreckage.   If he proposes to use it as his key to the acts of Wilson and his associates he will have to justify himself.   Neutrality cannot be taken for granted as an American doctrine.

NOTES

1. U.S. President, *A Compilation of the Messages and Papers of the Presidents* (New York, 1917?), XVIII, 8231.

2. *Congressional Record,* 65 Cong., 1st Sess., pp. 213–34.

3. John S. Bassett, *Our War with Germany* (New York, 1919); John B. McMaster, *United States in the World War* (New York, 1918–20).

4. Sidney B. Fay, "New Light on the Origins of the World War," *American Historical Review,* XXV (July, 1920), 616–39, XXVI (October, 1920), 37–53, XXVI (January, 1921), 225–54; Henry Morgenthau, *Ambassador Morgenthau's Story* (Garden City, N.Y., 1918).

5. Harry Elmer Barnes, *The Genesis of the World War* (New York, 1926; rev. ed., 1929), p. xii.

6. Sidney B. Fay, *The Origins of the World War* (2 vols., New York, 1928; rev. ed., 1930).

7. New York *Herald Tribune,* January 8, 1936.

8. Franklin D. Roosevelt, *Public Papers and Addresses,* V (New York, 1938), 10.

9. American Institute of Public Opinion, October 10, 1937.

10. F. D. Roosevelt, *Public Papers and Addresses,* VI (New York, 1941), 406–11.

11. Cambridge, Mass., 1935, p. 81.

12. Norman, Okla., 1939, p. 326.

13. That this existed, the writer remembers well from the early days of the Second World War, when there was an acute sensitivity,

among the newspapermen with whom he worked, to anything smacking of propaganda.   But perhaps the best evidence of this sensitivity is to be found in Dwight D. Eisenhower's *Crusade in Europe* (Garden City, N.Y., 1948).

In 1945, after the world had, one would have thought, been willing to accept almost any tale of terror, General Eisenhower encountered his "first horror camp" near Gotha:

"I visited every nook and cranny of the camp because I felt it my duty to be in a position from then on to testify at first hand about these things in case there ever grew up at home the belief or assumption that 'the stories of Nazi brutality were just propaganda.' Some members of the visiting party were unable to go through the ordeal. I not only did so but as soon as I returned to Patton's headquarters that evening I sent communications to both Washington and London, urging the two governments to send instantly to Germany a random group of newspaper editors and representative groups from the national legislatures.   I felt that the evidence should be immediately placed before the American and British publics in a fashion that would leave no room for cynical doubt." (pp. 408–9).

14. American Institute of Public Opinion, October 10, 1937.

15. Information supplied by American Institute of Public Opinion.

16. New York *Herald Tribune,* January 18, 1937.

17. Boston, 1944, pp. 37, 52.

18. Englewood Cliffs, N.J., 1955, p. 468.

19. New York, 1947, p. 206.   20. Chicago, 1952, p. 9.

AN INTERPRETATION OF
FRANKLIN D. ROOSEVELT

by Bernard Bellush

THE CITY COLLEGE

NEW YORK

"THE BIGGEST and finest crop of revolutions is sprouting all over the country," a farm spokesman informed a Senate committee only weeks before Roosevelt was inaugurated as President in March, 1933. Throughout the Middle West riots against mortgage foreclosures and forced sales indicated the temper of the farmers. Their situation was deplorable. Of the approximately thirty million persons dependent upon agriculture for their living, some 75 percent carried water from wells or other sources of supply, got along with outdoor toilets, and with kerosene or gasoline lamps; 93 percent had neither bath tub nor shower! 54 percent heated their homes practically or entirely with stoves and 33 percent with fireplaces; 48 percent had to do their laundry work out of doors.

Conditions all over the country were going from bad to worse. Typical was the Family Service of Akron, Ohio, which managed to handle 257 charitable cases in 1929, but found itself overwhelmed with 5,000 cases in 1932. Wage rates were falling faster than prices. Breadlines coiled around whole city blocks. Chicago and other cities defaulted on their employees' payrolls. Banks were shuttered, factory chimneys cold, and freight yards silenced. More than thirteen million were unemployed out of a total working force of almost fifty-two million.

It is difficult to imagine the despondency, the hopelessness, and the lawlessness threatening the nation. It is difficult for the present generation to appreciate and the older generation to recall the significant attraction of socialism and communism.   It is equally difficult to picture Hoovervilles of unemployed, like the one along Riverside Drive in New York, or a tottering middle class, reared on social Darwinism and the saintliness of business leadership, shamed into seeking relief handouts.

The world of the 1920s was shattered.   A handful of economists, and Norman Thomas, had warned the nation in 1928, but little attention had been paid them.

Was Franklin D. Roosevelt prepared, in 1933, to assume the leadership of a nation economically destitute, psychologically despondent, and politically discouraged?

As a student at Harvard and later as Assistant Secretary of the Navy, Franklin D. Roosevelt admired the character of executive leadership exhibited by Theodore Roosevelt and Woodrow Wilson, and was impressed by their devotion to progressive ideology and the stewardship philosophy.   Between these two periods he rode the tide of New York progressivism into the State Senate.   On several occasions he had come close to breaking with Tammany.   By 1920, however, he managed to establish permanently his ties as an organization man.   That year he crisscrossed the country as vice presidential nominee, met key party leaders, and was seen and heard by thousands.   Following his polio attack of 1921, F.D.R. exhibited strength and courage by refusing to retire to Hyde Park as a country squire.   He expanded his intellectual horizon and increased his depth of understanding by reading and by meeting such challenging personalities as Rose Schneiderman.   He also gained a stalwart ally in his wife, who blossomed forth during this critical period.   Thereafter, Eleanor Roosevelt would advocate positions on social welfare issues far in advance of her husband.

To political sophisticates, the polio attack signaled the end of Roosevelt's public career.   Ironically, subsequent events disproved this.   The years devoted to recovery kept F.D.R. out of political consideration during a period of Democratic apathy and inadequacy.   With Al Smith comfortably housed in Albany, Roosevelt might have run for the United States Senate.   But Congress was no longer a strategic jumping-off place for the White House.   By this time it was the governor who controlled the party machinery and the bloc of votes at the national nominating convention. Roosevelt would have to succeed Smith as the favorite son through the governorship.

F.D.R.'s retirement afforded him opportunity to communicate regularly with national Democratic leaders, urging revitalization of the party.   After the bitter and exhausting convention of 1924, it was at Roosevelt's Hyde Park estate that defeated Smith was reconciled with the party's compromise nominee, John W. Davis. Roosevelt had come to be viewed as a youthful elder statesman who had nothing personal to gain from party activities.   And yet it was F.D.R. who made the most vivid and lasting impression on convention delegates with his dramatic nominating address for the Happy Warrior. During the next four years, Josephus Daniels and others urged F.D.R. to seek the presidential nomination as they believed he was the one man who could unite the party and avert religious recriminations certain to be raised by Smith's Catholicism.   While insisting that Smith would garner more votes than he, Roosevelt knew that these were not Democratic years and was, therefore, unprepared to sacrifice himself upon the altar of Republican prosperity.

In 1928 Roosevelt was drafted for the gubernatorial race in New York to strengthen Smith's national ticket.   Whereas Smith suffered a traumatic defeat, particularly in his home state, Roosevelt squeezed through with a 25,000 vote plurality out of more than 4,000,000 votes cast.   F.D.R. was on his way.

Although his head remained high, he no longer looked down at the public over pince-nez glasses.   While governor, he continued to develop as a political tactician.   From 1920 on, he had studiously avoided offending any considerable portion of the public.   Having supported the League of Nations that year, he thereafter remained silent.   By 1932 even an isolationist could vote for him.   When imprisoned labor martyr Tom Mooney of California appealed to Roosevelt for support, the Governor refused for fear of alienating possible Hearst endorsement.   The Governor's original reluctance to indict pervading Tammany graft and corruption illustrated an appreciation of organization sup-

port. He also overlooked, for a time, obstructionism by the
banking world to badly needed legislation.   Though such tactics
temporarily lost him endorsement by such leaders as Walter Lippmann, Rabbi Stephen S. Wise, and Reverend John Haynes
Holmes, he was reelected in 1930 by the greatest plurality in the
state's history and retained overwhelming support of the voting
public thereafter.

As a developing politician, F.D.R. was not merely a student
of tactics and practical maneuver but also a pragmatist and experimentalist.   He gave evidence of these tendencies as early as
1926 when he informed the graduating class of Milton Academy
that unrest in the world was caused as much by those who feared
changes as by those who sought revolution.   Unrest in any nation, he felt, whether caused by ultraconservatism or extreme
radicalism, was in the long run a healthy sign.   In government,
in science, in industry, in the arts, inaction and apathy were the
most potent foes.

The critical depression which began late in 1929 saw Governor Roosevelt respond with an open-minded pragmatic approach in the field of economics.   Although some governors, like
John G. Winant of New Hampshire, also sponsored remedial
legislation, F.D.R.'s acts remained in the forefront, for he was the
chief executive of the richest and most populous state and a leading aspirant for the Democratic presidential nomination.

Immediately after the stock market collapse, Roosevelt believed that fundamental industrial conditions were still sound.
The following March he maintained that the depression would
be short-lived, and that it was due, amongst other things, to the
regular business cycle.   When he appointed a committee to investigate long-range solutions to the unemployment problem—
the first governor to do so—F.D.R. shortsightedly placed unquestioning faith in the ability, and in the desire, of industrialists generally to ease voluntarily the depression and aid the unemployed.
He was consistent, however, in urging his administrative agencies
to expand state construction projects to the maximum.   He was
the first governor, in 1930, to publicly urge adoption of some
form of unemployment insurance.

Toward the end of 1930, Roosevelt exhibited growing cognizance of the seriousness and extent of the depression when he suggested experimentation in an attempt to resuscitate the sickened economy. The following January he acknowledged that the depression had hurdled state boundaries and proclaimed the need for a regional approach to basic economic problems.

With belated support from the 1931 legislature, Roosevelt established the Temporary Emergency Relief Administration to make state aid available to localities for work and home relief. This brought Harry Hopkins onto the scene to direct the experiment which became a model for subsequent federal legislation.

The beginning of 1932 found Roosevelt extending his concept of governmental aid to the forty-eight states when he supported federal legislation for unemployment relief. During the months and years which followed, various Congressional sessions provided federal aid to states for work relief and direct federal participation in securing work for the unemployed on federal projects. These precedent-shattering enactments in the field of social welfare were justified, according to Roosevelt, because they were "carrying out the definite obligation of the government to prevent starvation and distress in this present crisis."

During his four years in Albany, F.D.R. amassed an outstanding record for remedial farm legislation. By his speedy appointment of farm authorities to an Agricultural Advisory Commission, he exhibited political acumen and administrative ability, for he appreciated the worth of experts and knew how to use them to greatest effect. By his persistent and wholehearted support of this nonpartisan commission, F.D.R. displayed an understanding of the problems confronting the rural community and of the urgent need for aid and reform.

In contrast to the national Republican administration, and to too many state executives, Governor Roosevelt actively initiated legislation which sought to ameliorate some of the most pressing difficulties of farmers. From the start his objective had been to raise the income and standard of living of farmers to that of city workers. He kept abreast of thinking among such agraraian specialists as M. L. Wilson and Henry A. Wallace. He knew of the

proposed domestic allotment principle on a voluntary basis before it was broached to him by M. L. Wilson, and subsequently
made it part of his 1932 campaign promises.

Roosevelt's farm record as governor, his receptiveness to new
proposals, and his evident leadership influenced many national
farm organizations, farm leaders, and farmers in general to support him for president in 1932.

From early in his public career Roosevelt had opposed the
unlimited acquisition of state-owned water-power sites by private
utilities.   In the process of his struggles with Republican-domi-
nated legislatures, Governor Roosevelt helped educate a majority
of the public to support the development of major water-power
resources by agencies of the government as the inalienable possession of the people; the marketing of power from such public
developments, if possible, through private agencies under contract; and the availability of public transmission and distribution as an alternative if the companies refused to make contracts
favorable to the public.

With the passing years Roosevelt learned he had to master
the power trust, not try to compete with it or outwit it in the
making of contracts.   The Niagara-Hudson Power Corporation
in New York would never be put in its place by the mere construction of a few state-owned power houses.   Only a yardstick in
the form of a government-owned and government-controlled
power industry, such as was created later in the TVA, supplemented by an effective independent regulatory commission, could
stimulate private utilities to reduce their high rates, improve their
services, and bring electric power to the rural areas.

Despite his inability to secure his water-power objectives during his governorship, because of Republican opposition in Albany and Washington, F.D.R. had opportunity to exhibit many
of the traits of leadership with which the nation generally was to
become familiar during his presidency.   He developed a more
educated public opinion by his radio and public addresses and
then activated it, when necessary, by means of organized campaigns.

Roosevelt's State Power Authority served him well, for this

group of experts and independent minds was used by F.D.R. to develop his power program for New York, and later for the nation, as it endeavored to attain Roosevelt's original objectives—cheap and plentiful power for the people.

Before assuming office as Governor, F.D.R. was aware that New York's Public Service Commission was neither an aggressive regulatory body nor independent of utility influence.   Before he left the governorship, however, the Commission veered in the direction of acting as a truly independent regulatory body after Roosevelt appointed Milo R. Maltbie as its new chairman.

Thus it appears that Roosevelt was prepared for the task of presidential leadership.   He was conversant with the realities of the situation, which were much more complex, much more encompassing, and much more threatening than those which had confronted T.R. and Woodrow Wilson.   Within a few days after his election F.D.R. remarked:

The presidency is not merely an administrative office. That is the least of it. It is preeminently a place of moral leadership. . . . That is what the office is—a superb opportunity for reapplying, applying to new conditions, the simple rules of human conduct to which we always go back. Without leadership alert and sensitive to change, we are bogged up or lose our way.[1]

The first two years of Roosevelt's presidency represent a contrast to his governorship.   During four years as chief executive of New York, F.D.R. had taken increasingly progressive steps in the fields of labor, agriculture, power, utility regulation, and banking, to the displeasure of many in the business community.   Although as President, Roosevelt continued to echo the phrases of a progressive, his first New Deal found him much less liberal than the governorship had prepared him to be.

To the left of Roosevelt in March, 1933, were many Congressional progressives who were anxious to press ahead with federal relief, enormous public works, and even economic planning councils.   But F.D.R. moved cautiously, disturbed that this program would mean higher taxes, an unbalanced budget, and increased business regulation.   During this period Roosevelt did not develop a program of radical reform.   He did not press for civil rights legislation nor for specific aid for sorely depressed tenant farmers and helpless sharecroppers. At no time during these two years did Roosevelt arrive at the point old Bob La Follette had reached in 1924. However, Roosevelt's speedy assumption of executive responsibilities, his boldness, his aggressiveness, and his self-assuredness, conveyed a feeling of confidence and hope to millions, especially to those who had been seeking a miracle.

During the dramatic, action-packed "first hundred days," President Roosevelt and a cooperative Democratic Congress pushed through emergency legislation to cope with such pressing problems as banking and finance, conservation and agriculture, the constructive use of unemployed youth, extended federal relief assistance, monetary reform, security regulation, loans to home owners and farmers, fair business codes, the right of labor to organize, public works, and a depressed seven-state area.

A year later F.D.R. devalued the dollar, established the Securities and Exchange Commission, pushed through the Reciprocal Tariff Act, and introduced the Federal Mediation Board to handle labor disputes under the NRA.

While these enactments established Roosevelt as an experimentalist, they also indicated that he had not yet become an ally of organized labor or of progressives. In fact, many labor spokesmen who supported F.D.R. grew uneasy and critical of the first New Deal's business leanings. By the time the Supreme Court declared the NRA unconstitutional in 1935, Roosevelt had permitted the business community to gain undue influence over the organizational development and interpretation of the NRA codes. Neither business, nor those responsible for administering the codes, would provide the opportunity for less-developed labor groups to become an equal partner in operating the NRA, as had been contemplated in the original act. Typical was the history of the drafting of automobile codes where, at every crisis in the relations between labor and management, President Roosevelt leaned in management's direction.

What about the Tennessee Valley Authority? Wasn't this a radical, if not socialistic, move in the direction of government ownership of the means of production and distribution of electricity? Yes, if taken out of the context of the times, and if we ignore the urgent need of millions in a depressed, barren seven-state area.

In supporting TVA, Roosevelt was merely reaffirming his philosophy that government must intervene when power utilities refuse—as in this instance—to meet the minimum needs of consumers, particularly in rural areas. Furthermore, it seemed to Roosevelt that when state governments could not cope with an untamed river which periodically destroyed lives, tore up the countryside, and depressed a great area of the nation, it was only logical that the federal government step in and take the initiative. Finally, TVA was the long-time brainchild of a progressive Republican from the heart of rural America, Senator George W. Norris of Nebraska. Norris had nourished this proposal for many years, but without success until 1933.

The needs of a region, the foresight of a rural spokesman, and the willingness of a pragmatist to experiment, insured the enactment, during those first hundred days, of probably the outstanding monument of the Roosevelt era. No longer would a flooded Tennessee destroy life and property. No longer would natives desert in droves. The harnessed river has insured immense commerce, an industrial revolution, cheap and plentiful electricity, expanding educational facilities, and heightened standards of living. Between 1933 and 1950, the TVA area annually increased its consumption of electricity at a rate almost double that of the nation. Per capita income in this area in 1955 was 61 percent of the national average, compared with 44 percent in the boom year of 1929. In 1933, individual federal income taxes from the seven states were 3.4 percent of the total of such taxes in the nation. Just short of two decades later they were 6.2 percent of the national total.

The first New Deal was a serious, nonradical attempt to save American capitalism from the impact of the depression. Presidential initiative and Congressional action reestablished faith and hope in the integrity of our system. Though unemployment never fell below five to six million, there was much less fear and tension about the future with the approach of the 1934 Congres-

sional elections.   Instead of producing the usual reaction against
the party in power, the mid-term elections reduced Republican
strength to 103 in the House and to 25 in the Senate, despite the
efforts of the American Liberty League.

Within a year of these elections Roosevelt began moving left
because of pressure from a progressive Congress and the cumulative impact of attacks from the Liberty League, the faltering
GOP, the Townsend pension movement, the right-wing populists,
such as Father Coughlin and Huey Long.

Composed of disenchanted "big business" Democrats and
their Republican counterparts, the Liberty League spearheaded
the rightist attacks against Roosevelt and the New Deal.   Dislike
and fear of New Deal spending and regimentation, and the conclusion that Roosevelt was still too independent of business, motivated the League to oppose him from 1934 through the presidential election two years later.

Speaking in behalf of thousands of depression-stricken, fearful
Americans, Father Charles E. Coughlin developed a tremendous
radio following through demagogic perorations for social justice
and against commercial banks, Jewish financiers, and the gold
standard.   Endorsing the devaluation of gold and the remonetiza-
tion of silver, Father Coughlin actively supported F.D.R. in 1932
and through much of the first New Deal.   Subsequently, he felt
that neither Roosevelt nor the Democratic Congress were seriously attempting to remove the control of gold from the hands of
private bankers.   After December, 1934, he vigorously opposed
the New Deal and eventually aligned himself with the Union
Party after promising to secure nine million votes for the Lemke
candidacy in 1936.

Huey P. Long, who had become absolute dictator of Louisiana by the time he went to Washington as Senator in 1932, soon
broke with the Roosevelt administration over patronage.   As
spokesman of the populist "Share the Wealth Movement," he
savagely attacked the inadequacies of the New Deal.   His movement, however, all but collapsed after he was assassinated in September, 1935.

Dr. Francis E. Townsend of California was even more popular

in his advocacy of federal monthly pensions of two hundred dollars to nonworkers over sixty years of age, on condition the money be spent within the month in which it was received. The despondent and elderly flocked to his banner. When neither party endorsed this extreme proposal by 1936, Dr. Townsend announced his support of the Lemke candidacy.

By 1935, "that man" Roosevelt found himself the brunt of increasing attacks from the Liberty League, the Republican Party, and right-wing populists. When much of this loose coalition adopted a negative, obstructionist role, they afforded Roosevelt little alternative but to look to labor and progressives for support of his experimental program and to help salvage those elements of the first New Deal which had survived Supreme Court rulings.

Roosevelt's move to the left—his second New Deal—eventually resulted in the passage of such progressive legislation as the National Labor Relations Act, the subsidiaries of the WPA, the Social Security Act, the National Housing Bill, and the Fair Labor Standards Act in 1938. The inspiration for many of these laws dated back to progressives and Socialists of the early twentieth century.

Despite this leftward move, Roosevelt remained at heart the enlightened conservative he had essentially been throughout his life, upholding personal property rights but believing in change "as essential to holding on to the values of national importance."

While rightist critics maintained that the Roosevelt administration became dominated by labor—"Clear it with Sidney"— F.D.R. always remained master in his own house. When faced with the task of filling the post of Secretary of Labor, for example, Roosevelt wanted to avoid involvement in labor's schisms. More important, he was not in accord with the theory that cabinet members should represent the clientele they were to serve. Roosevelt did not want his cabinet to contain spokesmen for organized labor, the business community, or farmers. He hoped that the heads of the administrative machinery would represent the "national interest." In this way he differed from other presidents. Although he opposed moves of business, labor, and agriculture to exert undue influence over the government, he willingly aided labor in becoming more of an equal partner with industry and agriculture on the economic and political levels.

Unlike their European counterparts, labor's spokesmen were overwhelmingly opposed to forming an independent party or seeking domination of either of the major parties. They did not want the responsibility of governing. In the Gompers tradition they desired labor to be a free and independent force, using its leverage primarily at the bargaining table. Even Walter Reuther, who represents the more dynamic, socially conscious elements within American labor, noted recently that during the New Deal, when labor had a favorable governmental climate, it made no significant progress on pensions and social security. What labor desired, and achieved, under Roosevelt was to attain a more favorable political atmosphere which enabled it to operate more effectively in its bargaining encounters with business. By 1958, when labor had grown in strength and effectiveness, Reuther could say that "our private negotiations [under President Eisenhower's administration] did more to accelerate progress and to make stronger our social security system than anything we ever did [under Roosevelt] through governmental action." [2]

Those who condemn the radicalism of the New Deal should further note that it was Roosevelt's experimental program, and the second New Deal in particular, which did more to dissolve the forces of American Socialism than the Liberty League and other right wing obstructionists. The New Deal achieved much that organized labor and reformist Socialism had been striving for these many decades. In the process, the American economy underwent certain basic changes yet remained essentially capitalistic. While the time-honored slogan of "free enterprise" was retained, the American economic system was forced to include the principles of public control, trade-union participation, and social responsibility. The extent to which these principles have been accepted and applied depends upon the character of the national administration and its appointments to that fourth branch of government, the regulatory agencies.

Before Roosevelt lost the initiative as legislative leader, the New Deal had gone far towards ameliorating many of the evils against which progressives, Socialists, and then Communists, had constantly harangued—low wages, long hours of labor, economic insecurity, child labor, and denial of educational opportunities. Virtually the entire traditional minimum program of the Socialist party became a reality—an eight-hour day, a minimum wage, unemployment and sickness insurance, old-age pensions, workmen's compensation, and abolition of child labor. Racial discrimination, however, continued to plague the country, but increased economic opportunities provided by relief and building works programs made their impact.

By 1936, the Socialist party began to disappear as a potent force, depriving the American scene of a badly needed catalytic agent. This inadequacy becomes all the more evident when the nation's press neglects its role of critic and impartial observer. Events in Europe, it is true, have affirmed the merits of the two-party system. Yet without an alert, responsible and independent citizenry, minority parties can, more often than not, play a constructive role as irritants and as the conscience of the body politic.

By 1936, the various New Deal agencies had brought governmental employment and relief assistance to millions. But the group which perhaps benefited most was the Negro. From the start of the depression Negro communities had suffered most severely. The expanding economic opportunities afforded by the New Deal had a greater impact upon the daily lives of Negroes throughout the nation than did the subsequent executive decree establishing the Fair Employment Practices Commission. By November, 1936, Negroes joined a powerful farmer-labor coalition to cut heavily into Republican middle-income strength and cast more than sixty percent of the total national vote for F.D.R.

Lemke's poor showing of less than a million votes indicated the end of the Union party, while the Socialist vote was the smallest since 1900.   Democrats increased their seats in the House to 333 out of a total of 435 and in the Senate to 75 out of 96.

Having received the greatest electoral mandate since James Monroe, F.D.R. was in an unusually favorable position to expand his second New Deal. Within the next two years, however, he was faced with a series of critical issues to which he was unable to respond with dynamic executive vigor and constructive leadership. The result was the loss of initiative on the legislative level and the steady retreat of the second New Deal.

In response to a series of split-decision vetoes of important New Deal legislation by the oldest Supreme Court in American history, whose personnel remained unchanged during F.D.R.'s first administration, Roosevelt unwisely invaded the "sanctity" of the Court. He lost his political touch when he sought to counter the conservative judiciary with "liberalizing" proposals which were suddenly thrust upon unsuspecting Congressional Democrats. Those who conclude that Roosevelt lost this battle but eventually won the war for judicial affirmation of New Deal legislation, overlook the chief executive's loss of legislative leadership. The Court issue split the Democratic party in Congress and the effects were evident in later years.

In addition, Roosevelt was suddenly confronted with an economic recession which lasted well on into 1938. He fumbled and was indecisive in responding to this setback, which indicated failings as an economist and thinker. Being uncommitted to any economic theory was, in this instance, a severe drawback. What Roosevelt needed at this time was a positive, dynamic program for the benefit of the common man. Had he solved the economic recession speedily and definitively, he would have been in an excellent position to retain legislative leadership and push on with the second New Deal.

Roosevelt compounded these setbacks by his unsuccessful attempts, in 1938, to "purge" conservative Congressional Democrats who criticized his policies. Master politician though he was, Roosevelt made a tragic blunder by personally taking the stump in primary contests against such well known Senate Democrats as Millard E. Tydings of Maryland and Walter F. George of Georgia. Their renomination was a sharp blow to his political prestige.

The extent of Roosevelt's decline can be observed by Congressional reaction to some badly needed legislation to modernize and increase the administrative efficiency of the executive branch. At the time that the President's Committee on Administrative Management issued its report, press and Congressional reaction was generally unfavorable to any proposals that might augment the power of "that man in the White House." Hence, the Reorganization Bill, embodying the recommendations of the President's Committee, was overwhelmingly defeated by Congress in 1938 on the issue of "Roosevelt's dictatorship."

The mid-term elections of 1938 also indicated a conservative trend when eighteen states turned against the Democrats. Republican membership in the House increased from 89 to 170 and in the Senate from 17 to 23. A bipartisan conservative bloc could now offer effective opposition to the President.

With the outbreak of the Second World War in Europe in September 1939, domestic issues receded into the background as Roosevelt devoted increasing attention to military preparedness at home and to strengthening a fighting coalition abroad.

In 1940, Republican amateurs overcame party regulars to nominate Wendell Willkie for the presidency. To the displeasure of conservative supporters of John N. Garner, Cordell Hull, and James A. Farley, who were opposed to a third term, the Democrats renominated F.D.R. With no other strong New Deal candidate in sight, organization Democrats felt that only Roosevelt could check the Republican tide. Still others insisted that this was not the time to swap horses. While accepting the major objectives of Roosevelt's foreign and domestic policies, Willkie warned that if F.D.R. was reelected "our democratic system will not outlast another four years."

Despite the third-term issue, and Willkie's evident sincerity and popular unorthodoxy, Roosevelt swept the electoral college 449 to 82. The victor's 54.7 percent of the popular vote, however, was lower than it had been in 1932 (57.3) and 1936 (60.2). The Democrats added slightly to their House majority but lost three Senate seats.

Politics was all but adjourned after the Japanese attacked Pearl Harbor on December 7, 1941. The mid-term elections of 1942 aroused slight interest, but resulted in sharp surprise. The Republicans gained ten seats in the Senate and forty-seven in the House, which they almost captured. Six key states went Republican in a vote that almost repudiated the administration.

The swing to the right was reflected in the continued decline
of Roosevelt's legislative leadership.   While the administration
had its way in nondomestic measures, a bipartisan bloc of Southern conservatives and Republicans consistently rejected Roosevelt's proposals on taxation, food subsidies, soldier voting, poll
taxes, and other progressive measures.

In the presidential year 1944 Republicans selected Governor
Thomas E. Dewey of New York because of their belief that he
was more popular than Governors John W. Bricker of Ohio or
Harold E. Stassen of Minnesota.   The great majority of Democrats felt that F.D.R. was their only choice.   Believing that this
was no time to swap horses, 53.4 percent of the voters cast their
ballots for F.D.R., but this gave him an electoral landslide of 432
to 99.   Roosevelt retained most of his labor and urban Negro
support in the North but lost ground in the farm belt.

Though both houses of Congress went Democrat by substantial margins, F.D.R. could not regain the legislative leadership
on domestic issues which he had lost during his second administration.   Southern Democrats, for example, showed their anger
at the removal of Jesse Jones as Secretary of Commerce when they
held up F.D.R.'s appointment of Henry Wallace to succeed the
Texan until the lending powers of the Reconstruction Finance
Corporation were separated from the Commerce Department.

During the war, Roosevelt could do little more on domestic
issues than bequeath a sort of last will and testament to the
American public in his State of the Union message of January 11,
1944.

While war was raging overseas, the President appealed to the
nation to plan immediately for a lasting peace and for higher
standards of living for all.   No longer could we permit anyone
to remain ill-fed, ill-clothed, ill-housed and insecure.   No longer
was it sufficient to provide the basic liberties established by our
founding fathers.   The impact of industrialization had proven
the inadequacy of these political rights to assuring equality.
True individual freedom, he maintained, could not exist without
economic security and independence.   "We have accepted," the
President insisted, "a second Bill of Rights under which a new

basis of security and prosperity can be established for all regardless of station, race, or creed."

The President's objectives included the right to a useful and remunerative job; adequate food, clothing and recreation; a decent home; adequate medical care; adequate protection from old age, sickness, accident and unemployment; and a good education.

How shall we sum up Franklin D. Roosevelt and the New Deal? With the aid of an activated Congress, and the cooperation of administrators on all levels, F.D.R. reinstilled hope, courage, and self-respect in the people and reaffirmed faith in their government as an institution concerned with their welfare. On the other hand, he did not go far enough in remedying the basic economic ills of our society, mishandled judicial reform plans, resorted to a tactless political purge, and lost the legislative leadership necessary to maintain the second New Deal. In the process of saving American capitalism by fostering a mixed economy, Roosevelt sounded the death knell of effective radical movements.

The epitaph to the New Deal might well be in Roosevelt's own words, which he addressed to the State Legislature in August, 1931:

The duty of the State toward the citizen is the duty of the servant to its master. The people have created it; the people, by common consent, permit its continual existence. . . . In broad terms I assert that modern society, acting through its government, owes the definite obligation to prevent the starvation or dire want of any of its fellow men and women who try to maintain themselves but cannot. . . . To these unfortunate citizens aid must be extended by government—not as a matter of charity but as a matter of social duty. . . . When . . . a condition arises which calls for measures of relief over and beyond the ability of private and local assistance to meet—even with the usual aid added by the State—it is time for the State itself to do its additional share.[3]

Within thirteen years of the death of Franklin D. Roosevelt,[4] social scientists and former associates have attempted to interpret F.D.R. and the New Deal on a scale unmatched in American history. The researcher has been aided in his task by F.D.R.'s foresight in establishing the Franklin D. Roosevelt Library at Hyde

Park, New York, which now houses his vast collection and those of Henry Morgenthau, Jr., John G. Winant, Louis Howe, and other New Deal personalities. Withheld from the public, but certain to provide at least valuable supplementary information, are the memoirs of Henry A. Wallace, Frances Perkins, and many others, tape-recorded by the Oral History Research Project of Columbia University which was founded by Allan Nevins.

For those seeking insights into the personality of F.D.R., one of the most perceptive studies remains that of Frances Perkins, *The Roosevelt I Knew* (New York, 1946). The former Secretary of Labor draws upon her great wealth of experience, beginning with Alfred E. Smith and F.D.R. as state legislators in 1911. She concludes that Roosevelt developed through the years into a great tested leader and contributed significantly to the development of American liberalism. She concedes not only personality conflicts within F.D.R. but also that "he was the most complicated human being I ever new." In *Working with Roosevelt* (New York, 1951), Samuel I. Rosenman writes of the processes of speechmaking from the 1928 gubernatorial campaign through the presidential report on the Yalta conference. F.D.R.'s speeches were his true secret weapons, through which he established a close rapport with public opinion and which held the support of his following. Despite minor foibles, Roosevelt will rank in history with George Washington. *This I Remember* (New York, 1949), by Eleanor Roosevelt is the work of the most active first lady in our nation's history, who was far in advance of her husband on social welfare issues. Its pages indicate her keen, intelligent, and humane interest in people and the New Deal. John Gunther's *Roosevelt in Retrospect* (New York, 1950) is a journalistic, laudatory work, with some keen insight into the period of recuperation following the polio attack.

Those books which seek to encompass the broad perspective of the New Deal include the monumental project by Frank Freidel, who has produced three of seven projected volumes. His works are primarily biographical in nature, sympathetic in orientation, yet objective and dispassionate in treatment, and extensive in scope and information. *The Apprenticeship* (Boston, 1952) traces Roosevelt's career as a local politician in the State Senate, as a campaigner for Wilson's election in 1912, and as Assistant Secretary of the Navy during the First World War. *The Ordeal* (Boston, 1954) brings F.D.R. through the 1920 elections, the polio attack, the inadequacy of the Democratic party in the 1920s, and his efforts to revitalize the party which helped insure his nomination and election to the governorship. *The Triumph* (Boston, 1956) describes F.D.R.'s "superb administration" as governor, his constructive response to the depression, and his masterful building up of a political machine to insure his nomination and then election as President.

Arthur M. Schlesinger, Jr., in the first of his four projected volumes, *The Age of Roosevelt: The Crisis of the Old Order, 1919–1933* (Boston, 1957), seeks to interpret the political, social, economic, and intellectual life of this period, particularly the devastation of the depression. He grants to Hoover success in breeching the walls of social Darwinism but takes him to task for his unwillingness, or psychological inability, to proceed further along these lines. In contrast to Richard Hofstadter who, in the *Age of Reform* (New York, 1955), views the New Deal as a "new departure" in American reform movements, Schlesinger maintains that the roots of the New Deal go back to Populism, and more especially to T.R.'s Square Deal. Schlesinger holds that "modern science and technology render political centralization inevitable; one must either accept power or reshuffle it," and concludes that "the best hope for individual freedom lies in the chinks and fissures created by the reshuffling process." Offering a progressive's criticism of F.D.R. is James M. Burns in *Roosevelt: the Lion and the Fox* (New York, 1956). His lament is that F.D.R. was too conservative and was remiss in exhibiting "creative leadership" in critical periods of his administration. A basic hypothesis of Burns is "the central findings of social scientists that leadership is not a matter of universal traits but is rooted in a specific culture." While tracing Roosevelt's conservatism from his first administration, Burns contends that F.D.R. moved left because of pressure from a progressive Congress and the impact of attacks from the right. "Creative leadership" was lacking because Roosevelt permitted the United States to drift in foreign affairs, mishandled judicial reform and the political purges, and was indecisive in combatting the recession of 1937 and 1938. Burns, however, does characterize F.D.R. as having "courage, joyousness, responsiveness, vitality, faith, and above all concern for his fellowman."

The conservative critics of Roosevelt have yet to attain the quantity, and quality, of works produced by more sympathetic observers, despite that giant of American historians, Charles A. Beard.   A serious indictment of the New Deal, and a useful antidote to the standard works, has been developed by Edgar Eugene Robinson's *The Roosevelt Leadership, 1933–1945* (Philadelphia, 1955).   Robinson concedes that F.D.R. provided the people, "for a time," with such practical results as they desired because of the initial crisis and because "radical elements" repeatedly returned him to power.   In the process of developing an all-powerful government and executive, F.D.R.'s tactics and accomplishments injured American democracy.   Robinson's measuring rod appears to have been former President Hoover's philosophy of individualism.

While not devoted exclusively to Franklin D. Roosevelt, Clinton L. Rossiter's *The American Presidency* (New York, 1956) is important as the work of an observant political scientist, who writes of the impact of presidents upon the office of the chief executive.   Rossiter places Roosevelt just below Washington and Lincoln as one of the greatest presidents in our history.   He took the baton of strong leadership from Woodrow Wilson and strengthened the presidency to a degree unmatched since Lincoln. To the ancient doctrines of our democracy F.D.R. added the principles of modern liberalism, carrying on the work of T.R., Wilson, La Follette, and Norris to a logical conclusion.   It was Roosevelt's task to remind us of the hollowness of liberty for man who lacks security—political, social and economic.   According to Rossiter, Roosevelt's major contribution to constitutional progress was his successful fusion of Jeffersonian humanitarianism with Hamiltonian nationalism.   To Roosevelt, the real duty of the president was "the leadership of this great army of our people dedicated to a disciplined attack upon our common problems."

There are many important works by Roosevelt's advisers and associates. In *The Memoirs of Cordell Hull* (2 vols., New York, 1948) F.D.R.'s Secretary of State and long-time associate within the Democratic party views Roosevelt as an "extreme liberal" surrounded by semiradicals. He laments F.D.R.'s frequent assumption of State Department reins, typified by direct dealings with Winston Churchhill throughout the war years. While seeking to prove how much greater wisdom he had than his chief, Hull also felt that he might have ventured into the presidential circle by 1940. One of the most independent members of Roosevelt's cabinet was Harold Ickes. *The Autobiography of a Curmudgeon* (New York, 1943) and *The Secret Diaries of Harold L. Ickes* (3 vols., New York, 1953–54) may be filled with trivia and illustrate his personal reactions to individuals but add color and vividness to the New Deal era. Robert E. Sherwood, who worked closely with Harry Hopkins and the President during the war years, mustered his great talents into an illuminating work, *Roosevelt and Hopkins: an Intimate History* (New York, 1948). He seeks to convey the dual impact of environment and daily events upon the President, and vice versa. The rise of Roosevelt to power was due more to the extraordinary circumstances of the times than to any clever conspiracy. The way to a Roosevelt audience was via Hopkins, and even in Europe Hopkins was often catered to in critical moments as the power nearest the throne. Hopkins was the trained spokesman of F.D.R. This book is also essential reading for an understanding of the handling of the domestic problem of relief. As political organizer from 1928, James A. Farley was master of them all. Since his parting with Roosevelt in 1940, Farley remained a frustrated office seeker. To this day he cannot appreciate the fact that New Deal progressives view him as a conservative because of his refusal to perceive that politics is a shabby game when not directed to larger and nobler ends. In *Jim Farley's Story: The Roosevelt Years* (New York, 1948) he eventually paints the picture of a seemingly sinister individual leading the Democratic party.

Cutting across the three categories mentioned thus far is Rexford G. Tugwell, *The Democratic Roosevelt* (New York, 1957).

Written by an original brain truster and political scientist, the early part of this important work is devoted to psychological insights into F.D.R.'s childhood and youth, in an effort to interpret motivations behind Roosevelt's subsequent decisions as politician and statesman.   F.D.R. was propelled by an inner drive of tremendous power.   His aristocratic background, his schooling, and the impact of T.R., turned F.D.R. into a patrician reformer. Power was to be used to build, to use the democratic political processes to husband the nation's material and human resources, and to broaden social and economic opportunities for the individual.   Although an experimenter, F.D.R. was more conservative and much more prone to compromise than the author. While seeking to attain his general objectives, Roosevelt made many inglorious compromises.   Had he lived, however, F.D.R. would have gone building toward a closer approximation of his conception of a just and kindly world.

Other works and scholarly articles which have been helpful in the preparation of this article include: Raymond Moley, *After Seven Years* (New York, 1939), which gives an excellent, though critical, picture of the period 1933–35; Basil Rauch, *History of the New Deal* (New York, 1944), a useful summary; John T. Flynn, *The Roosevelt Myth* (New York, 1948), which castigates Roosevelt unfairly; John P. Frank, *Mr. Justice Black* (New York, 1949); Kenneth E. Trombley, *The Life and Times of a Happy Liberal* (New York, 1954); Bernard Béllush, *Franklin D. Roosevelt as Governor of New York* (New York, 1955); Gordon R. Clapp, *Tennessee Valley Authority* (Chicago, 1955); Daniel R. Fusfeld, *The Economic Thoughts of Franklin D. Roosevelt and the Origins of the New Deal* (New York, 1956), which brings F.D.R. to the presidency as knowledgeable on things economic; Dexter Perkins, *The New Age of Franklin Roosevelt, 1932–45* (Chicago, 1957); and Irving Howe, *The American Communist Party, a Critical History, 1919–1957* (Boston, 1958); Henry Brandon, "A Conversation with Walter Reuther: 'How Do We Live With Bigness?',", *New Republic,* CXXXIX (July 21, 1958), 13–18; Sidney Fine, "President Roosevelt and the Automobile Code,"

Mississippi Valley Historical Review, XLV (June, 1958), 23–50; Will Herberg, "What Happened to American Socialism?," *Commentary,* XII (October, 1951), 336–44; Marian D. Irish, "The Organization Man in the Presidency," *Journal of Politics,* XX (May, 1958), 259–77; Bruce B. Mason, "Why Roosevelt Moved Left," *Institute of Social Studies Bulletin,* II (Fall, 1954), 78–81, and "Coughlin and Roosevelt, The National Union for Social Justice," *Institute of Social Studies Bulletin,* III (Fall, 1955), 33–36.

NOTES

1. Arthur M. Schlesinger, Jr., *The Age of Roosevelt: The Crisis of the Old Order, 1919–1933* (Boston, 1957), pp. 483–84.

2. Henry Brandon, "A Conversation with Walter Reuther: 'How Do We Live with Bigness?' " *New Republic,* CXXXIX (July 21, 1958), 15.

3. Franklin D. Roosevelt, *Public Papers and Addresses,* I (New York, 1938), 458–59.

4. This paper was completed in 1958.

INDEX OF NAMES